Governing
New Mexico

Governing
NEW
MEXICO

EDITED BY

F. Chris Garcia
Paul L. Hain
Gilbert K. St. Clair
Kim Seckler

University of New Mexico Press
ALBUQUERQUE

PRINTED IN THE UNITED STATES OF AMERICA

YEAR   PRINTING
10 09 08 07 06   1 2 3 4 5

Library of Congress Cataloging-in-Publication Data

Governing New Mexico / edited by F. Chris Garcia.
    p. cm.
  "This version is a revision of the third edition (1994) of New Mexico
Government [ed.] by Paul L. Hain."
  Includes bibliographical references and index.
  ISBN-13: 978-0-8263-4128-0 (pbk. : alk. paper)
  ISBN-10: 0-8263-4128-4 (pbk. : alk. paper)
  1. New Mexico—Politics and government. I. Garcia, F. Chris. II. Hain,
Paul L., 1939– III. New Mexico government / ed. by Paul L. Hain. 1994.
3rd ed.
  JK8016.N48 2006
  320.9789—dc22
                            2006011885

Book design and composition by Damien Shay
Body type is Minion 10.5/14
Display is Bellevue and Belwe

Contents

List of Illustrations

Preface

This version is a revision of the third edition (1994) of *New Mexico Government* by Paul L. Hain, F. Chris Garcia, and Gilbert St. Clair. The primary changes to the third edition materials are the welcome addition of a new editor and major contributor, Kim Seckler; the updating of most of the information; and a consolidation and update of the two chapters on the executive branch in the third edition. Several contributors to earlier editions have given their permission to continue to use their materials without specific attribution. We thank them. We are especially indebted to David Abbey, David Hadwiger, and William Taylor of the New Mexico Legislative Finance Committee staff for their extensive revision of "The Fiscal Structure of New Mexico." We would also like to thank Meg Edwards, Tali Gluch, Xavier Medina, Olivia Stockman, James Timberlake, John Todsen, and Esteban Torres for their assistance in the preparation of this draft.

We also extend our gratitude to the University of New Mexico Press, publisher of the three previous editions, for its permission to produce and distribute for class use unpublished draft versions of the fourth edition, and for its continued support of this endeavor.

As we have worked on this fourth edition, we are ever reminded of the constancy and continual change in New Mexico government and politics. Since the publication of the third edition in 1994, New Mexico has participated in yet another decennial census. The turn of the century was marked by the presence of more than 1.8 million New Mexicans, continued growth in the Rio Grande corridor, and continued population decline in the state's rural eastern and western border communities. The decade was also marked by significant political change, as both the governor's office and the top legislative posts welcomed new occupants. The new occupants continue to make their mark on the contours of New Mexico government.

Though many of the political faces have changed, many of the issues have not. New Mexicans and their governments continue to wrestle with issues as diverse as water and the environment, DWI, education, crime and drugs, and economic development. In the pages that follow, we attempt to present descriptions and explanations of the structures and environments in which some of those efforts occur.

Chapter One

New Mexico: The Setting

New Mexico is a state of great beauty and fascination, one whose
geography, climate, and people are very diverse and complex. A
broad range of distinctive cultural, geographic, and climatological elements impinge upon and interact with one another to produce an intrigu-
ing mosaic of people and places. The state is aptly nicknamed the Land
of Enchantment.

One basis for the great diversity of the state is its natural character-
istics. The state is very large—ranking fifth in size among the fifty United
States; its land area consists of 78 million acres, or 121,666 square miles.
This is equal to the combined land area of Maine, New Hampshire,
Massachusetts, Rhode Island, Connecticut, New York, New Jersey, and
Delaware. This expansive land provides a grand stage for the interaction
of the varied cultures and natural phenomena that make the state's pol-
itics particularly interesting. Much of the land is publicly owned. The
United States federal government owns one-third (33 percent) of the state,
or 25.6 million acres. The state itself owns 12 percent, or 9.4 million acres.
Native Americans have been allotted 7.9 million acres (10.23 percent).
This leaves about 35 million acres (45 percent) under private ownership;
of this total, 1.4 percent, or 500,000 acres, is owned by foreign investors.

New Mexico is a state of unsurpassed natural beauty. One major reason for this is its great geographical variety. Within its boundaries are

found six of the seven life zones existing on the North American continent. Pine-forested mountains reaching above thirteen thousand feet are found in the northern part of the state. The mountains of the southwestern and south-central part of the state are equally impressive, even though they rise from a lower base elevation. The cool and comparatively moisture-laden mountains provide a great contrast to the vast arid areas of the state. The Great Plains roll westward from the central United States into the eastern part of New Mexico. These plains, known as the *llano estacado*, or "staked plains," extend down to an altitude of some three thousand feet above sea level in the southeastern part of the state. The southwestern and southern parts of the state are primarily rolling hills of rather sparse vegetation, at three to four thousand feet above sea level, along with some rugged mountainous areas. The west-central and northwestern parts of New Mexico are a high, arid plateau, shaped by considerable volcanic activity and featuring high and dramatically sculptured mesas, plateaus, and stone formations.

New Mexico's lack of moisture is difficult to appreciate. Only 0.2 percent of the land surface is water. This is the lowest proportion of surface water to surface land of any state in the nation. New Mexico has a few major rivers, and although they might be considered no more than streams in most other parts of the country, the Rio Grande, San Juan, Chama, and Pecos rivers historically have provided the lifeblood for the state's population centers. The runoff from the melting snows of the high mountains through these rivers is essential for both agricultural irrigation and the replenishment of the water table for industrial and consumer utilization. An average of only ten inches a year falls on most of the state, although the mountain areas receive considerably more precipitation. This high and dry climate produces an atmospheric freshness and clarity that is found in few other places in the United States. The skies over the state are usually clear, crystal azure, and strikingly expansive.

NEW MEXICO'S PEOPLES

If New Mexico's population were evenly distributed across the state, one would find about fifteen people living in each square mile. It is, however, highly concentrated. Almost one-third of the state's total population lives in the Bernalillo County (Albuquerque) metropolitan area. One-half of the population (including that in Bernalillo County) can be

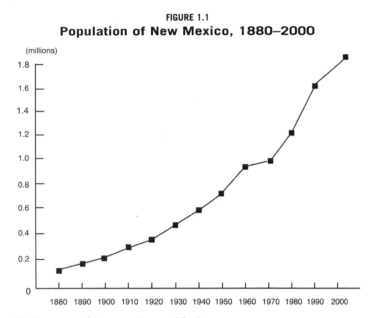

FIGURE 1.1
Population of New Mexico, 1880–2000

Source: U.S. Department of Commerce, Bureau of the Census

found along the Rio Grande and its tributaries. The only other population centers are those that have sprung up around the mining and petroleum industries of the northwest Four Corners area and the southeastern quadrant of the state. In 2000 the state's population stood at 1,819,406 and was growing steadily.

Through the 1990s the state gained population at a higher rate than the national average—20 percent compared to the national average of 13.2 percent. This increase was primarily due to in-migration, since the birth rate decreased substantially after 1966, and the death rate remained fairly stable. In the 1970s the state had been "discovered" by those Americans seeking to escape the crowded conditions of metropolises in the East and Midwest. The most recent in-migration seems to be taking place from the West Coast, with people who had originally moved to California from the East and Midwest coming back into an area they had only passed through on their way to the coast. Indications are that in addition to the newcomers from the snowbelt and California, the greatest number of immigrants to New Mexico has come from the adjoining states of Texas, Colorado, and Arizona, as well as from Latin America, particularly Mexico.

The recent decades of migration to New Mexico are changing the unique configuration of cultures that for so long has been distinctive to the state. Due to relatively decreasing fertility rates among non-Hispanics, improving mortality rates among minority groups, and a significant rate of in-migration from Mexico and other Latin American countries, in 1990 ethnic "minorities" in New Mexico became the majority. In 1990 about half (some 49.1 percent) of the residents of New Mexico were "Anglo."[1] By 2000 the percentage of Anglos or "whites" had decreased to 44.7.[2] The Native American Indian (9.5 percent in 2000) and Hispanic (42.1 percent) populations had been decreasing in proportion to the Anglo population over the previous several decades, but increased slightly between 1980 and 2000. "Others" comprised 3.7 percent of the populace. A mid-decade report based on July 2004 population estimates placed the Hispanic population at 43 percent and the American Indian population at just under 10 percent. Thus, New Mexico became the first contemporary "majority-minority" state (in which ethnic and racial "minority" groups are in the majority) on the United States mainland. (Prior to World War II Hispanics had been in the majority). By 2010 it is projected that the Hispanic community alone (43.3 percent) will once again outnumber the Anglo population (42.5 percent).[3]

This pluralistic ethnic composition has had major effects on the state's politics and government. New Mexico's political and social relationships have long included an integral involvement of Spanish Americans that is unique among the states of the Southwest.[4] Because of the relatively large proportion of distinctive ethnic groups in the state, and because of these cultures' long history in the area, ethnic relations have probably been closer to the model of cultural pluralism here than those found in any other part of the country.[5] While there have occurred some hostilities, various instances of discrimination, and some antagonism between the cultures, by and large New Mexico has as good a record of peaceful relations between ethnic groups as any other state. New Mexico prides itself on its multicultural conditions. Rather than strive toward a "melting pot," in which all cultural distinctions are mixed and merged, the state may be more accurately described as a cultural mosaic; each piece separate and distinct, but when placed side by side with other individual pieces, forming an integrated, composite whole. This diversity, while inevitably producing some conflict, again illustrates the heterogeneity

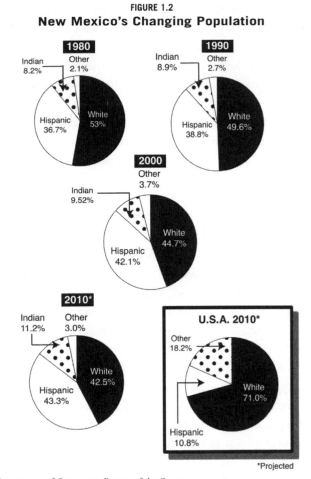

FIGURE 1.2
New Mexico's Changing Population

Source: U.S. Department of Commerce, Bureau of the Census

that produces a fascinating mix in the social and political relationships among New Mexico's peoples.

ECONOMY

New Mexico is often described as a poor state. This phrase is accurate if applied to the average capital assets of the total population, but it is not descriptive of the state's natural and human resources and potential riches. The state's relative income position in per capita personal income has remained fairly stable over the past four decades. In 1978 New Mexico ranked forty-third; this figure generally has sunk lower from the late 1970s onward. In 1990 the per capita personal income was 76.4 percent of the national average and ranked forty-eighth in the United States. In 2000, New Mexico ranked forty-ninth in per capita income, above only the state of Mississippi. The per capita personal income in New Mexico was $21,833, which was 74.3 percent of the national per capita income of $29, 451. A 2003 estimate revealed that New Mexico's ranking had risen slightly to forty-sixth, but the Census Bureau ranked the state forty-ninth in 2004. In 2003 it was reported that New Mexico had the lowest wages paid to its workers of any state in the nation.

As is often the case, averages do not give the total picture, since New Mexico has its share of the very wealthy and more than its share of economically very depressed citizens. In 2003 at the high end in average individual incomes were Los Alamos County at $48,541, Santa Fe County, $32,378, and Bernalillo County, $30,064. At the lower end were the counties of Guadalupe, $14,455, Mora, $15,867, and McKinley, $16,437. These bottom three counties have large Hispanic and Indian populations, an indication that the non-Anglo groups of the state tend to gather at the bottom of the socioeconomic scale.

Perhaps most disturbing is the high rate of poverty—one of the highest in the nation. In 2002, 17.7 percent of New Mexico's population was impoverished compared to 12.1 percent of the nation. Only Mississippi had a higher proportion of poverty. Child poverty in New Mexico is especially bad. It rose from 26.6 percent in 1989 to about 32 percent in 1995 and at the beginning of the twenty-first century was reported to be the highest in the nation at 28 percent.

Being one of the poorer states of the Union, New Mexico receives substantially more money from the federal coffers than it contributes. In 1988 New Mexico was second in the ranking of states based upon the per capita amount of federal aid received; in 2002 it ranked fifth. However, New Mexico's citizens are taxed at a fairly high rate; that is, the tax effort per capita is quite high, when based on personal income. In 1987 New Mexico ranked fifth in the nation in the percentage of personal income paid for taxes and other governmental fees. In 2004, the ranking for total tax burden was eighteenth. Yet residents' incomes are so low that even a great tax effort does not produce enough revenue to make federal assistance less necessary.

FIGURE 1.3
Comparative State Per Capita Incomes

	1990		1995		2000		2003 /r	
	Dollars	Rank*	Dollars	Rank*	Dollars	Rank*	Dollars	Rank*
United States	$19,477	N/A	$23,076	N/A	$29,847	N/A	$31,459	N/A
Arizona	$17,005	35	$19,929	37	$25,661	37	$26,931	38
California	$21,638	8	$23,203	13	$32,466	8	$33,403	10
Colorado	$19,575	18	$23,004	14	$33,371	7	$34,510	7
Connecticut	$26,504	1	$31,045	1	$41,495	1	$43,292	1
Idaho	$15,724	41	$18,707	39	$24,076	42	$25,583	45
Mississippi	$13,089	50	$16,291	50	$21,007	50	$23,343	50
Montana	$15,448	43	$17,861	45	$22,932	46	$25,775	44
Nevada	$20,346	13	$23,772	9	$30,438	14	$31,487	18
New Mexico	**$14,924**	**46**	**$17,631**	**46**	**$22,134**	**47**	**$25,502**	**46**
New York	$23,523	3	$25,785	4	$34,900	4	$36,296	5
Oklahoma	$16,187	37	$18,374	42	$24,410	41	$26,567	39
Texas	$17,421	31	$20,189	34	$28,313	23	$29,076	29
Utah	$14,913	47	$17,566	47	$23,878	43	$25,230	47
Washington	$19,865	16	$22,938	16	$31,780	11	$33,264	12
Wyoming	$18,002	25	$20,498	29	$28,463	21	$32,235	15

Most of the revenues for New Mexico state government come from the gross receipts ("sales") and personal income taxes. In 2002, 34 percent of the state's general fund came from the gross receipts tax and 27 percent from personal income taxes. Other sources included: oil and gas taxes, rents and royalties—13 percent; investment income—12 percent; "other income"—11 percent; and the corporate income tax—4 percent. These had changed little in the preceding four years.

Historically, New Mexico's economy has been somewhat underdeveloped and problematic, because of a stubbornly high rate of underemployment and unemployment, a weak manufacturing base, and a heavy dependence upon governmental spending. However, recent efforts in economic development, including higher than average population and employment growth as well as increases in the construction, petroleum, health care, and social assistance areas have brightened the outlook.

Out of the $18.8 billion of total personal income generated in the state in 1988, $3.5 billion was paid to individuals working for governmental institutions at all levels, including the schools. This constituted 26.1 percent of the nonagricultural civilian workforce of 540,400. In 2003, 25.2

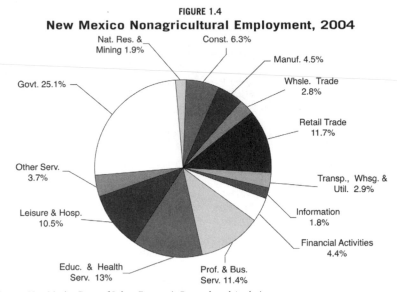

FIGURE 1.4
New Mexico Nonagricultural Employment, 2004

Nat. Res. & Mining 1.9%

Const. 6.3%

Manuf. 4.5%

Govt. 25.1%

Whsle. Trade 2.8%

Retail Trade 11.7%

Other Serv. 3.7%

Transp., Whsg. & Util. 2.9%

Leisure & Hosp. 10.5%

Information 1.8%

Financial Activities 4.4%

Educ. & Health Serv. 13%

Prof. & Bus. Serv. 11.4%

Source: New Mexico Dept. of Labor, Economic Research and Analysis

percent of the nonagricultural workforce was employed by governments in New Mexico compared to 16.6 percent of the national workforce. The percentage of government workers in our counties ranges from 13.1 percent in Lea County to 64.5 percent in Los Alamos County and 65 percent in Mora County. Governmental expenditures are not spread evenly throughout the state but instead are concentrated in the federally funded city and county of Los Alamos; in the state capital, Santa Fe; and in the Albuquerque metropolitan area.

In 2003, after public-service employment, services (38.6 percent, including professional and business services, leisure and hospitality, and others) and wholesale and retail trade (14.5 percent) constituted the next largest employment sectors. In 2003 wholesale and retail trade provided over $2.8 billion in personal income. The services (including personal and private household services; business and repair services; amusements and recreation; hotels and other lodging; and professional, social, and related services) contributed more than $4 billion to personal income. Contract construction employed 6.1 percent of the state's workforce in 1988, adding $2.2 million to the total production income of New Mexico, and it has continued to grow at a healthy rate.

New Mexico has a relatively small manufacturing base; 4.7 percent of the nonagricultural population is involved in the sector (2003), compared to a national average of 11.2 percent. Computer and electronic production was the largest subsector in 1997 (26.7 percent of total manufacturing in the state).

Although in 2000 only 16.5 percent of the total civilian workforce was engaged in agricultural production, New Mexico's farms and ranches sold $1.7 billion worth of agricultural products in 2002. The total personal income from farming was $677.5 million. The leading agricultural producers are Chaves, Doña Ana, Union, Curry, and Roosevelt counties. There has been a decline in the number of farms over the last few decades and a corresponding increase in the size of farms. The top commodities in 2002 were dairy products (38 percent of total farm receipts) and livestock (30.3 percent of the state's total farm receipts). Most of the state's agricultural effort is devoted to livestock rather than produce. Seventy percent of commodity cash receipts are from livestock, mostly cattle, and from field crops.

Mining, formerly a major sector, has played a decreasing role in the economy; only 1.8 percent of the workforce was engaged in this sector in 2002 compared to 2.8 percent in 1988 and 5.5 percent in 1978. New Mexico still ranks seventh among the states in its mineral resource value, however, particularly with respect to petroleum, coal, natural gas, and uranium. The state also has significant amounts of copper, potash, lead, zinc, and molybdenum.

After several years in which there was a decreased interest in and demand for the energy resources of New Mexico, the twenty-first century has brought renewed interests. In addition to ferrous and nonferrous minerals, the state has major petroleum fields and vast quantities of uranium and coal, plus a great abundance of solar and geothermal energy sources. Although there are uncertainties regarding the development of the latter in the near future, there is increasing realization that these will be very important in the long run.

The state's natural beauty, favorable climate, and wide-open spaces increasingly appeal to out-of-state vacationers and filmmakers. Efforts are being made to further develop these two industries—tourism and moviemaking—both of which are making noticeable contributions to the economy of New Mexico.

Because of the relatively small employment opportunities in the manufacturing and industrial sector, the state historically has had a relatively high rate of unemployment. In non-recessionary times, New Mexico typically has an unemployment rate slightly higher than the national average. For example, in 1987 unemployment was 8.9 percent in New Mexico, compared to the national average of 6.2 percent; in February of 1990 the state's jobless rate was 6.1 percent, and the national rate was 5.8 percent. However, in the twenty-first century the state's unemployment rate diminished steadily each year until it was lower than the national rate in 2004. In 2003 the New Mexico unemployment rate was 6.4 percent compared to the 6 percent national rate. Throughout the year 2004, the unemployment rate in the state remained between 5.1 and 5.6 percent, close to the national average. In early 2005 the unemployment rate in New Mexico and the United States were the same—5.8 percent. Because its employment rests on relatively stable bases such as agriculture, mining, and, most importantly, government expenditures, New Mexico's level of employment is much less subject to the ups and downs of the economic cycle than many other states. Consequently, during hard times or the export of jobs to other nations, when manufacturers and other producers are forced to lay off great numbers of employees, New Mexico remains relatively unaffected.

One of the biggest events to affect the economy of New Mexico was its transformation into a major gambling ("gaming") state in the mid-to-late 1990s. One of the first major events was the establishment of a state-sponsored lottery in 1995, when New Mexico joined several other states that had long-standing lotteries. Prior to that time, pressures for a lottery and for new and different types of gaming had been resisted by state government, as well as by the defense of the status quo by the courts. Legitimized gambling was restricted primarily to horse racing and to bingo games sponsored by churches. In 1988 federal legislation had allowed casinos in the states. A few Indian tribes began to have bingo halls on their pueblo grounds, and they expanded this in both size of winnings and the variety of the types of games played, which came to include pull-tabs and slot machines in the bingo halls.

In 1995, a giant leap was taken by Governor Gary Johnson, who negotiated compacts with Indian tribes that allowed slot machines on Indian reservations. The legality and propriety of these actions were challenged and ruled unconstitutional by the state supreme court because the legislature had not given its approval. However, the governor and the tribes (the latter acting on their claims to sovereignty and freedom from state regulation) continued with the compacts, regardless of the court's ruling. The Indian gaming activities expanded to Las Vegas-style casinos with table games of chance. The legislature, at first upset by what it saw as a usurpation of its legislative and regulatory powers, in 1997 gave its approval to these already ongoing gaming activities. The House of Representatives approved the compacts between the state and Indian tribes for casinos and legalized a limited number of slot machines at racetracks and fraternal and veterans clubs. These compacts sought to impose some restrictions on gaming activities and to levy some taxes on the profits of the tribes. In addition, the voters of New Mexico formally approved the institution of a state-run lottery system, most of whose profits were directed toward funding education, primarily higher education tuition scholarships. By 2005, there were thirteen tribes operating fifteen Indian gaming sites in the state, which were earning millions of dollars, plus state lottery games that also earned huge amounts of state revenues. Although detailed information is not available, cloaked in the prerogatives of tribal sovereignty and compacts with the state that promise secrecy, estimates are that gaming earnings in the state approached $600 million in 2005.[6] The many effects of this surge of gaming activity on the state's economy are unknown. Certainly it has, at the very least, greatly affected the internal redistribution of wealth within the state but in ways about which there is much speculation and little substantial data. The lottery has undoubtedly increased the number of students enrolling in New Mexico's institutions of higher education.

EDUCATION

New Mexico was historically late in developing a statewide system of public education, and because of this and its weak economic base, many problems exist in the area.[7] However, considering the relative scarcity of revenues, New Mexico has made a noteworthy effort to support its educational establishments and in 1990 ranked second among the states in the percentage of state funds spent on its elementary and secondary schools. In 2004–5 New Mexico had a total of 998 precollegiate educational institutions, 80 percent of which were public schools. Included among the 795 public schools were 117 senior high schools, 151 junior high and middle schools, 447 elementary schools, and 80 other specialized schools, including charter schools. The state has six graduate-degree-granting public universities, each with branches, as well as almost two dozen community colleges and several private colleges. New Mexicans attend school for an average of 12.5 years, a figure close to the national level. In 2000, 78.9 percent of the state's population twenty-five years of age or older had completed high school. New Mexico has the largest number of Ph.D.s proportionate to its population of any state in the union, and ranked tenth in 2004 in the percentage of population having a graduate or professional college degree. In contrast, New Mexico ranked ninth in the nation in the portion of its population (9.25 percent) having less than a ninth-grade education. The state also ranked forty-sixth among the states in high school graduates and in college bachelor's degrees. These contrasting averages also point out the great disparities in educational attainment among the state's varied population groupings. For example, the poor, Hispanics, and Indians average significantly less educational attainment than other groups.

In spite of its weak economic base and the difficulties of such varied educational attainment among its ethnic groupings, New Mexico has been one of the nation's leaders in its attempts to provide equal educational financing for all areas of the state. Its equalization funding formula and centralized state-level funding of schools have served as models for attempts by other states to reform their educational finance systems. More will be said about this in the chapters on state governance of education and state finance.

RELIGION

No one religion dominates in the state. While the Catholic Church has exerted a significant force historically, at present its influence is not disproportionate to that of any other major religious grouping. An early offshoot of the church, lay confraternities called the Penitentes (*Los Hermanos Penitentes*), was important to the social and political development of Hispanic communities in the northern part of the state. The Native Americans in the state also continue to worship in their traditional manner, while adopting and sometimes adapting various Christian denominations, as the result of the work of missionaries. Among the

Hispanic population, Roman Catholicism is the predominant religion, with perhaps 80 to 90 percent of the state's Hispanic population being of this faith. Among the Anglo population can be found all major and many minor religious denominations.

Pluralism also extends to the religions of the state. The 2000 Census reported the following religious affiliations: Protestant—44 percent; Catholic—37 percent; Other Christian—4 percent; Other Religions—1 percent; and "Non-religious"—11 percent. Among Protestants, the largest denominations were Baptists (12 percent), and Methodists (7 percent).

Only estimates, including surveys, of denominational church memberships are available, but by far the largest single denomination is Catholic (about 37 percent of the population), followed by Baptists and Methodists. Other churches having sizable memberships are (roughly in descending order): Presbyterian, Church of Christ, Lutheran, Episcopal, Church of Jesus Christ of Latter Day Saints, Assembly of God, Christian Disciples, Church of the Nazarene, and United Church of Christ. The Jewish community, estimated in 1990 to number from 8,000 to 10,000 people, has also played a significant role in the state.[8] These, plus several other smaller denominations, constitute a total church membership of some 672,000 New Mexicans.

Although almost all of these religions are actively involved in social activities and have entered the political arena on particular issues of concern, no single religious sect continually dominates the state's political or social relationships.

HISTORY

Probably the most significant feature of New Mexico's social history is that it includes some of the oldest continuously inhabited settlements in North America. What are recent immigrants or distinctive ethnic minorities in other parts of the United States are in New Mexico the primary inhabitants of the area. The Native American Indians who settled in this area occupy much the same villages and pueblos as they did hundreds or even thousands of years ago. Unlike the Indians of other states, New Mexico Native Americans by and large have not been uprooted from the area of their choice and moved to other parts of the country, but instead continue to inhabit their older areas of settlement. Some New Mexicans of Spanish and Mexican ancestry claim that they can trace their origins back to the seventeenth century. The present capital city of Santa Fe, for example, had already been established for a decade by the time the Pilgrims landed at Plymouth Rock.

Archaeologists tell us that New Mexico is the site of some of the earliest remains of the first humans in America.[9] In the caves of the Sandia Mountains near Albuquerque, relics and remnants have been found pointing to the existence of people in that area perhaps as far back as twenty-five thousand years ago. In 1991 a handprint believed to be between twenty-eight and thirty-five thousand years old was discovered near Orogrande. More concrete and direct evidence of New Mexico's first inhabitants was found in the eastern area of the state, near Clovis. The famous "Clovis Man" may have existed here as long as thirteen thousand years ago. The most accepted theory holds that these and other early people who settled in New Mexico were the descendants of those prehistoric migrants who crossed the land bridge across the Bering Strait some twenty thousand to thirty thousand years ago. The descendants of these early peoples in turn produced the Hohokam cultures, which developed irrigated farming in southwestern New Mexico, and the Ancestral Puebloan cultures of northwestern New Mexico. Many Indian pueblos, several hundred years old, are still vital and viable communities located throughout the state. Because of drought, depletion of resources, and perhaps disease, these earliest villages were reduced in number and became concentrated along the northern and central river valleys. The survivors of these early cultures still live in the nineteen Indian pueblos of modern New Mexico. They have brought to the state the heritage of some forms of government that are in some ways at least as democratic as that of European cultures, as well as their philosophy of people living with and as part of nature.

Sometime after the ancestors of today's Pueblo Indians had settled in the state, another wave of early Americans descended into the area. These people are known as Athabascans; they later evolved into the Navajo and Apache tribes. The Athabascans engaged in considerable and long-lasting conflict with the Pueblo peoples.

Spain, through its viceregal government in Mexico City, explored the area of the present American Southwest beginning in 1539, with the reconnaissance of the Franciscan friar Márcos de Niza and his black guide, Estévan. Francisco Vásquez de Coronado led a major exploratory expedition up the Rio Grande Valley and east and west across New Mexico from 1540 to 1542. Forty years later some small groups, headed by friars and soldiers such as Brother Agustín Rodríguez and Captain Francisco Sánchez Chamuscado, in 1581–82, and Father Bernardino Beltrán and Antonio de Espejo, in 1582–83, explored through the state. In 1598 a caravan of 400 men (130 brought families), 83 wagons and carts, and more than 7,000 head of stock made its way up the Rio Grande Valley to settle in northern New Mexico. The expedition was led by Don Juan de Oñate, who had contracted with the Spanish crown to colonize northern New Mexico.

Along with the expedition's soldiers came Roman Catholic priests, Franciscan fathers, seeking souls for the church. While some conflict with the Indians was inevitable, by and large Spanish contact with and conquest of Native Americans was probably less violent than was that of the English settlers with Indians on the eastern seaboard. This was probably due in part to the fact that Roman Catholic theologians in Spain decided that the American Indians were human beings with souls; consequently they had certain God-given rights and privileges and were accorded relatively humane treatment as well as legal protection. Also, the Spaniards had a long history of contact with Islamic culture in Spain and with the indigenous peoples of the Caribbean as well as the American mainland. Consequently, relations between the Spaniards and the Pueblo Indians could be described as relatively peaceful, although there were some violent conflicts and some situations involving slavery. The Spanish and Mexican explorers and settlers consisted mainly of males; therefore a substantial amount of intermarriage took place between them and Pueblo Indian women, especially during the eighteenth century, creating a mestizo culture.

Oñate moved up the Rio Grande Valley to its confluence with the Chama River and established camp at the Tewa village of Ohke north of present day Española. This settlement he renamed San Juan de los Caballeros, New Mexico's first mixed cultural capital. A few months later he moved across the Rio Grande and founded San Gabriel. The capital was moved to Santa Fe in the year 1609, a year after Oñate was removed as governor.

The period from 1610 to 1680 was one of increased Spanish colonization along the central and northern Rio Grande Valley. Sporadic but continual conflict occurred between civil and religious authorities, between the Pueblos and the colonies, and between both of these and increasing numbers of Plains Apaches. In 1680 some of the Pueblo Indians decided to revolt against their Spanish rulers. The revolt was primarily planned in Taos Pueblo and led by the San Juan Indian, Popé. Greatly outnumbered, the Spanish, assisted by some Indian allies, retreated down the Rio Grande Valley to El Paso. Twelve years later, in 1692, the Spaniards returned under the leadership of Don Diego de Vargas, in what is sometimes known as the Bloodless Reconquest. However, attempts to resettle Santa Fe were resisted by Indian leaders, and sporadic fighting continued throughout that area until 1696.

Tony Hillerman describes the subsequent century and a half as "one of poverty, government mismanagement and neglect, and sporadic combat between the Spanish and their pueblo Indian allies on the one hand and Navajos, Apaches and Comanche-Kiowa war parties on the other."[10] The major features of life in the northernmost colony of Spain were isolation (from Europe and Mexico, as well as from the developments on the eastern seaboard of the United States) and a struggle for survival against the elements and hostile Indians. Although the territory had been administered by governors responsible to the Spanish crown, the fall of Spain to Napoleon was hardly noted in this distant corner of New Spain. When Mexico won its independence from Spain in 1821, this also had little if any impact on the government of New Mexico. For most people it meant little more than changing the flag over the governor's palace.

When New Spain won its independence in 1821, the outlying areas of the viceroyalty, including New Mexico, also became part of the Mexican nation. While Mexico as a whole entered a long period of national turmoil, the administration in Santa Fe enjoyed fairly stable conditions. With the adoption of the Mexican Constitution of 1824, New Mexico became a territory ruled by a governor (usually a native New Mexican), an advisory legislature, and the traditional local mayors and councils.

During the Mexican period, lasting twenty-five years, the territory of New Mexico was opened to foreign trade. The Santa Fe Trail helped bring more Anglo-American and French-Canadian trappers and traders into the area. Indians were granted full citizenship, and the general policy of protecting their lands was continued. Although discoveries of gold and silver provided some revenue, the government was constantly forced to struggle for survival, due to inadequate finances. When a new ruling group took over Mexico in 1836, an attempt was made to gain tighter federal control over the states and the territory of New Mexico. The result was a revolution in 1837 by some in northern New Mexico. However, the insurrection was quickly crushed, and the central authorities in Mexico again paid little attention to New Mexico. The 1840s were characterized by increased attacks and raids by Indians as well as by Anglo marauders from the Republic of Texas. In 1841 Texas soldiers invaded New Mexico and claimed all the land east of the Rio Grande. Their efforts were thwarted by Gov. Manuel Armijo and an army of volunteers, and the Texan invaders were captured and sent to Mexico City.

The war between Mexico and the United States, which began in 1846, brought the Anglo-American culture into New Mexico in full force. General Stephen Kearny took over Santa Fe without much resistance in August of 1846. Although most New Mexicans had accepted willingly, or at least resigned themselves to, the change in government, at least two revolts, one at Taos and one at Mora, were attempted. In 1847 a rebellion against the U.S. military broke out in Taos. Governor Charles Bent was killed, but the rebellion failed, as it did in Mora. New Mexico became part of the United States under the Treaty of Guadalupe Hidalgo, signed in 1848. Under the terms of the treaty, residents could choose either Mexican or U.S. citizenship. All property and civil rights of the inhabitants were to be protected by the U.S. government. A final portion of New Mexico was added to the United States in 1853, when southwestern New Mexico and Arizona were purchased from Mexico (the Gadsden Purchase). Anglo-American political, economic, and social institutions were superimposed onto the two "native" cultures, but lightly so, as New Mexico did not have the attractions of wealth that might bring in hordes of Anglo-American settlers.

In 1850, New Mexico (which at that time included present-day Arizona, southern Colorado, southern Utah, and southern Nevada) made a first attempt at a constitution and statehood, but this plan did not get anywhere and was nullified by the Compromise Bill of 1850 that gave New Mexico territorial status. Several other attempts were made to make the territory a state. New Mexicans voted against two proposed constitutions in 1872 and 1889, but it was usually the rejection by the U.S. Congress that kept the territory from statehood. New Mexico kept at it, however, and finally, on June 20, 1910, President William H. Taft signed an Enabling Act that authorized the territory to call a constitutional convention in preparation for statehood. On October 3 of that year, one hundred delegates elected from every county in the territory gathered in Santa Fe and drafted a constitution that was approved by voters on January 21, 1911. On January 6, 1912, President Taft signed the proclamation admitting New Mexico as the forty-seventh state. It had taken New Mexico over fifty years and many attempts to attain statehood. After the signing, the president turned to the New Mexico delegation and said, "Well, it is all over. I am glad to give you life. I hope you will be healthy."

New Mexico's role in the Civil War was minor and brief. Confederate troops did try to take over territory in New Mexico, moving up from Confederate Texas through the southeastern part of the territory, up the Rio Grande Valley and on into the north. The cities of Albuquerque and Santa Fe were briefly under Confederate occupation in 1862. This advance was halted when the Confederates were met by Union forces in a battle at Glorieta Pass, between Santa Fe and Las Vegas. The Confederate campaign was curtailed; the Southern forces retreated into Texas, suffering more defeats along the way.

One by one, bands of Navajo and Apache Indians, who had continued their raids and forays against the pueblos and non-Indian villages, were defeated by Colonel Kit Carson and his forces. Many of the Navajos were rounded up and forced on the tragic "Long Walk" to Fort Sumner; others went voluntarily. They were kept there under harsh conditions until 1868, when Congress established the Navajo reservation in northwestern New Mexico and northeastern Arizona, to which the Navajos were relocated. The Apaches were the last Indians to come under the governance of the United States. It was not until 1886 that the last famous Chiricahua chief, Geronimo, was captured.

With the Indians now swept off the eastern plains of New Mexico, the land was seized by Texas ranchers and land-hungry immigrants from the Confederate states who had been displaced by the war. The Hispanic ranchers who had managed to survive in the area were moved out by the southern Anglo immigrants. Some of the hostility between Hispanic ranchers and Texas and southern cowboys who brought their racial perceptions with them lives on even today.

The Mexican and Spanish governments had donated large grants of land to the settlers of northern New Mexico. These grants were given to both villages and individuals and were communally owned and managed. Because the grants were often vague in specifying boundaries and were not properly surveyed according to Anglo-American standards, many of them were lost through legal as well as extralegal means in the U.S. court system. For instance, property taxes were imposed on land-grant inhabitants, and when they were ignored (often the settlers did not even realize the taxes were imposed), the lands were snapped up at bargain prices by Anglo-American lawyers and other entrepreneurs. The fact that great plots of land were taken over by Anglo Americans, often through illegal means, only exacerbated the conflict between the Spanish-American and Anglo-American cultures in northern New Mexico.

The turn of the nineteenth to the twentieth century saw a period of great mining activity, as mining boomtowns sprang up in northern and central New Mexico. These were primarily Anglo-American-owned enterprises, although they were worked by many natives and based upon mining techniques developed by Spanish and Mexican miners.

After unsuccessfully petitioning several times for statehood, New Mexico had become the forty-seventh state of the Union in January 1912. At that time the state had a population of some 330,000 and was a relatively peaceful and quiet area composed of small farms, a few big ranches, and some mining activities. The population was still overwhelmingly composed of the native peoples of the state.

It was not until World War II and the development of atomic energy and defense-related industries that New Mexico became a modern, technologically developed area. Los Alamos was established by the federal government as a secret facility for the development of atomic explosives, and Sandia Base in Albuquerque was charged with developing the weapons for military use. These two centers have brought into the state a great many people who are skilled in technical and professional areas and in management. They have settled primarily in the Los Alamos area and in Albuquerque. The impact of the federal government's programs can be seen in the growth of Albuquerque in Bernalillo County, the state's most urbanized area. In 1940 the population of the area was 35,500. By 1950 the city's population reached 96,815. In 1960 it was 201,190, and the population pushed 300,000 in 1975. The population of the

Albuquerque metropolitan area was 485,431 in 1980 and 589,131 in 1990. The population of the Albuquerque Metropolitan Statistical Area (MSA—Bernalillo, Sandoval, and Valencia counties) was estimated by the Census Bureau at 748,067 residents as of July 2003. That was an increase of 1.7 percent from a year earlier and an increase of 5 percent since the 2000 Census (712, 738).

The historical influx of very different people and cultures has resulted in an interesting pattern of political subcultures in the different geographic areas of the state.[11] Northern and central New Mexico, areas of original Spanish-Mexican settlement, have retained a very distinctive political culture. This area is one of the few places in the United States where individuals of Mexican-Spanish ancestry control the governmental and political institutions of their communities. This pattern has remained the same for the past three hundred years. The people tend to be fairly liberal on socioeconomic matters and conservative or cautious on sociocultural issues. Participation in politics is quite high, and competition between the parties historically has been intense. Another distinct political subculture exists along the eastern side of the state, particularly in the southeastern corner. This part of the state is ideologically, politically, economically, and even geographically tied to the states of Texas and Oklahoma. Ideologies tend to be "southern Democratic," that is, conservative. The northwestern corner of the state, primarily the counties of McKinley and San Juan, has a heavy proportion of New Mexico's Indian population. Indian social, political, and economic systems are, of course, unique. Indian participation in the larger culture's affairs has been minimal, although it is increasing at present. The Anglo population in that area includes a large number of residents who originally came from the southern part of the United States, west Texas, and Oklahoma. They again tend to be fairly conservative on political matters. Los Alamos, being a city and county created by design through actions of the federal government, is sometimes said to possess a unique scientific political culture. The high socioeconomic and educational level of the predominantly Anglo population accounts for the high level of political participation and awareness among area residents. The state's most urbanized area, Bernalillo County, features a very mixed political culture, with a sampling of elements from other parts of the state. In many ways it is a microcosm of the state's political culture, including elements of traditional Hispanic culture, Indian culture, a relatively large black population, an industrial-scientific sector, and some conservative mining and ranching interests. The combination and interaction of all these groups in the state has imparted an interesting and unique flavor to New Mexico's government and politics.

To the outside observer, New Mexico's politics would not seem particularly unusual. With the exception of 1976, New Mexico has always given a plurality of its votes to the same presidential candidate who has received a plurality of the national popular vote, usually in proportions very close to that of the national electorate. It is only when one examines closely the internal workings of New Mexico politics that the full flavor and distinctive quality can be fully appreciated, although perhaps never completely understood.

The very factors that combine so distinctively to produce New Mexico government and politics are certainly not duplicated in any other state in the union. The ethnic mix and institutionalized historical influence of its diverse population are probably the most outstanding features. Nevertheless, from an external perspective New Mexico has often paralleled national trends. Its politics were largely Republican from statehood until the New Deal era. However, party competition in this period was intense, and New Mexico could most accurately be described as a two-party state during that time. As the country turned to the Democratic party during the Great Depression of the 1930s, so did New Mexico. Although the state has remained predominantly Democratic at the local level, it appears to be becoming more Republican in its state and national offices. The state's governors were mainly Democratic until the 1950s, when the governorship again became a two-party contest. In sum, the political history of New Mexico can best be described as modified one-party (Democratic) but changing toward a more Republican and competitive two-party system currently.

PREVIEW

The factors discussed in this chapter provide a setting for the political and governmental life of New Mexico. The following chapters will outline the essence of the state's structure of governance. Finally, a brief overview and conclusion are offered by F. Chris Garcia, Paul Hain, Gilbert St. Clair, and Kim Seckler. Throughout the book we will compare New

Mexico's governmental institutions and practices with those of other states of the Union.

NOTES

1. A southwestern term applied indiscriminately to non-Hispanic, non-Indian, non-black people of the region.
2. Source: U.S. Census Bureau, Census 2000. Unless otherwise noted, the population and economic data in this chapter is from the U.S. Census Bureau, U.S. Department of Commerce, the U.S. Department of Labor, or the University of New Mexico, Bureau of Business and Economic Research.
3. Bureau of Business and Economic Research, "Projection of the Population of New Mexico by Age, Sex, and Race, 1985 to 2010" (Albuquerque: University of New Mexico, 1989).
4. F. Chris Garcia and Robert D. Wrinkle, "New Mexico: Urban Politics in a State of Varying Cultures," in Robert D. Wrinkle, ed., *Politics in the Urban Southwest* (Albuquerque: University of New Mexico, Division of Government, Research Publication no. 81, 1971).
5. Nancie L. Gonzalez, *The Spanish Americans of New Mexico: A Heritage of Pride* (Albuquerque: University of New Mexico Press, 1968).
6. See the series of articles in the *Albuquerque Journal*, January 2–9, 2004.
7. John B. Mondragón and Ernest Stapleton, *Public Education in New Mexico* (Albuquerque: University of New Mexico Press, 2005).
8. Estimates provided by the New Mexico Inter-Church Agency and the Jewish Community Council. Survey evidence comes from the National Survey of Religious Identification, 1989–90, by the City University of New York Graduate School.
9. Frank Hibben, *The Lost Americans* (New York: Thomas Y. Crowell, 1968).
10. Tony Hillerman and David Muench, *New Mexico* (Portland, Ore: Graphic Arts, 1975), p. 37.
11. Jack Holmes, *Politics in New Mexico* (Albuquerque: University of New Mexico Press, 1967).

FOR FURTHER READING

Beck, Warren, *Historical Atlas of New Mexico*. Norman: University of Oklahoma Press, 1969.

Bureau of Business and Economic Research. *New Mexico Business: Current Economic Reports*. Albuquerque: University of New Mexico. [monthly]

Chávez, Fray Angélico. *My Penitente Land*. Albuquerque: University of New Mexico Press, 1974.

———. *Origins of New Mexican Families*. Santa Fe: Historical Society of New Mexico, 1954.

Chávez, Thomas E. *An Illustrated History of New Mexico*. Albuquerque: University of New Mexico Press, 2002.

Dutton, Bertha. *Indians of New Mexico*. Santa Fe: New Mexico Tourist Division, Department of Development, 1973.

Ellis, Richard, ed. *New Mexico Past and Present: A Historical Reader*. Albuquerque:

University of New Mexico Press, 1971.

Etulain, Richard W., ed. *Contemporary New Mexico, 1940–1990*. Albuquerque: University of New Mexico Press, 1994.

Gonzalez, Nancie L. *The Spanish Americans of New Mexico: A Heritage of Pride.* Albuquerque: University of New Mexico Press, 1968.

Hillerman, Tony, and David Muench. *New Mexico.* Portland, Ore.: Graphic Arts, 1975.

Horn, Calvin. *New Mexico's Troubled Years.* Albuquerque: Horn and Wallace, 1963.

Jenkins, Myra Ellen, and Albert H. Schneider. *A Brief History of New Mexico.* Albuquerque: University of New Mexico Press, 1974.

Pearce, T. M., ed. *New Mexico Place Names.* Albuquerque: University of New Mexico Press, 1965.

Price, V. B. *A City at the End of the World.* Albuquerque: University of New Mexico Press, 1992.

Reeve, Frank. *New Mexico: A Short Illustrated History.* Denver: Sage Books, 1964.

Rosner, Hy, and Joan Rosner. *Albuquerque's Environmental Story.* Albuquerque: Albuquerque Public Schools and the City of Albuquerque, 1985.

Scurlock, Dan. *From the Rio to the Sierra: The Environmental History of the Middle Rio Grande Basin.* Fort Collins, Colo.: U.S. Department of Agriculture, Forest Service, Rocky Mountain Research Station, 1998.

Simmons, Marc. *Hispanic Albuquerque, 1706–1846.* Albuquerque: University of New Mexico Press, 2003.

_____. *New Mexico: An Interpretive History.* Rev. ed. Albuquerque: University of New Mexico Press, 1991.

———. *Spanish Government in New Mexico.* Albuquerque: University of New Mexico Press, 1968.

Twitchell, Ralph E. *Leading Facts in New Mexico History.* Cedar Rapids: The Torch Press, 1911–17.

Vigil, Maurilio E., Michael Olsen, and Roy Lujan. *New Mexico Politics and Government.* New York: University Press of America. 1990

Weber, David J. *Foreigners in Their Native Land.* Albuquerque: University of New Mexico Press, 1973.

Weigle, Martha, and Peter White. *The Lore of New Mexico.* Albuquerque: University of New Mexico Press, 1988.

Williams, Jerry L., ed. *New Mexico in Maps.* 2d ed. Albuquerque: University of New Mexico Press, 1986.

Wolf, T. Phillip. *A Bibliography of New Mexico State Politics.* Albuquerque: Division of Government Research, University of New Mexico, Albuquerque: 1974.

Chapter Two

The New Mexico Constitution

Any discussion of the Constitution of New Mexico must start with the acknowledgement that it is a frequently changed document. Like the United States Constitution, the New Mexico Constitution is supposed to be the fundamental framework of government. Unlike its federal counterpart, New Mexico's fundamental structure has undergone a slow but steady remodeling.

The first three editions of this book contain a comprehensive history of the creation of the New Mexico Constitution and changes in the document (and unsuccessful attempts to change it) in its first sixty-odd years, through 1976. The author of that history, Ms. Dorothy Cline, was professor of political science at the University of New Mexico for some three decades and was an elected delegate and a vice president of the 1969 constitutional convention. An abbreviated version of that comprehensive history appears below to provide the reader with insights into the politics involved in the creation of the state constitution and of many of the proposed changes to it. Dick Folmar and Kim Seckler pick up where Professor Cline left off as they detail constitutional changes of the subsequent thirty years. The New Mexico Constitution has changed significantly since Professor Cline's history was written. However, the underlying questions and the pressures on state government have remained surprisingly constant.

CONSTITUTIONAL POLITICS IN
NEW MEXICO, 1910–1976

THE PEOPLE AND THE CONSTITUTION

The purpose of the government of the state of New Mexico is to serve the people of the state and perform its vital functions in the federal system. The shape of the state constitution determines the degree to which all the organs of the state respond effectively, responsibly, and sensibly to human needs in the immediate present and the foreseeable future. What the constitution says, does not say, or says very poorly, facilitates or thwarts the state in carrying out its many and constantly changing tasks.[1] Frank P. Grad, a constitutional expert, writes:

> The least we may demand of our state constitutions is that they interpose no obstacles to the necessary exercise of state powers in response to state residents' real needs and active demands for service. A constitution which meets these needs and demands must be an instrument of government that will enable the state to play its part not only in the traditional activities of state government, but also in accepting and advancing the new functions... that grow out of the increasingly close partnership between the state and federal governments.[2]

New Mexicans have a chronic problem with their organic law, as we shall see. President Taft proclaimed New Mexico a state in January 1912, and within the year, the voters started on a steady course of altering the document.[3] Constitutional politics, beginning with the 1910 constitutional convention, encompasses amendment politics, and the only attempt since statehood to rewrite the constitution in a convention.

THE ENABLING ACT AND THE 1910 CONSTITUTION

New Mexico's constitutional convention, authorized by the 1910 Congressional Enabling Act, consisted of one hundred delegates, elected on a party ballot, whose per diem could not exceed sixty days. Congress required the proposed constitution to be submitted to the voters between sixty and ninety days after the convention adjourned and, if rejected, it directed the governor to call another convention within twenty days.

The Convention: Partisan and Conservative

The convention, meeting on October 3, was firmly controlled by the Republicans (seventy-one delegates, as opposed to twenty-nine Democrats) whose leaders were called the "Old Guard." The body included the most influential territorial leaders in both parties, for as Jack E. Holmes observed: "Party leaders who never before, and never again, held elective office made sure they would be on hand to shape the framework of the new state."[4] The convention, occupationally, was dominated by lawyers and stockmen, joined by merchants, farmers, saloonkeepers, bankers, physicians, newspaper editors, county officers, a sawmill operator, and a college president. One-third were native-born of Spanish descent.

The overriding political goal of the Old Guard was to join the Union, and in order to succeed, they had to write a charter acceptable first of all to the voters, and lastly to a conservative president and a wary Congress. The men who had governed the territory for thirty years, built towns, secured eastern capital, and founded fortunes in banking, mining, railroading, ranching, land speculation, and merchandising, were equal to the delicate and awesome task.

The Old Guard, through a caucus chaired by Holm O. Bursum, elected officers, drafted rules, employed staff, established twenty-seven committees, and arranged committee assignments with the Democrats receiving minority representation. They did not start with the draft of a proposed constitution; however, they knew what they wanted and how to proceed; several delegates had served in an earlier constitutional convention held in 1889.

The battle lines were drawn between the conservative Republicans and the progressive Democrats from the beginning to the end of the convention. The division was prophesied by Holm Bursum, chairman of the Republican Central Committee during the contest for delegate seats: "The line of cleavage will hinge more on politics as advocated by what has become commonly known as conservatives and radicals or progressives. The dividing line will be whether or not the constitution should contain prohibitions and limitations as well as providing for definite policies with reference to various interests."[5] Determined to stimulate economic development, the Old Guard proposed to write a constitution that would encourage corporations to come into the state and protect those already in existence. The central theme of Harvey B. Fergusson, the eloquent minority leader, was "the struggle of the poor and the humble against their oppressors."[6] The villains were the trusts, Wall Street, the corporations, and the big bosses of Valencia, San Miguel, Socorro, and Colfax counties, who were writing a constitution, "made for the benefit not of the whole people of the state, but for special interests, especially those who desire to escape their share of taxation."[7]

The Republicans, using "gag rules" (rules imposing limits on debate) turned back every attempt to adopt some of the progressive reforms appearing in other state constitutions. They struck down the initiative (a means whereby the people can initiate legislation) after a great debate; rendered the referendum (the submission of a proposed law to a direct popular vote) unworkable; approved the nomination and election of judges and district attorneys on a party ballot; adopted the long ballot requiring the governor to share power with eight executives; created a weak corporation commission; and placed rigid and detailed restrictions on taxing, borrowing, and spending powers. The document included a mass of legislative and transitory material; prohibitions, limitations, prescriptions, and definitions fixing the powers of state government, executives, legislators, judges, boards, commissions, institutions, officials of local government, school districts, and the voters. The Amendment Article was intended to make the constitution impervious to change but the provisions were so repugnant to Congress that the voters were given an opportunity to alter the article. (The "blue ballot" amendment was adopted in November 1911, marking the first change in the pristine constitution.)

Unique Features of the Document

Party leaders were keenly aware that the constitution could not win a majority vote unless it accommodated the deeply rooted, cultural, and traditional values of the citizens of Hispanic ancestry. So, for the first and only time in the convention, the Democrats, champions of "the common man," joined with the Old Guard, to write a document, unique among the states, for the extraordinary civil, religious, and political rights granted to a group of people. Holmes believes that "New Mexico can perhaps take credit for being the first to have given Calhoun's doctrine of the concurrent majority a formal expression that governs a major aspect of politics *within* a state."[8]

The most significant provisions were written into Articles II, VII, XII, and XX:

II. Bill of Rights
The rights, privileges and immunities, civil, political and religious, guaranteed to the people of New Mexico by the Treaty of Guadalupe Hidalgo shall be preserved inviolate. (sec. 5)

VII. Elective Franchise
Every male citizen of the United States who is a legal resident of the State and is a qualified elector therein, shall be qualified to hold any public office in the state.... (sec. 2)

   The right of any citizen of the State to vote, hold office, or sit upon juries, shall never be restricted, abridged or impaired on account of religion, race, language, or color, or inability to speak, read or write the English or Spanish languages, except as may otherwise be provided in this constitution.... (sec. 3)

XII. Education
The legislature shall provide for the training of teachers in the normal schools or otherwise so that they may become proficient in both the English and Spanish languages...; and shall provide proper means and methods to facilitate the teaching of the English language...to such pupils and students. (sec. 8)

   No religious test shall ever be required as a condition of admission into the public schools or any educational institution of this state, either as a teacher or student, and no teacher or student... shall ever be required to attend or participate in any religious service whatsoever. (sec. 9)

   Children of Spanish descent in the State of New Mexico shall never be denied the right and privilege of admission and attendance in the public schools or other public educational institutions... and they shall never be classed in separate schools..., and the legislature shall provide penalties for the violation of this section. (sec. 10)

   The Spanish American School at El Rito is confirmed as a state educational institution. (sec. 11)

XX. Miscellaneous
For the first twenty years after the constitution goes into effect all
laws passed by the legislature shall be published in both the English
and Spanish languages. (sec. 12)
    The use of wines solely for sacramental purposes under
church authority at any place within the state shall never be
prohibited. (sec. 13)

The desire to protect the document from radical changes in the future
caused the delegates to freeze four sections into the constitution, since
called the "unamendables." This was achieved by requiring extraordinary
majorities for proposing and ratifying an amendment, that is, the approval
of the proposed amendment by three-fourths of the members elected
to each house of the state legislature, and ratification by at least three-
fourths of the electors in the state voting on the question and at least a
two-thirds majority of the voters in each county. (See sections 1 and 3,
Article VII, Elective Franchise; sections 8 and 10, Article XII, Education.)
They forestalled changing section 1, Article VII, by subjecting it to conditions laid down in sections 1 and 5, Article XIX, Amendments.
    President Charles Spiess, the presiding officer of the convention,
underscored the significance of these measures when he told the delegates: "You have by its provisions guaranteed the equal protection of the
law to every citizen of New Mexico; you have preserved the religious, political, social and civil rights to every one of our citizens, and placed them
beyond the power of assault from any source whatsoever."[9]
    The convention completed its work on November 21—well short of
the sixty-day deadline; the constitution, running to 21,227 words, was
signed by all but six delegates—dissident Democrats. President Spiess
hailed it as "one of the grandest documents ever written for a people."[10]

REFERENDUM CAMPAIGN AND ADOPTION

When the delegates left Santa Fe, they had two months to campaign.
The victorious Republicans had money, a superb statewide organization, an abundance of party workers, and the support of most of the
press. The Democratic party was feeble, poverty-stricken, and divided
on ratification. Fergusson favored statehood but argued a second convention would produce a more progressive constitution. Many

Democrats, however, refused to risk statehood and joined the ratification movement.

The Republicans portrayed the constitution as steering a safe course between "socialist" and "reactionary" politics. It offered the people stability, order, a limited government, and economic development, and they said, it would be acceptable to the president and Congress. According to the Albuquerque *Morning Journal*, it was a "safe and sane" constitution. Fergusson countered by firing a volley of shots at the Old Guard:

> I am fighting this constitution because I saw the crowd who made it, and how they made it . . . the men who have ruled our legislatures in the past, the bosses who came out of the counties with power built on discrimination and favoritism . . . that explains why the vital safeguards for the people were left out, it explains why there is a joker in almost every passage relating to the essential matters of public welfare . . . [11]

The constitution was ratified on election day, January 21, 1911, by a thumping three to one majority (31,742 to 13,399), and in all counties except Roosevelt, Lincoln, San Juan, and Sierra.

STATE GOVERNMENT AND THE CONSTITUTION UNDER PRESSURE

The first serious discussion of the constitution emerged thirty-seven years after statehood and the adoption of thirty amendments. In 1949, Governor Thomas J. Mabry, a "Founding Father," disturbed about the increasing number of piecemeal amendments, stated: "We can't go too long now without calling a convention to rewrite the constitution. This patchwork system . . . is not working well. The people are not sufficiently interested and often not sufficiently informed."[12]

The governor was reacting perhaps not so much to the amending process as to the terrific impact of World War II developments in New Mexico originating with the Manhattan Project at Los Alamos. State officials were inundated with unprecedented problems: the rise of boom towns, a burgeoning population, rapid growth of scientific and military facilities, the multiplication of federally funded programs, dwindling counties, and at the same time, the emergence of the state's first metropolitan area, Greater Albuquerque. Demands mounted for schools, highways, playgrounds, hospitals, and homes. City and county governments grappled with urban sprawl, annexations, planning, zoning, refuse disposal, traffic, public safety, and fire protection.

Little Hoover Committee Initiates Reform

The pressures prompted Governor Edwin L. Mechem, elected in 1950 with a "good government" image, to support the creation of the State Reorganization Committee to study New Mexico government and make recommendations intended "to promote greater efficiency and greater economy of effort and money in the exercise of state government."[13] The Little Hoover Committee, as it was called,[14] submitted a report a year later[15] that was remarkable for its substantial influence over the years on research, constitutional revision, and reorganization of state government. The committee was the first to apply the "principles" of reorganization developed in the 1930s to New Mexico state government, and it laid the groundwork for later studies, legislation, piecemeal amendments, the 1969 constitutional convention, and efforts by successive governors to reorder the executive branch. The core principles consisted of: centralizing administrative responsibility and authority in the governor as chief executive; establishing sound personnel, budget, and fiscal programs; grouping together all the executive agencies performing similar and related functions; and consolidating the latter into a small number of departments with heads appointed by the governor and serving as a cabinet. The committee offered a long list of recommendations, most of which could be implemented by the legislature or the governor, while others could not be achieved without amending the constitution. The latter included the proposal to consolidate 134 executive agencies into 12 departments under the governor which, of course, impinged upon the legal powers of the independently elected state executives.[16] Over the next ten years, many of the committee's proposals were implemented by legislation, executive orders, and amendments.[17] At the same time, many reform leaders, anxious to achieve more basic changes in the executive department, pursued the idea of calling a convention.

Constitutional Revision Commission Established

By 1963, newly elected Democratic governor Jack M. Campbell declared it was time to make "essential changes" in the constitution, and persuaded the legislature to establish the state's first Constitutional Revision

Commission,[18] which was authorized to conduct research, recommend changes in the constitution, and *draft implementing legislation and proposed constitutional recommendations.* [Italics added]

Fourteen months later, the commission reported to Governor Campbell, listing several recommendations for "immediate attention:" a referendum on calling a convention; extending the commission for two years; repealing section 1, Article XIX, and, if approved, repealing section 5 of Article XIX; extending the governor's time to sign bills; amending the constitution to provide for reapportionment, a legislative post-audit, a judicial commission, a court of appeals, and an appointive system for district and supreme court judges.[19]

Granted a two-year extension, the Revision Commission pushed ahead with hearings, research, and analysis, and sent its final report in January 1966 to incoming Republican governor David F. Cargo.[20] The commission again urged the calling of a convention and recommended specific provisions for the Enabling Act.

Voters Approve a Convention

The 1967 legislature approved the convention proposal and set the referendum for the November 8, 1968, general election. The pro-Call campaign was spearheaded by the State League of Women Voters, while the New Mexico Livestock Bureau opposed the Call.

The reformers won easily—by a better than two to one majority. However, those who approved the Call represented only 18 percent of the eligible voters. Subsequently, the 1969 legislature passed an Enabling Act[21] that provided for the nonpartisan election of seventy delegates on June 17, 1969 (one from each legislative district), meeting August 5, 1969, for no more than sixty calendar days.

There was a light vote on June 17, 1969. The elected delegates included forty-eight Democrats, twenty-one Republicans, and one Independent ranging in age from twenty-four to seventy-two. There were fifty-three Anglos, sixteen Hispanos, one Native American, and nine women. The delegates were well educated, pursued twenty occupations with the largest number (57 percent) engaged in law, ranching, farming, and education. No more than three or four had a power base in state politics for, unlike 1910, the post failed to attract influential party leaders, former state officials, governors, university presidents, or congressmen, although former speaker of the House of Representatives Bruce King served as president.[22]

The Explosive Issues

All but a very few of the convention proposals were thrashed out in committees[23] and on the convention floor without party considerations. The important, certainly the most controversial, questions were decided on ideological grounds. At one end of the spectrum were those few delegates who insisted on keeping the constitution intact, and at the other were those who advocated drastic reforms. The former might be described as ultraconservative while delegates who championed substantial changes in the *form and structure* of state government could not always also be classified as liberals on social and economic issues. The overriding purpose of convention leaders was to forge compromises with moderate conservatives, moderate liberals, and reformers. Urban representatives tended to be more liberal and reform-minded than those from rural areas and small towns. Delegates from the second (southern) congressional district were less liberal and wanted fewer major changes than those from the first. While Hispanos voted with the liberals on many issues, they opposed reform measures that contravened traditional values and political customs. The hotly contested proposals that came perilously close to ending the convention reflected the enormous changes that had swept across New Mexico and the nation since the early 1900s and produced the New Deal.

The convention's most divisive proposals sought fundamental changes in the executive and judicial articles. The legislative, local government, and education articles contained significant but easily understood reforms while modest or technical changes appeared in the remaining articles.[24] The Executive Committee focused on the basic fault in the constitution—New Mexico's plural executive. (The 1910 delegates adopted the long ballot for pragmatic reasons: the patronage flowing from the offices fortified Republican party control of state and local government; and it was a popular arrangement with the voters.) Witnesses verified what had been known for many years: that each elective official not only had separate and autonomous legal powers, but independent personal party ties, organizational and factional alliances, campaign organizations, and constituencies.

The committee majority concluded that taxpayers could no longer afford to "support a horde of conflicting, overlapping, uncoordinated agencies, or a government that cannot deliver services that are essential to their well being.... The plain fact is the governor of this state is not able to govern under a system of divided and irresponsible government."[25] To remedy the situation, the convention recommended eliminating the elected offices of secretary of state, attorney general, and state treasurer, permitting the governor to consolidate agencies, appoint directors, and form a cabinet. The convention retained the State Corporation Commission until changed by the legislature, and provided the executives with two four-year terms. After a heated battle over appointed versus elected state judges, the delegates voted two to one for continuing the election of state judges.

The reports of other committees contained proposals that became highly contentious on the convention floor: reducing the voting age to eighteen; the right to bear arms for hunting and recreation; prohibiting the denial of civil rights on account of economic condition; including education as a basic right; constitutionalizing the Human Rights Commission; home rule for cities; and transferring the budgetary control of the public schools from the executive to the State Board of Education.

The majority report of the Bill of Rights Committee provoked a stormy debate after which the convention, for the first and only time, rejected the report and accepted the minority report, consisting of Article I of the existing constitution with slight modifications.

A divisive tactical question arose throughout the convention: whether to offer the voters alternatives by placing the "three or four" most controversial issues on the ballot apart from the main body of the document. The single package won by default since the matter was too complicated to explore after the convention got under way.

The Shape of the Document

The delegates tried to follow expert advice by writing a short, precisely worded, well-integrated document, omitting legislative material. Most of the objectives were accomplished by removing outmoded, unnecessary provisions, sharpening the language, and rearranging and synthesizing sections and articles. The failure to confine the document to fundamental law was due to the history of constitutional revision in New Mexico, entrenched special interests, and the delegates' understandable inability to make a realistic distinction between "fundamental" and "legislative" material. The 1910 document with twenty-three articles, seventy-two amendments, and twenty-four thousand words was transformed into fourteen articles with fifteen thousand words.

The Referendum Campaign: Voters Say No

The striking feature of the forty-seven-day campaign was the weak position of the constitution's supporters and the gathering strength of the opponents. The proponents moved into the final stretch without money, leadership, or campaign materials. For some reason, early and influential backers of constitutional reform failed to establish a citizens' coalition and a statewide public information program. Opposition leaders had different reasons for defending the status quo: Democrats fearful of losing patronage and longtime control of state government; businesses regulated by the Corporation Commission, fearful of losing established relationships; sportsmen, fearful of losing the independency of the Game and Fish Commission; key legislators, fearful of a strong executive; elected executives, fearful of losing a power base in state politics. Those with the most to lose tapped grassroots organizations and county courthouses, mounted a full-scale attack on the short ballot while gaining additional support from Hispanos who thought the document undermined the extraordinary rights guaranteed in 1910. On December 9 the proposal lost by a hair's breadth with one-third of the eligible voters making the eventful decision.

TRENDS SINCE STATEHOOD

The 1910 delegates produced a document that could only respond to twentieth century developments in science, technology, urbanization, and federalism by undergoing continuous revision. Six generations of New Mexicans have attempted to make these adjustments, with varying degrees of success.

By 1974 the constitution contained ninety-one amendments with only four of the original twenty-three substantive articles intact. The Legislative Article had been most frequently changed with eighteen amendments, followed by Taxation and Revenue with thirteen revisions, the Executive, Judicial, and Education with eight amendments each. Those most impervious to change were the Bill of Rights and Elective Franchise—four each, and Corporations, Public Lands, Irrigation and Water Rights, Mines and Mining, each with a single amendment.

An election without an amendment on the ballot is becoming a rare phenomenon for New Mexicans. In the 1970s, 1980s, and 1990s every general election had proposed constitutional amendments on the ballot. Close to half of the 188 amendments submitted to the voters from 1912 to 1974 became a part of the constitution. During the first twenty-nine years of statehood, the voters adopted 40 percent of the proposals while approving 51 percent over the last thirty years. The trend is more impressive for ten-year intervals. The voters in the elections held during the 1920s accepted 26 percent of the proposals, while those in the 1960s ratified 52 percent of the amendments and voters in the 1980s adopted almost 67 percent of proposals put forth by the legislature.

Politics in General and Special Elections

Whether to place an amendment on the ballot in the general election or in a special election is an important legislative decision since the distinctive political features of the two elections leave their imprint on the constitution. The essential differences relate to the size of the vote, the nature of the campaigns, and the characteristics of the men and women who move into the political arena for each event.

Political parties, fighting for the control of offices and public policy making, activate the party machinery, and corral hard-core workers who, with masses of campaign materials and door-to-door canvassing, turn out the voters on election day. Since more people participate in a general election, it is not surprising that an amendment has a 14 percent better chance of being adopted than in a special election. Even so, the fate of the proposal often depends on the wishes of a minority of general election voters. An evaluation of election returns for the 1960s and '70s show that 52 percent to 64 percent of those who voted for governor failed to express any opinion about the amendment. Yet, paradoxically, these voters have less information about the issues than those who go to the polls in a special election since political parties concentrate on the election of candidates and sidestep amendments for fear of alienating potential supporters. An exception is noteworthy: if the party per se has a vital stake in the adoption or rejection of an amendment, it has the influence and resources to determine the outcome of the election.

Special elections, on the other hand, are dominated by private organizations and special interest groups who move onstage for the single purpose of adopting or defeating an amendment or tax levy. Fewer workers, compared with party activists, conduct intensive campaigns for a smaller-sized electorate, appealing to those voters who are strongly attached to issues and causes. One of the distinguishing features of the two elections is that the individual who votes in a special election carries more weight in shaping the constitution than the person who votes in a general election because of the smaller number of voters participating.

The "Unamendables"

The section of the 1910 constitution requiring "extraordinary majorities" for the passage of amendments has blocked continuous efforts by state officials and public interest groups to adjust the document to changing times. Allowing New Mexicans to vote by absentee ballot is a superb example of the serious impediment placed in Section 1, Article VII. An amendment providing absentee voting first appeared on the ballot in 1919 and, after failing to pass, it reappeared in eleven subsequent elections. When the actions of two legislatures, designed to void the "extraordinary majorities" provisions, were declared unconstitutional, it seems these could only be changed by a constitutional convention. However, the New Mexico Supreme Court issued a landmark decision in 1968, legalizing absentee voting by declaring the passage of the amendment constitutional despite its failure to achieve the two-thirds majority in twelve counties.[26] After forty-nine years, this specific issue was resolved, and by the court, but the case may or may not set a precedent when future courts are asked to determine the outcome of an election on other issues or amendments requiring the majorities. In the absence of court rulings, the only recourse is to rewrite the sections in a convention and secure their adoption.

The Executive

The only valiant endeavor since statehood to alter the basic provision in the Executive Article failed in 1969 for the chief reason that many New Mexicans have a deep and emotional attachment to the long ballot. To be sure, the features of the office of governor altered through the years as governors assumed increasing responsibilities for budgeting, financial administration, personnel, planning, purchasing, and federally funded programs, and on occasions, employed political means to set policy, control boards and commissions, and coordinate key agencies. Nevertheless, the branch is headed by a plural executive and the legal structure will be retained until the voters are convinced they are ill served by a galaxy of agencies that compete among themselves and with the governor for political power, programs, allegiances, and tax dollars.

Constitution Writing

New Mexico voters have actually served as delegates to a continuing constitutional convention since statehood, writing and rewriting fundamental law every two or four years, while giving scant thought to the political realities of the revision process. There can be little doubt that piecemeal revision, as practiced in the state, has thrust enormous burdens on the citizens. In just the last few years, they have grappled with a cornucopia of tough problems, such as banking, taxes, indebtedness, the courts, the legislature, powers of municipalities and counties, and whether to foster stability and continuity in state government or create new centers of political influence. It is presumed, of course, that the individual citizen is fully capable of making these judgments, has ready access to reliable information,[27] the time to study each proposal, and a compelling desire to be a "good citizen" by voting. We know that only a minority exhibit these qualities, and they do remarkably well under the circumstances.

The piece-by-piece approach poses yet another problem for legislators and voters. A constitution must be viewed as a *whole* statement, written in a clear, compact form—as were the early, model state constitutions—with all the parts meshed into the total document. Piecemeal revision encourages people to think of the charter as merely a shapeless collection of separate, unrelated sections and articles. Hence, it is no wonder the constitution embodies superfluous, antiquated, verbose, and contradictory provisions or that the attorney general and the courts have been asked frequently to interpret the document. While the legislature turns on the flow of piecemeal proposals and conditions the qualitative features of the constitution, it has neither arranged for a continuous review of the condition of the constitution, which was a convention recommendation, nor deliberately fostered the passage of *whole* articles as single

amendments.[28] One authority offers the more general and inclusive "comprehensive" amendment as a practical option lying midway between a
convention and piecemeal revision.[29]

The future of constitutional revision in New Mexico is unclear. While
piecemeal revision has a firm hold in the state, customs are broken and
bent by unusual events and perspicacious leaders. Voters may yet be persuaded to approve a convention and a newly written constitution.

Recent Constitutional Activity

Since Dorothy Cline penned this original chapter in 1974, the New Mexico
Constitution has continued to undergo steady piecemeal change. From
1970 to 2005, the legislature submitted over one hundred proposed
amendments to the New Mexico Constitution for approval or rejection
by the voters. A majority (approximately 64 percent) of those proposals were adopted by the voters and constitute additional change to the
basic 1910 document.[30] Many of these amendments have made fundamental changes to the basic structure and operation of state government.
Others affected the actual amendment process. Some of the more significant are presented below.

CONSTITUTIONAL REVISION

Perhaps in light of the state's steady piecemeal constitutional revision,
the 1993 legislature authorized the creation of a temporary, appointed
Constitutional Revision Commission. The commission was charged with
examining the Constitution of New Mexico and the constitutions of
other states and making recommendations for change.[31] Working
through most of 1994 and 1995, the commission concluded its work in
December 1995, ultimately making a number of findings and recommendations. The recommended changes were prioritized by the commission from highest to lowest priority. The highest priority changes were
both procedural and substantive. They included establishing an additional mechanism for amendment that would include more than
piecemeal revision but less than an entirely new document (as would
occur with a constitutional convention); clarifying the 75 percent affirmative vote requirement necessary to amend the historic "unamendable"
sections while abolishing the two-thirds affirmative vote in each county
requirement;[32] and authorizing the secretary of state to engage in voter

education for proposed amendments but removing legal notice requirements. These proposals were approved by the voters in the 1996 general election. The Constitutional Revision Commission also
recommended a number of substantive changes to legislative and executive provisions of the constitution. Legislative proposals included the
establishment of legislative compensation, more time for governors to
view bills passed by the legislature, and the establishment of an independent auditor general. By and large these proposals have yet to be submitted to the electorate. Proposals related to the executive branch have
been more successful with legislators agreeing to propose and voters
approving changes to utility regulation, the State Board of Education,
and investment of permanent funds.

While the efforts of the Constitutional Revision Commission were
extensive and comprehensive, their work represents only a portion of the
constitutional change that has occurred in the last thirty years. Gradual
change, in the form of piecemeal amendments approved by the voters,
has affected the executive, legislative, and judicial branches, education,
local government, and public finance.

EXECUTIVE BRANCH

New Mexico continues to experiment with length of terms for its elected
officials. In the beginning of statehood, the constitution provided a four-
year term for state officials. In 1914 it was amended to reduce the terms
to two years, with the right of succession for one additional term. In 1970
the voters approved one four-year term with no immediate right of succession. The lieutenant governor was the only state officer allowed to run
immediately for another state office, the office of the governor.[33] In 1986
Constitutional Amendment No. 11 was adopted by the voters to permit
state officers elected in 1990 and thereafter to serve two consecutive four-
year terms. It also permits a state officer to hold another elective state
office immediately after the term of the original office has expired. With
his election to a second term in 1998, Governor Gary Johnson became
the first governor in the history of the state to serve eight consecutive
years in office.

One long-standing problem with respect to the governor's power
to remove appointed officials was corrected by the adoption of
Constitutional Amendment No. 2 in 1988. Previous to this change, Article 5,

Section 5, of the New Mexico Constitution stated that the governor could only remove gubernatorial appointees by charging "incompetency, neglect of duty or malfeasance in office." In the case of most removals, governors are only trying to place their own people in these jobs, and it was patently unjust and unfair to charge otherwise honest and capable officials as required by the constitution. Under the 1988 amendment, most (though not all) appointees serve at the pleasure of the governor; they may now be removed without stating a reason for doing so.

LEGISLATIVE BRANCH

In 1976, Constitutional Amendment No. 7 for the first time in the history of the state placed a limitation on the size of both houses of the legislature. Under the change the House of Representatives was restricted to a maximum of seventy members and the Senate to a maximum of forty-two. The importance of that amendment went beyond guaranteeing the adequacy of seating in the respective chambers and the availability of office space. It also reduced the flexibility of the legislature in reapportionment legislation; previously, political deadlocks in creating districts could be sidestepped by increasing the memberships by one or more seats.

Legislative compensation continues to be an oft-considered subject. A 1982 amendment increased the allowed per diem for each member from forty to seventy-five dollars; the mileage reimbursement was also increased; and the payment of per diem and mileage to legislators for service on interim committees was authorized.[34] This section was amended again in 1996 to remove specific per diem and mileage standards in favor of the more flexible and ever-increasing federal IRS standards. As of 2005, voters have failed to approve legislative compensation in excess of per diem and mileage reimbursements. New Mexico remains one of only a handful of states that fail to provide a legislative salary or compensation for legislative expenses.

Though the constitution prohibits legislators from receiving a salary for service, legislators have authorized a legislative retirement plan by statute. Article 4, Section 3, of the constitution authorizes the legislative payment of per diem and mileage and no other compensation, perquisite, or allowance. It is that constitutional provision on which Attorney General Hal Stratton based his 1988 challenge to the twenty-five-year-old legislative retirement plan. In an effort to validate the statutory plan and to authorize a maximum six-thousand-dollar annual retirement annuity, Constitutional Amendment No. 1 was submitted to the voters at the November 8, 1988, general election. It was the only one of seven proposed amendments rejected by the voters. Though voters failed to approve the amendment, the retirement benefit continues as Stratton eventually lost his challenge when the New Mexico Supreme Court upheld the validity of the statutory retirement plan.[35]

Though voters have failed to authorize legislative salaries, they have authorized additional interim work. Constitutional Amendment No. 6 (1986) allowed the Senate to designate an appropriate standing committee to operate as an interim committee for the purpose of conducting hearings and taking testimony on the confirmation or rejection of gubernatorial appointees. This committee is then charged with the responsibility of making its recommendations to the Senate at the next succeeding session. Not surprisingly, the Senate named its Rules Committee to perform this function.[36]

JUDICIAL BRANCH

After rejection by the voters in 1952 and 1982, as well as being turned down by the 1969 constitutional convention, the concept of a merit system for the selection of justices of the Supreme Court and judges of the Court of Appeals, district court, and metropolitan court was approved by voters in 1988. After voters approved the change, the amendment was challenged by Benjamin Anthony Chavez, a successful candidate for the Court of Appeals, and Petra Jimenez Maes, a state district judge. The petitioners argued that submission of the constitutional amendment by the even-year legislature violated Article 4, Section 5, of the constitution, which limits the subject matter of the even-year regular sessions to (1) budgets, appropriations, and revenue bills; (2) bills drawn pursuant to special messages of the governor; and (3) bills of the last previous regular session vetoed by the governor. The petitioners also argued that the authority under Article 19, Section 1, for the legislature to submit proposed constitutional amendments at regular sessions did not extend to even-year regular sessions, since at the time Article 19 was adopted, regular annual sessions were not contemplated, and further, that Section 5 of that article prohibited any change in Section 1 except by constitutional convention.[37]

All but one of the sitting members of the Supreme Court recused themselves; the petition was ultimately heard by Justice Richard Ransom and four appointed district judges. The importance of the Court's decision was not to be underestimated. At stake was not only the fate of the judicial reform provision that had been adopted by a margin of 43,552, or 56 percent of the vote, but also the possible validity of twenty-one other provisions of the constitution previously submitted by even-year regular sessions of the legislature.[38]

In a unanimous decision the Court disagreed with petitioners Chavez and Maes holding that the term "regular session" in Article 19, Section 1, has consistently been interpreted to mean "other than a special or extraordinary session." It said that the purpose of the framers was to limit the introduction of amendments to regular as opposed to special sessions, rather than to limit amendments to odd-numbered regular sessions. As for the argument that Article 4, Section 5, precludes the introduction of constitutional amendments in even-year sessions, the Court said that the petitioner's argument "fails to take into account the limited scope of Article IV." In other words, when the legislature submits amendments to the voters, it does so under the provisions of Article 19, Section 1, and not Article 4.[39]

The *Chavez* decision cleared the way for implementation of a new method for the selection of judges. Under the modified merit selection system, judicial candidates are selected by the governor from a list of qualified candidates. New judges then run in a partisan election—in the first general election following their appointment. Once elected, however, they do not face an opposing candidate in subsequent elections. Instead, the only name on the ballot is that of the sitting judge, and the object of the election is the question of his or her retention or rejection. A 1994 amendment raised the bar on retention, requiring that all judges receive at least 57 percent of the votes cast to retain their seat. If for any reason the office becomes vacant, a nominating commission composed of judges, lawyers, and lay people submit the names of qualified successors to the governor, from which he or she must fill the position by appointment until the next succeeding general election. The amendment also increased the age and legal-practice requirements for justices and judges. The amendment does not apply to most of New Mexico's limited jurisdiction trial courts, namely the magistrate, municipal, and probate courts.

Finally, a 2002 amendment (Constitutional Amendment No. 3) to the constitution repealed the constitutional limitation on the number of judicial districts. For many years the legislature had authorized by statute more judicial districts than constitutionally permitted. The 2002 repeal brought the constitution into conformance with actual practice.

EDUCATION

In 1986 voters approved Constitutional Amendment No. 7, to change the structure of the State Board of Education. The change provided staggered four-year terms for the ten elected members of the board. It also allowed the governor to appoint, with the advice and consent of the Senate, five additional members to the board for staggered four-year terms. The addition of the five appointed members was in the way of a compromise, to compensate for the loss of the governor's authority over functions relating to the distribution of school funds and financial accounting for public schools. The 1986 amendment transferred fiscal control from the Office of Education in the Department of Finance and Administration (under the authority of the governor) to the State Department of Education.

Between 1986 and 2003, the fifteen-member board oversaw the State Department of Education, determined educational policy, and appointed the chief administrative officer, the superintendent of public instruction. Nonetheless, the relative autonomy of the state board and the inability of the governor to hire or fire the superintendent of public instruction proved a steady irritant to some occupants of the governor's office. In 2003, in a now rare special election, voters were asked to amend Article 12, Section 6, to return control of the Department of Education to the governor's office. The few voters voting in the special election obliged and in November of that year, the state board became a public education commission and the position of state superintendent was abolished in favor of a secretary of education within the governor's cabinet. At the same special election voters were also asked to allow the state to dig deeper into the state permanent fund, increasing the annual distribution for public schools. Fewer voters approved of this, the only other question on the ballot, but proposed Constitutional Amendment No. 2 did pass with a margin of victory of less than two hundred votes.[40]

In addition to changes to state education governance, voters have been asked to consider local school-board changes as well. In 1973, the voters adopted Constitutional Amendment No. 3, which provided for the recall elections of local school-board members. A later (1986) amendment allowed the legislature to provide the procedures for such recall by law.

LOCAL GOVERNMENTS

Constitutional Amendment No. 1, adopted by the voters in 1970, conferred upon municipalities the right to adopt a charter of home rule. Under such a charter, a municipality was given the authority to exercise all legislative powers and perform all functions not expressly denied by general law or charter. That grant of power did not include the power to enact private or civil laws governing civil relationships except as part of the exercise of independent municipal power, nor did it include the power to provide for a penalty greater than a petty misdemeanor.[41]

Thirty years later the legislature proposed a related constitutional amendment, this one allowing voters to adopt home-rule status for Bernalillo County. The proposed constitutional amendment (Constitutional Amendment No. 1) called for a vote and enabled any registered voter in Bernalillo County to vote on the question of whether the county should become an "urban" county. The constitutional amendment authorizing the vote passed in November 2000. However, when Bernalillo County voted in December 2001 to decide whether or not to adopt "urban" status, few people turned up at the polls, and those who did turned down the proposal. A second part of Constitutional Amendment 1 authorized a separate vote on a companion proposal, one providing for the consolidation of Albuquerque city and Bernalillo County governments in a "unification" move. This, too, was defeated by Bernalillo County voters in 2003.

While many of the constitutional amendments relating to local government have dealt with issues of governance, others have addressed election issues. Under the provisions of Constitutional Amendment No. 7, adopted in 1988, the board of county commissioners of any county could, by unanimous vote, adopt a five- instead of a three-member board. If a five-member board is adopted, the members run from single-member districts for staggered terms of four years (two years prior, the voters authorized local governing bodies to elect their members from single-member districts).[42] Before the adoption of this amendment, the constitution had authorized five-member boards of county commissioners only for counties having certain valuations and populations. In 1992, Article 10 was again amended to provide for uniform, staggered four-year terms for all county officers. A 2000 proposed amendment to remove term limits for county officials failed by a substantial margin and a 1996 amendment authorizing recall of county officials passed by an equally substantial margin.[43]

In November 2004, voters approved a constitutional amendment to allow municipalities to provide by charter or by ordinance for municipal runoff elections. Prior to the change, New Mexico courts had determined that municipal runoff elections were not supported by then existing constitutional language.

INDEPENDENT CONSTITUTIONAL ENTITIES

Since the early days of statehood, the adjudication of workers' compensation claims was deemed to be a matter solely for the courts. A 1957 state Supreme Court decision held that any administrative (that is, executive) determination of such claims was a violation of the separation of powers doctrine of our state constitution. Through the years, New Mexico remained one of only two states in the country where an administrative determination of such claims was not permitted. In 1986, however, two events changed this position. The Supreme Court reversed the 1957 decision, and the voters adopted Constitutional Amendment No. 10. This amendment to Article 3, Section 1, explicitly authorized the legislature to establish by statute an administrative body with statewide jurisdiction to decide workers' compensation actions. As a result, the 1987 legislature enacted the Workers' Compensation Law.

Like many western states, New Mexico's 1910 Constitution created a State Corporation Commission to regulate developing industry. Over the years, the State Corporation Commission regulated insurance, transportation, and telecommunications. Eventually the legislature created, by statute, the Public Utility Commission to regulate other industries in the state. Advocates for reform recommended restructuring the State Corporation Commission and, in 1996, voters obliged by abolishing the three-member, elected-at-large State Corporation Commission and replacing it with the five-member, districted Public Regulation Commission (PRC). The PRC is a combination of the State Corporation Commission and the Public Utility Commission. It is granted broad constitutional regulatory authority over all public utilities, business corporations, transportation companies, transmission and pipeline companies, and insurance companies.[44]

Finally, in a change of semantics more than function, voters in 2002 agreed to change the name of the powerful State Highway Commission, replacing it with the more modern moniker—the State Transportation Commission—also renaming the Highway Department the Department of Transportation.[45]

PUBLIC FINANCE

Though other portions of this text address New Mexico's public-finance structure, we would be remiss not to mention the considerable recent changes to the constitution in this area. These changes cover many areas and include distributions from state permanent funds, valuation of property and property tax exemptions, and county borrowing authorizations.

Perhaps most significant of these amendments was Constitutional Amendment No. 1, passed in 1996, that changed the way the state invests and makes distributions from its permanent funds. The permanent funds, New Mexico's multi-billion-dollar "rainy day" funds, had strict investment prohibitions (no foreign companies, only companies that had paid consistent dividends, etc.) and had traditionally distributed only earnings on investments. In 1996, voters approved proposals to expand and modernize investment options and to allow annual distributions of a portion of the corpus of the fund based on a rolling average of fund value. In the special election in 2003, voters were asked to expand the 1996 amendments to allow for a greater percentage of earnings to be distributed annually—theoretically for the purpose of paying for education reforms.[46] The amendment was approved by a very narrow margin.

Property taxes have also been the focal point of numerous proposed amendments in recent years. In 1998, voters approved limits on residential property valuation, making limited exceptions to the rule that property taxes be in proportion to value. This was an attempt to limit property tax increases in resort areas that have seen skyrocketing property values. Voters have also expanded property tax exemptions for disabled veterans.[47]

Changes to public finance have not been limited to state agencies. County borrowing possibilities have steadily expanded with the passage of constitutional amendments in 1980 to include water and sewer systems, sanitary landfills, and airports, and in 1988, 1991, and 1994 to allow county borrowing for building repairs, library resources, and open space.

BILL OF RIGHTS

Article 2, Section 13, provided for the right of every person to bail, except in the case of capital offenses where the proof is evident or the presumption great. In 1980 Constitutional Amendment No. 3 permitted the district courts to deny bail for a period of sixty days after the incarceration of a defendant, if that person had a past record of conviction for two or more felonies, or for one felony if accused of committing another felony with the use of a deadly weapon. This sixty-day period can be extended to any period of time during which the trial is delayed because of a motion of continuance on behalf of the defendant. In 1988 the right of bail was further restricted by the adoption of Constitutional Amendment No. 5. This change denies the right to bail to a person convicted of a crime who is awaiting the result of an appeal for that conviction. It should be noted that there is no federal constitutional right to bail after a defendant has been convicted; this is a matter that has been left to the individual states.

In the special election of 1971, the voters approved Constitutional Amendment No. 3, which prohibited the enactment of any law that would abridge the right of a citizen to keep and bear arms for security and defense, for lawful hunting and recreational use, and for other lawful purposes. However, the amendment did not appear to authorize the carrying of concealed weapons or any local control of the issue. Nonetheless, in 2001 the legislature passed the Concealed Handgun Carry Act authorizing the carrying of concealed weapons by permitted individuals. The law was challenged by Albuquerque Mayor Jim Baca. The challenge was successful and in June 2002 the New Mexico Supreme Court held that the legislation was defective on the basis that local municipalities could "opt out" of the law, in violation of the constitutional provision. Legislators were not deterred and in the subsequent legislative session (January 2003), the New Mexico Legislature enacted another law authorizing the carrying of concealed weapons, this time minus the offending "opt out" provision. The 2003 act also faced a constitutional challenge though this time opponents of the act were unsuccessful. The court upheld the validity of the act in January 2004.[48]

In 1972 the voters of the state adopted the "Equal Rights Amendment," providing that equality of rights under the law shall not be denied on account of the sex of any person.

Twenty years later, in 1992, voters agreed to add a victim's rights amendment to the constitution. This most recent addition to New Mexico's bill of rights grants victims of violent crimes some basic notification, information, and participation rights in the criminal justice system.[49]

CONCLUSION

The New Mexico Constitution continues to grow by piecemeal amendment, in order to adjust to the demands of the evolving social and economic conditions of the state. There is an apparent reluctance on the part of the legislature and the voters of this state to call a constitutional convention to rewrite the basic document. In the single instance since statehood where such a convention was held (1969), the voters rejected the proposed new constitution by the close margin of 3,702 votes. Proposals for a new convention have been treated negatively by the legislature and have generally been greeted with an absence of enthusiasm on the part of the public. For the foreseeable future, at least, it is apparent that piecemeal amendment of the document will continue to be the primary means of effecting change in the state's supreme law.

NOTES

1. See Ernestine D. Evans, *The Constitution of New Mexico as Adopted January 21, 1911, and as subsequently Amended by the People in General and Special Elections 1912 through 1974* (Santa Fe: Office of the Secretary of State, January 1975). Also see Richard H. Folmar, *Piecemeal Amendment of the New Mexico Constitution 1911 to 1975*, 7th rev. ed. (Santa Fe: The Capitol, New Mexico Legislative Council Service, July 1, 1975).
2. Frank P. Grad, *The State Constitution: Its Function and Form for Our Time* (New York: National Municipal League, repr. from *Virginia Law Review* 54, no. 5. [June 1968]).
3. In November 1912, the voters repealed the section of the Congressional Enabling Act requiring state officers and legislators to read, write, and speak English without an interpreter. Jack F. Holmes, *Politics in New Mexico* (Albuquerque: University of New Mexico Press, 1967), pp. 50–52.
4. Ibid., p. 49.
5. Ibid., pp. 176–77.
6. Harvey Fergusson, *Home in the West* (New York: Duell, Sloan and Pearce, 1944).
7. Letter from Harvey B. Fergusson to J. Floersheim, Dec. 19, 1910. Dorothy I. Cline collection.

8.   Holmes, *Politics in New Mexico*, p. 51.
9.   *Proceedings of the Constitutional Convention of the Proposed State of New Mexico* (Albuquerque: Press of the *Morning Journal*, 1910), p. 288.
10.   Ibid.
11.   Frank W. Clancy, *Letters and Addresses Relating to the Constitution of New Mexico* (Santa Fe, 1911), pp. 39–40.
12.   The *Albuquerque Journal*, Sept. 14, 1949.
13.   Chapter 14, Laws of 1951.
14.   Governor Mechem appointed (Republicans) *Chairman*, E. L. Moulton, Ilfeld and Company; Rupert Asplund, Director, New Mexico Taxpayers Association; Edward Hartman, State Comptroller; (Democrats) *Vice-Chairman*, Virgil McCollum, Carlsbad Potash Company; *Secretary*, Dr. Thomas C. Donnelly, Government Department, University of New Mexico; State Senator Horace De Vargas and Waldo Spiess, House Majority leader (son of Charles Spiess).
15.   *Report, New Mexico State Reorganization Committee* (Santa Fe: The Capitol, June 30, 1952).
16.   The proposed departments consisted of: Agriculture, Revenue, Finance and Administration, Police and Public Safety, Justice, Personnel, Education, Highways, Labor, Commerce, Game and Fish, Health and Welfare.
17.   These included: adoption of a personnel system; creation of a Department of Finance and Administration, and a Board of Educational Finance; the demarking of funds; establishment of a Legislative Finance Committee and the post of legislative fiscal analyst; the start of legislative interim committees.
18.   Chapter 222, Laws 1963, provided for appointment by the governor of one member from each of the eleven judicial districts with two senators and representatives serving as legislative advisers. Appointed were (Republicans) Charles M. Tansey, lawyer; Tony Sanchez and Sherwood Culberson, ranchers; D. D. Monroe, businessman; (Democrats) Edward E. Triviz and Manfred W. Rainwater, lawyers; Ellis L. Stout, staff member, Los Alamos Scientific Laboratory and county commission chairman; Doyle Balko, businessman; John Burroughs, businessman and former governor; Mrs. Joe Pino, League of Women Voters. Tansy, Rainwater, Sanchez, and Burroughs were former legislators. Legislative advisers were: Senators Ed V. Mead, R. H. Wamel, Jr.; Representatives Roy W. Davidson and David L. Norvell. The commission elected Triviz chairman; Stout, vice chairman; Tansey, secretary.
19.   *1964 Report of the Constitutional Revision Commission* (Santa Fe: The Capitol, Sept. 29, 1964).
20.   *Report of the Constitutional Revision Commission State of New Mexico*, 1967. Adopted November 5, 1966, Harry L. Patton, Chairman. (Santa Fe: The Capitol, 1967).
21.   Chapter 134, Senate Bill No. 166, approved Apr. 1, 1969.
22.   The Convention officers were (Democrats) King, President; Sedillo, first vice president; Cline, fourth vice president; Martin, coordinator. (Republicans) Hughes, second vice president; Lewis Cox, third vice president.
23.   *Substantive committees:* Bill of Rights (Aragon, D), Elections (Irick, R), Legislature (Leyendecker, D), Executive (Tansey, R), Judiciary (Carmody, D), Education (O'Donnell, D). Revenue (Bigbee, R), Local Government

(Sanchez, D), Natural Resources (Sahd, R); *Procedural:* Rules (Parker, D), Public Information (Garcia, D), Style (McCormack, D).

24. Most of the provisions could be traced to the Little Hoover Committee, the Bluebook, and the Governor's Committee on Reorganization of State Government. *Interim Report*, Nov. 15, 1967. *Final Report—New Mexico's Statutory Executive Agencies and How They Grew*, Jan. 1, 1970 (Santa Fe: The Capitol).

25. *Ratio Decidendi*—Addendum to the Executive Committee Majority Report. New Mexico Constitutional Convention, 1969.

26. *State of New Mexico ex rel Boston E. Witt v. State Canvassing Board*, 78 NM 682, (1968).

27. For the first time, the legislature in 1975 memorialized the secretary of state to publish the full texts of amendments, indicating new and deleted material.

28. A new article may be proposed as a single amendment if the provisions relate to the subject. See Attorney General Opinion No. 65–23, February 4, 1965, *City of Raton v. Sproule*, 78 NM 138, 429 P.2d 336 (1967) and *State ex rel. Chavez v. Vigil-Giron*, 108 NM 45 (1988) *but see State ex rel. Clark v. State Canvassing Board*, 119 NM 112 (1995).

29. G. Theodore Mitau, "Partial Constitutional Revision through Piecemeal and Comprehensive Amendments: Reform Patterns of the 1960s," *Contemporary Approaches to State Constitutional Revision* (Vermillion, S.D.: Governmental Research Bureau, Report No. 58, University of South Dakota, 1970), pp. 49–61.

   In fact, the legislature has set the stage for this to occur through the addition of a constitutional amendment in 1996 that authorized the creation of an independent revision committee that could propose constitutional amendments to the legislature. The independent commission would comprise a third method of amendment and would be a middle ground between piecemeal amendment and a constitutional convention.

30. As found in Office of the Secretary of State, State of New Mexico, *State of New Mexico Official Returns*, General and Primary Returns, 1970 through 2003. Also see Richard H. Folmar, *Piecemeal Amendment of the New Mexico Constitution, 1911 to 2005*, 16th rev. ed. (New Mexico Legislative Council Service, 2005).

31. Laws 1993, Chapter 271.

32. This section was declared unconstitutional in 1968 by the New Mexico Supreme Court, which determined that the provision violated the federal equal protection clause. See *State ex rel Witt v. State Canvassing Board*, 78 NM 682 (1968).

33. Constitutional Amendment No. 3 (1970).

34. A history of proposals pertaining to legislative compensation submitted to the voters since statehood is as follows:

Submitted	C. A. No.	Per Diem Request	Date Adopted
1925	1	$7.00	
1927	1	$10.00	
1937	6	$7.00	
1943	1	$10.00	Nov. 7, 1994
1949	9	Annual Salary	

Submitted	C. A. No.	Per Diem Request	Date Adopted
1951	7	$20.00	
1953	5	$20.00	Sept. 15, 1943
1961	6	Set by Statute	
1971	2	$40.00	Nov. 2, 1971
1974	1	Set by Commission	
1978	4	Annual Salary	
1980	6	$60.00	
1982	5	$75.00	Nov. 2, 1982
1988	1	$75.00 + $6,000 retirement annuity	
1990	3	$100 + monthly salary	
1992	4	Create Legis. Compensation Commission	
1994	14	IRS rate + extra days for expenses	
1996	5	IRS rate	

35. Though Attorney General Hal Stratton filed the suit, the case was ultimately decided during the term of Attorney General Tom Udall, hence the citation *State ex rel. Udall v. Public Employees Retirement Board*, 120 NM 786 (1995).

36. The Senate Rules Committee is the standing committee assigned during the session the responsibility for conducting hearings and making recommendations to the Senate on the confirmation of gubernatorial appointees subject to the advice and consent requirements of state law.

37. *State ex rel. Chavez* v. *Vigil-Giron*, 108 NM 45 (1988).

38. Jean Peters, New Mexico Legislative Council Service, *Constitutional Amendments during Even-Year Regular Sessions*, Information Memorandum No. 202.72401, Nov. 29, 1988. Those parts of the constitution included Article 6, Section 10, pertaining to municipal home rule; Article 2, Section 18, providing for equality of rights without regard to a person's sex; Article 9, Section 14, authorizing loans to students of the healing arts; Article 4, Section 3, limiting the size of each house of the legislature; and Article 5, Section 10, allowing state executive officers two consecutive four-year terms beginning January 1, 1991.

39. *State ex rel Chavez v. Vigil-Giron*, 108 NM 45 (1988).

40. Only a fraction of the eligible voters turned up to vote in the special election with only 186,570 votes cast. The voter registration in the state at the time of the election showed more than 900,000 registered voters. On Constitutional Amendment No. 1 the vote was 101,542 (For) and 83,155 (Against). On Constitutional Amendment No. 2 the vote was 92,198 (For) and 92,003 (Against).

41. *Constitution of New Mexico*, Article 10, Section 6.

42. According to some legal opinions, the constitution prohibited the election of

most local governing boards from single-member districts (see *Gibanny v. Ford*, 29 NM 621, 225 P.577 1924); therefore the amendment was written as permissive, in order to validate 1985 statutes requiring the creation of such districts in all but certain small jurisdictions.

43. Constitutional Amendment No. 2 (2000), Constitutional Amendment No.1 (1996).

44. Constitutional Amendment No. 5 (1996).

45. Constitutional Amendment No. 9 (2002).

46. Constitutional Amendment 2 (2003).

47. Constitutional Amendment 5 (1998); Constitutional Amendment 1 (2002).

48. The court was interpreting the provision of Article 2, Section 6, of the New Mexico Constitution that states "No law shall abridge the right of the citizen to keep and bear arms for security and defense, for lawful hunting and recreational use and for other lawful purposes, but nothing herein shall be held to permit the carrying of concealed weapons. No municipality or county shall regulate, in any way, an incident of the right to keep and bear arms."

49. Article 2, Section 24, Constitution of New Mexico.

FOR FURTHER READING

Bebout, John. "The State Constitutional Convention," *Covering the Illinois Constitutional Convention: An Orientation Seminar for Newsmen*. Urbana, Ill.: College of Communications and the Institute of Government and Public Affairs, June 1, 1970. See information concerning New Mexico's 1969 convention.

Bingaman, Jeff. *Comparison of Proposed and Present Constitution*. Santa Fe: Office of the Attorney General, n.d.

Clem, Alan L., ed. *Contemporary Approaches to State Constitutional Revision*. Addresses and commentary by David Fellman, John Bebout, and G. Theodore Mitau. Vermillion, S.D.: Governmental Research Bureau, Report No. 58, University of South Dakota, 1970. See Bebout for references to New Mexico's 1969 constitutional convention.

Cornwell, Elmer E., Jr., and Jay S. Goodman. *The Politics of the Rhode Island Constitutional Convention*, pp. 82–92. New York: National Municipal League, 1969. See the typology employed in studying New Mexico's 1909 convention.

Cornwell, Elmer E., Jr., Jay S. Goodman, and Wayne R. Swanson. *Constitutional Conventions: The Politics of Revision*. New York: National Municipal League, 1974. See information concerning New Mexico's 1969 convention.

Dishman, Robert B. *State Constitutions: The Shape of the Document*. Rev. ed. New York: National Municipal League, 1968.

Donnelly, Thomas C. *The Government of New Mexico*. Albuquerque: University of New Mexico Press, 1953.

Evans, Ernestine D. *New Mexico Constitutional Convention, August 5, 1969*. Santa Fe: Office of the Secretary of State, 1969. See biographical data for delegates and the Enabling Act.

Kelleher, Sean, Jay S. Goodman, and Elmer E. Cornwell, Jr. "Political Attitudes of Activists in the American State: Some Comparative Data." *The Western*

Political Quarterly (March 1973). See data pertaining to the delegates to New Mexico's 1969 constitutional convention.

Larson, Robert W. *New Mexico's Quest for Statehood, 1846–1912.* Albuquerque: University of New Mexico Press, 1953.

League of Women Voters of New Mexico. *What Have We Here: A Brief Look at the New Mexico Constitution.* Washington, D.C.: League of Women Voters Education Fund, February 1968.

Proposed New Mexico Constitution (as adopted by the Constitutional Convention of 1969). Santa Fe: Office of the Secretary of State, 1969.

"State Government Modernization." *State Action 1974: Building on Innovation.* Washington, D.C.: Advisory Commission on Intergovernmental Relations, February 1975.

Sturm, Albert L. *A Bibliography on State Constitutions and Constitutional Revision 1945–1975.* Englewood, Colo.: The Citizens' Conference on State Legislatures, August 1975.

———. *Thirty Years of Constitution-Making: 1938–1968, with an Epilogue: Developments during 1969.* New York: National Municipal League, 1970.

Chapter Three

The Legislature

The state of New Mexico is a vibrant body politic and sitting in the center of that body is the New Mexico State Legislature. It is from the legislature that all statutory law and constitutional change emanates and its description as a part-time, citizen legislature belies the truth of its power. Like many powerful institutions, the legislature draws its strength from both its institutional structure and its membership. This chapter will attempt to describe both.[1]

The New Mexico State Legislature is established, empowered, and limited by Article 4 of the Constitution of New Mexico. Like the national government and all but one state, New Mexico has a bicameral legislature. The seventy members of the House of Representatives are elected to two-year terms. The forty-two members of the Senate are elected for four-year terms. All members are elected on a partisan basis from single-member districts.[2] New Mexico operates a "part-time" legislature convening legislative sessions for only a portion of each year. Per the state constitution, the legislature convenes annually on the third Tuesday of January. In even-numbered years, the legislature remains in session for thirty consecutive days (the "short session"). In odd-numbered years, the legislature stays in session for sixty consecutive days.

In addition to regular sessions, the constitution authorizes the legislature to meet in special session. Special sessions, a phenomenon that has increased in frequency in recent years, may be called by the governor. The legislature may request that the governor call a special session. The governor is required to call a special session upon the receipt of a

petition signed by three-fifths of the membership of each house requesting a session. If the governor refuses, the legislature may call itself into
extraordinary session during which it may conduct business for up to
thirty days. An extraordinary session has been convened only once; that
session was held in June 2002, the result of a budget showdown between
the Democratic legislature and a Republican governor.[3]

The brevity of the legislative session should not mislead one into
thinking that legislators only work ninety days every two years. The legislative session is merely the intense period of a legislator's duties. During
the interim (the period of time between sessions), legislators serve on a
large number of interim legislative committees, deal with constituents,
meet with interest groups, participate in national legislative organizations, and act as local government emissaries to state government.

POWERS OF THE LEGISLATURE

The legislature draws its power to act from the Constitution of New
Mexico. It is that document and the U.S. Constitution that set forth the
limits on the power of the legislature. While both these documents limit
what the legislature can do, it is probably easier to understand those limitations if one first looks at the power of the legislature.

Clearly the most identifiable powers of the legislature are to enact
laws and propose constitutional amendments to the electorate. The legislature also has the power to judge the qualifications of its membership; to determine its own rules of procedure; to confirm executive
appointments; to investigate and remove (through impeachment) certain executive and judicial officials; and to establish budgets and authorize the expenditure of funds. The constitution also recognizes certain
emergency powers enabling the legislature to act in times of national
emergency or disaster.

The power to enact legislation is the most visible of legislative powers. When the legislature convenes each year, legislators are asked to con-
front a wide variety of issues. As the breadth and depth of those issues
has changed, legislators have been forced to meet more often. Up until
1964, the state legislature only convened once every other year in odd-
numbered years. The legislature would meet for sixty days to consider
legislation and pass a biennial budget. In 1963, legislators proposed a
constitutional amendment allowing for the addition of a regular short

session (thirty days) in even-numbered years. The voters authorized such a change to the constitution at the general election in 1964 and since then the legislature has met in regular sessions on an annual basis. Though the legislature meets in regular session each year, the annual sessions are different in odd and even years. During the short session (even years), the constitution limits what may be considered by the legislature to budgets, appropriations and revenue bills, bills drawn pursuant to special message of the governor, and bills of the previous session vetoed by the governor.

In addition to annual regular sessions, the constitution authorizes the legislature to meet in special session upon the call of the governor. When a governor calls the legislature into special session, he issues a session proclamation asking all legislators to come to Santa Fe at a specific date and time. The proclamation limits the subjects to be considered during the special session. Particularly in recent years, governors have crafted very narrow areas of consideration in an attempt to curtail and guide the activities of legislators meeting in special session. Once the governor calls a special session, he cannot limit how long legislators stay. The constitution authorizes legislators to remain in session for up to thirty days once convened in special session.

While legislators in all states have the power to enact legislation, many states also grant that power to the people, through the process of initiative. The New Mexico Constitution does not grant such a power to the people and initiative does not and never has existed in New Mexico. Unlike states such as California, the constitution does not authorize citizens to petition and then seek a vote of the electorate to enact new legislation. The lack of an initiative process is the result of constitutional convention fights of many years ago. Framers of New Mexico's 1910 constitution were anxious to secure statehood and felt that the most likely way to achieve that goal was to pass a relatively conservative founding document. Conservative votes at the 1910 constitutional convention prevailed and the initiative process was excluded from the 1910 constitution. It has not been added since.

While voters of the state do not have the power to enact legislation through initiative, they do have a limited ability to disapprove legislation enacted by the legislature. This limited referendum, a compromise concession to progressives at the 1910 constitutional convention, provides that voters may secure petition signatures from registered voters in an effort to repeal a law passed by the legislature. The number of petition signatures required is significant—10 percent of the votes cast in the last general election.[4] Signatures must be obtained statewide and in three-fourths of the counties. Once the requisite petition signatures are obtained, the secretary of state places the question of approval or rejection of the law on the ballot at the next general election. If a majority of voters vote to reject the law, and those votes total not less than 40 percent of the votes cast at the election, the law is deemed repealed. While this provision has been used to place questions on the ballot (in 1950, 1964), petitioners have always been unsuccessful. Even though the repeal question may garner an overwhelming majority of votes, the 40 percent of votes cast requirement has been too high a hurdle. Many voters simply failed to vote on the question.[5]

In addition to its lawmaking authority, the Constitution of New Mexico grants the legislature significant administrative and investigative powers. Some of these powers are internal to the administration of the legislative body and some powers operate as a check and balance on the powers of the executive and judiciary. Internally, each chamber of the legislature determines its own rules of procedure and each selects its own officers and employees and fixes their compensation. The legislature's rules of procedure are subject to certain constitutional constraints. These include such things as the constitutional definition of a quorum, a requirement that each house keep a journal of its proceedings and votes, and a provision that neither house may adjourn for more than three days without the permission of the other house.

The constitution also protects the authority of each chamber to judge the election and qualifications of its members. Any question about an individual's election or whether that individual meets the constitutional qualifications for membership is to be settled by that member's (or prospective member's) chamber. Each chamber also has the authority to discipline its members. A member may be expelled from the body on a vote of two-thirds. Most recently (in 1992), this provision was utilized to discipline Rep. Ronald Olguin (D- Bernalillo). Rep. Olguin was accused of soliciting and receiving a bribe. After review and consideration by the House Ethics Committee and significant floor debate, the members of the House voted to censure rather then expel Representative Olguin. In a dramatic ceremony, Representative Olguin was summoned to the well of the House (in front of the Speaker's dais) and publicly rebuked for his behavior. At the time of the House investigation, Olguin was also under criminal investigation for bribery. Subsequent to his House censure, he was charged and convicted of soliciting a bribe, eventually serving a prison term for that conviction.

In addition to policing its own membership, the constitution grants to the legislature the authority to investigate and impeach members of the executive and judicial branches. All state officers and judges of the district court are subject to impeachment for "crimes, misdemeanors and malfeasance in office".[6] Much like the United States Congress, it is the state's House of Representatives that has the sole power of impeachment, upon a majority vote of the entire membership. Impeachments are tried by the Senate. If the governor or lieutenant governor is on trial, the chief justice of the New Mexico Supreme Court presides. A two-thirds vote of the elected membership of the Senate is required for impeachment. Upon such a vote, the officer is removed from office and is prohibited from holding any office of honor, trust, or profit with the state. Whether convicted or acquitted, the accused may be subject to civil or criminal prosecution.

Finally, the legislature possesses a gentler means of oversight of the executive branch, that of confirmation authority. By constitution and by statute, the New Mexico Senate is charged with advice and consent responsibilities for many gubernatorial appointments. From cabinet secretaries to members of the boards of regents to the members of the board of medical examiners, the legislature is asked to investigate and confirm the governor's appointees. While this endeavor is a time-consuming and usually uneventful process, the occasional clash of political goals is to be expected and, in the past, confirmations have been considered a viable political battlefield.

While the powers of the legislature are extensive, one should be aware of the limitations on those powers. These limitations derive from four specific sources: (1) the United States Constitution and those provisions of the Bill of Rights made applicable to the states through incorporation of the Fourteenth Amendment; (2) limitations set forth in the state constitution; (3) the veto power of the governor; and (4) the reliance of the legislature on the executive branch for implementation of laws passed by the legislature.

The United States Constitution limits states in their ability to legislate prohibiting the enactment of ex post facto laws and the passage of bills
of attainder. The federal Bill of Rights also prohibits the passage of legislation that impinges on certain fundamental rights such as the rights of
expression, religion, and association. While such limitations were not originally applied to states (as the Bill of Rights was seen only as a limitation
on the federal government), court opinions in the twentieth century have
held that states may not take away fundamental freedoms guaranteed by
the federal Bill of Rights on the premise that the Fourteenth Amendment
makes some of those rights enforceable against the state. As such, the legislature must be mindful of the protections of the United States
Constitution and the Bill of Rights when crafting state law.

In addition to the protections of the U.S. Constitution, the state legislature is also limited by the New Mexico Constitution. The New Mexico
Constitution, a document that is significantly longer than its federal counterpart, places many limitations on the legislature. These protections range
from the substantive twenty-four-section Bill of Rights (which discusses
everything from the Treaty of Guadalupe Hildalgo to concealed weapons
and victims rights) to the many procedural restrictions of Article 4, the
legislative chapter.

Once the legislature successfully navigates the restrictions placed on
it by the state and federal constitutions, it must still navigate the political waters of gubernatorial authority. The Constitution of New Mexico
affords the governor the veto power—a power by which the governor
may veto legislation passed by the legislature. Using this power, the governor may prevent a bill passed by the legislature from becoming law.
For most pieces of legislation, the governor must veto or accept the entire
bill. However, if the bill is an appropriation bill, the constitution affords
the governor a line-item veto with which he can selectively line-out parts
of the legislation that he does not want to become law. The power of the
governor is not absolute; the legislature may override a veto with a two-
thirds vote of each chamber.

Finally, one must remember that it is the job of the legislature to enact
law, not to administer it. After legislation is crafted and voted, it is passed
on to the executive administration for implementation. On more than
one occasion, the governor and the legislature have been at odds over
the implementation of legislation. Unfortunately for the legislature, a

part-time body with a small permanent staff is limited in its ability to oversee the implementation process. And of course, changes in legislation must generally wait until the next year's regular session.

LEGISLATIVE LEADERS

As is the case in the United States Congress and forty-eight other states, the New Mexico Legislature is customarily organized along party lines. At statehood, Republicans led both chambers, but since 1933 Democrats, with few exceptions, have been the majority in both houses. Prior to the beginning of a legislative session, party members meet in caucus and select, by secret ballot, the party leadership. The minority party selects a minority leader, a minority whip, and a caucus chairman. The majority party also selects a majority leader, a majority whip, and a caucus chairman. The majority party caucus also votes on the chamber leader—the President Pro Tem in the Senate and the Speaker of the House in the House of Representatives. Though the official election for these posts does not occur until the first day of the session, the majority party nominee normally has enough votes in caucus to make the opening day vote a foregone conclusion. Once elected, leaders generally serve for an entire legislature (a two-year term including a short and long session). On occasion, political struggles within a body have prompted a mid-term election of new leaders, as was the case in 1986 when Democratic leaders retook leadership of the Senate during a special session.

The election of party leadership is not a mundane task in the legislature. Historically, party discipline has ensured that such an election would be a mere formality. The practice of forming coalitions between one party and dissident members of the other party, however, has made it increasingly uncertain that all members of the party will vote for their parties' caucus choice for Speaker or President Pro Tem, as had been expected in the past. This shifting party loyalty has led to significant upheaval in both chambers in recent years.

In 1979, the tradition of party discipline was shattered by the House. In the Democratic caucus, the incumbent Speaker, moderately liberal Walter Martinez, defeated Gene Samberson by a healthy 30–11 vote (which was much greater than the 26–22 caucus margin by which he had retained the Speakership in 1977). The dissident conservative Democrats, mostly representatives from the southern and southeastern parts of the state, refused to accept defeat. They formed a coalition, joining twenty-nine Republican representatives to elect Representative Samberson as Speaker of the House. This cross-party coalition was the first, but not the last, of its kind in New Mexico. The House coalition lasted until 1983 when loyal Democrats regained the Speaker's post with the election of Raymond G. Sanchez. In 1985, the coalition again asserted its strength, reelecting Samberson as Speaker. He held that office until 1987, when Raymond G. Sanchez was once again elected Speaker. Representative Sanchez held the Speaker's post continuously until 2000 when he lost his general election bid to serve a sixteenth term in the House. Speaker Sanchez's lengthy term set a record; to date he is New Mexico's longest serving Speaker of the House.

Coalitions have also played an important role in the Senate. In 1988, five Senate Democrats joined with twenty-one Republicans to take control of the Senate. This time the dissident Democrats were from varying parts of the state and the cross-party coalition elected a liberal, Senator Manny M. Aragon (D-Albuquerque) to be President Pro Tem. The 1988 coalition was brief, however, and in 1989 the loyal Senate Democrats returned with a solid majority, including the former dissidents. Ironically, the Democrats reelected the former coalition leader, Manny Aragon, to his post as President Pro Tem. Senator Aragon held that post for twelve years, before being ousted by a different Democratic–Republican coalition in 2001. The 2001 coalition, on a vote of three Democrats and nineteen Republicans, elected a different Democrat to the Pro Tem post—Senator Richard Romero (D–Albuquerque). Senator Romero held that post until 2004, when he chose to run for the United States Congress. Interestingly, the 2002 Senate amended its rules to prohibit future Presidents Pro Tem from serving in that office for more than four consecutive regular sessions.

While party membership plays an important role in the selection of legislative leaders, the Speaker and President Pro Tem are both elected by their entire respective chambers. As in Congress, seniority usually plays a role in who will be President Pro Tem, but not in who will be Speaker. The post of President Pro Tem usually (but not always) goes to the most senior member of the majority party. On occasion the senior Democrat has declined the post to remain chairman of the Senate Finance Committee. On other occasions the senior member was not elected, as was the case in 2001 when Senator Richard Romero was elected to the post, ousting a more senior member, Senator Manny Aragon.

While the Speaker and President Pro Tem are both elected by their entire chambers, they differ significantly in their legislative roles and powers. The greatest difference between the two legislative leaders is that the Speaker of the House has broad discretionary authority as presiding officer of the House; this power is denied the President Pro Tem. The Speaker administers the order of business as provided by the rules, answers parliamentary inquiries and questions of procedure and order, and makes rulings, subject to appeal to the House membership. The Speaker also controls the use of all electronic and public-address equipment installed in the House chamber. The Speaker assigns introduced bills to the committee(s) he deems appropriate. By House rule, bills containing appropriations must be referred to the House Appropriations and Finance Committee. The Speaker also appoints a member to preside whenever the House chooses to sit as a committee of the whole.[7]

In the New Mexico House of Representatives, the Speaker has significant power.[8] One of the most important powers, in terms of ability to determine policy, is the authority to appoint the chairs and members of all standing (permanent) committees of the House at the beginning of each regular session. The Speaker can seek advice from a committee on committees of his or her own choosing, but he retains appointing authority. The only time the Speaker does not select committee members is when a special committee is established by resolution and the motion to create the committee designates the committee membership. Each House member is limited to service on two substantive (subject-matter) committees, but may serve on other special or procedural committees. With care, the Speaker can align the membership of certain committees to meet his or her legislative goals. Since the Speaker also controls the referral of most bills to committees, this leader can have a great impact on the fate of many bills and can to a large extent predetermine the outcome, at the committee stage at least, of certain policy decisions. The exercise of these powers, of course, is limited by the political necessity of satisfying the legislators who elected him or her Speaker.

The President Pro Tem, in contrast, does not preside over the New Mexico Senate; the state constitution makes the lieutenant governor the president of the Senate and its presiding officer. But the lieutenant

governor is a member of the executive branch of government, not the legislative branch, and can vote only in case of a tie. Because this leader is
imposed on the Senate from the outside, the lieutenant governor (like the
vice president at the national level) seldom has much power in the Senate.

Although the Senate President Pro Tem has fewer formal powers than
the House Speaker, this post in the New Mexico Senate (unlike that in
the U.S. Senate) is actually a position of substantial power. The President
Pro Tem has some powers in relation to presiding over the Senate and
assigning senators to committees, but they are decidedly inferior to those
possessed by the Speaker of the House. Whenever the lieutenant governor is not presiding over the Senate, the President Pro Tem is entitled
to preside or to appoint another senator to preside. This leader can also
preside or appoint a member to preside when the Senate resolves itself
into a committee of the whole. The President Pro Tem also chairs the
Senate Committees' Committee, which makes all Senate committee
assignments and exercises most of the procedural and administrative powers held by the Speaker of the House. Unlike the authority of the Speaker,
the committee as a whole is responsible for decisions and the committee's discretion is sharply limited by the Senate's seniority system (see
the following section). The presiding officer in the Senate does not possess the Speaker's power to refer bills to friendly or hostile committees.
Unless another senator objects, bills introduced by senators are referred
to the committee requested by the sponsor. If there is an objection, the
Senate as a body determines the committee referral. As in the House, however, Senate rules require that bills containing appropriations must, at
some stage, be referred to the Senate Finance Committee.

The Speaker of the House and the Senate President Pro Tem are generally elected in a partisan manner; thus, they are expected to look out
for their party's interests. Still they are elected by the entire chamber and
therefore have a responsibility to the House or the Senate as an institution, unlike the majority and minority floor leaders and whips. The latter are party officers whose responsibilities are primarily to their
respective parties. Often, too, they speak for the governor when that leader
is of their party.

In the House the majority floor leader is the majority party's leader
on the floor and normally is second to the Speaker in the legislative party
hierarchy. The floor leader looks out for the party's interests in the House,

plays a major role in the scheduling and conduct of debate, and usually serves as a traffic manager for the conduct of business. Usually the Speaker and the majority leader assist their party colleagues in the House when they can and, in return, expect support when they need it. The relationships between these officers and their fellow party members can be complicated by cross-party coalitions; in the 1979–80 sessions the floor leader and the Speaker were from different party factions. The Speaker and the other ten Democratic representatives who joined in the coalition with the Republicans were actually expelled from the House Democratic caucus.

The majority whip assists the majority leader and acts for the latter when the leader is absent from the chamber. The whip communicates the leadership's position on issues to party members in the House and attempts to keep track of the positions of party members on major issues. It is this knowledge of voting strength on the floor that allows the party leadership to maneuver more effectively to achieve legislative goals.

In the House, the duties of the minority floor leader and minority whip are similar to those of their majority party counterparts, although the minority floor leader is the minority party's actual leader in the chamber. The minority floor leader and minority whip plan minority party strategy, seek to form a winning coalition with dissident members of the majority party on certain legislation, attempt to build a legislative record for the party, and when possible, seek to embarrass the majority party for its action or inaction on certain issues. It is important to note here that the minority party leader does not formally control the committee assignments of minority party members—the Speaker does. However, through political accommodation with the Speaker, the minority leader often achieves informal control of minority member committee assignments.

In the Senate, the majority and minority floor leaders and whips have duties similar to the House party officers, except that Senate officers also serve on the Committees' Committee. They are elected by their respective party caucuses. Although these positions are not awarded on the basis of seniority, junior senators are unlikely to be elected.

The preceding discussions should not mislead the reader into overestimating the strength or power of party organization in the New Mexico Legislature. Party members do not always agree on all issues, and members do not always vote the party line. Indeed, the fact that cross-party coalitions seized control of the House in 1979 and 1985 and of the Senate in 1988 and 2001 suggests that party loyalty in the New Mexico Legislature may not be the glue it is supposed to be.

LEGISLATIVE COMMITTEES

As is true of other American legislatures, the New Mexico Legislature does most of its work in committee. Because a plethora of proposals are introduced during each session, it would be impossible for the entire membership of each chamber to consider in detail the merits of each proposal. In the sixty-day session, for instance, over two thousand bills are introduced; most die. Some die because of strong opposition, some because opponents control a key committee, and others because they are not important enough to compete successfully for the attention of busy legislators. Both chambers, therefore, appoint committees to consider proposed legislation. By legislative rule, party strength on each committee roughly reflects the chamber-wide party ratio.

In the House, as noted above, the Speaker appoints the committee members and officers (committee chairs and vice chairs). Once appointed by the Speaker, House committee members and chairs can be removed only by a two-thirds vote of the House. Committee chairs have sufficient power and flexibility in guiding committee business and delaying or expediting certain bills that they are figures of substantial authority and prestige in the legislature.

Subject to approval by the entire Senate, committee assignments in that body are made by the Committees' Committee. That committee is composed of the President Pro Tem, the majority and minority floor leaders, the majority and minority whips, five members of the majority party, and one member of the minority party appointed by the President Pro Tem. The Committees' Committee is obligated to make Senate committee assignments on the basis of members' preferences and chamber seniority whenever possible. The Committees' Committee also appoints the chair and vice chair of each committee. No chair or vice chair of a standing committee (other than the Committees' Committee) may serve in either position on any other committee; and no member of the Senate Finance Committee may chair one of the six other substantive committees. Each senator is limited to service on two standing committees, not counting the Committees' Committee. The majority floor leader is regularly appointed to only one standing committee, but is an ex officio member entitled to participate in the deliberations of all other standing committees. Though the floor leader can vote in committee deliberations, he is not counted for quorum purposes in committees on which he serves ex officio.

Committees play a very important role in the legislative process and seniority plays a very important role in committees. Senate Rule 9-1-4 reads:

> Seniority of the members of the Senate shall prevail at all times
> in committee assignments, and chairmen of committees shall be
> appointed by request of the senior members. All committeemen shall
> be placed on committee by rank of seniority. Should a vacancy occur,
> the next ranking member of the Senate shall have priority on the
> requested committee. Seniority will be governed by continuous
> service in the New Mexico Senate. This rule can only be repealed
> or suspended by a three-fourths vote of the elected Senate.

This rule, unique among the state senates, severely limits the discretion of the Committees' Committee. It has also been the target of past Senate coalitions. Senate Rule 9–1–4 was removed from the Senate rules in 1988 when a coalition of Democrats and loyal Republicans seized control of the chambers. It was reinstated one year later when loyal Democrats regained control.

It should be noted that the seniority rule in the New Mexico Senate does not operate in the same manner as the seniority system in the U.S. Congress. In both chambers of the national legislature, factors other than chamber-wide seniority influence who becomes a committee chair. In Congress, party seniority on a given committee is important. Despite all the well-publicized ills of the congressional seniority system, it does ensure that a person becomes familiar with a committee's business before assuming the role of committee chair. This is not necessarily the effect of the New Mexico Senate's seniority rule. The existing seniority system in the New Mexico Senate reproduces most of the negative features of the congressional seniority system, including giving independent power to committee chairs who are not sympathetic to the policy goals of their colleagues and giving disproportionate power to areas that repeatedly reelect the same person to the Senate. It is not unusual for senior senators to be chairs of a committee on which they have never served and with whose subject matter they are not familiar.

The House has fifteen standing committees. The twelve that consider legislation and report bills to the floor of the chamber for a vote are called substantive committees. The other three are procedural committees. Each representative normally serves on two substantive committees and may also be appointed to a procedural committee as well as a special committee. Normally committee chairs and vice chairs are members of the majority party. The Senate, with its smaller membership, has only eight committees, in addition to the Committee's Committee. All of New Mexico's Senate committees are substantive committees.

Figure 3.1 outlines the structure of the two chambers by listing the 2005 Senate and House committees, along with their number of members. Each Senate committee is coupled with the House committees or committees whose general functions it performs, although the overlap is not perfect. In addition, a bill with the same subject matter will not always be sent to the same pairing of committees in the House and Senate. Although each substantive committee normally receives certain types of bills, legislative tactics and the balancing of committee workloads often lead to the referral of an "alien" bill to a committee. As mentioned above, however, all appropriations bills must be referred to the Senate Finance Committee and the House Appropriations and Finance Committee.

Since most important bills require the expenditure of state funds for their implementation, state priorities are decided in a very real sense in the finance committees. Consequently, the chairs of these committees are very powerful figures. As Figure 3.1 indicates, the Senate Finance Committee has comparable responsibilities to the House Appropriations and Finance Committee. The House Taxation and Revenue Committee has historically also been an important finance-related committee. For a number of years, the Senate created a comparable Senate Ways and Means Committee. However, that committee was abolished in 2001. The importance of these appropriation and revenue committees is indicated by the fact that they are the largest ones in their respective chambers.[9]

The procedural committees also perform vital tasks for the legislature. The Enrolling and Engrossing Committee in the House puts into final form bills passed by both houses.[10] The House Committee on Printing and Supplies, as its name suggests, awards contracts for printing and

FIGURE 3.1
Standing Committees of the New Mexico Legislature, 2005
(number of members in parentheses)

HOUSE	SENATE
Appropriations and Finance (18)	Finance (10)
Taxation and Revenue (16)	—
Energy and Natural Resources (13)	Conservation (9)
Agriculture and Water Resources (7)	—
Education (14)	Education (9)
Judiciary (11)	Judiciary (10)
Enrolling and Engrossing-(11)	—
Business and Industry (13)	Corporations and Transportation (9)
Transportation (12)	—
Consumer and Public Affairs (7)	Public Affairs (9)
Labor and Human Resources (9)	—
Government and Urban Affairs (7)	—
Rules and Order of Business (18)	Rules (9)
—	Indian and Cultural Affairs (9)
Voters and Elections (14)	—
—	Committees' (11)*
Printing and Supplies (14)	—

*The Senate Committees' Committee also exercises the Speaker of the House's appointment powers.

Source: "State of New Mexico Forty-Seventh Legislature First Session, House Standing Committees" (Santa Fe: New Mexico Legislative Council Service, 2005); and "State of New Mexico Forty-Seventh Legislature First Session, Senate Standing Committees" (Santa Fe: New Mexico Legislative Council Service, 2005).

approves the purchase of supplies and equipment. In addition, its members hire House employees for the legislative session. The House Rules and Order of Business Committee is responsible for considering proposed changes in the House rules and making recommendations to the entire chamber. During thirty-day and special sessions, this committee determines whether bills are germane; that is, whether they fall into the limited categories the legislature can consider in those sessions. If the rules committee determines that a bill is germane, the legislature may appropriately consider the bill during the short or special session.

Like the House, the Senate has certain procedural matters that require attention. As one would expect, consideration of proposed changes to the Senate rules is a responsibility held by the Senate Rules Committee. That committee, however, has substantive duties as well, including jurisdiction over election laws, constitutional amendments, and recommendations on gubernatorial appointees requiring Senate confirmation. Unlike the House Rules Committee, the Senate Rules Committee does not rule on germaneness; that determination is made by the Senate Committees' Committee. The Senate Rules Committee is the only standing committee of either house permitted to sit during the interim period. The duties performed in the House by the Committee on Printing and Supplies are performed in the Senate by the Committee's Committee. Enrolling and engrossing are duties assigned to the Senate Judiciary Committee.

THE LEGISLATIVE PROCESS

A recounting of the steps in the legislative process is somewhat misleading because such a description omits the excitement and uncertainties involved in negotiating, compromising, rounding up support, and making moves at just the right time. Nevertheless, one cannot understand all the activity without knowing the basic mechanics of the process.

The legislature considers three types of measures; these are memorials, resolutions, and bills. A fourth type of measure, a capital outlay request, is a fairly new invention in the legislative process. It is designed to allow legislators to submit their requests for capital outlay (brick and mortar projects) without the necessity of a formal bill. Successful requests are eventually rolled together in one or more comprehensive capital outlay bills.

Each type of measure serves a different purpose in the legislative arena. A memorial is an expression of legislative desire, usually addressed to another governmental body in the form of a petition or declaration of intent. For instance, a memorial may ask the Department of Transportation (formerly the Highway Department) to give high priority consideration to building a road in a certain part of the state. Either chamber may pass a memorial without regard to the other chamber or the governor. Joint memorials are those passed by both the House and the Senate. Memorials are not signed by the governor and do not have the force of law. A resolution is a formal declaration by the legislature concerning a subject that it either cannot or does not wish to control by law. A joint resolution is a declaration by both houses and is the vehicle used to propose state constitutional amendments to the electorate. Like memorials, resolutions are not signed by the governor. A bill is the form used to propose laws. In order to become a law, the bill must be passed by the House and the Senate (in exactly the same form) and be approved by the governor or passed over a gubernatorial veto.

To become law, a bill must traverse a route through the legislature, a route that is complex and full of obstacles. The process tends to give the advantage to the bill's opponents, who need only block it at one point (or just delay it long enough near the end of the session) to kill it. The bill's sponsor (the legislator who introduced it) must devote much time and effort in the legislative session to getting the bill approved. Most legislators find that as sponsors they can give proper attention to only a handful of bills each session.

A bill may be introduced in either the House or the Senate. There are time limits on introduction; only certain types of bills may be introduced after the midpoint (the fifteenth or thirtieth day) of a regular session. Each bill introduced is given a number, read twice by title, ordered to be printed, and referred to the proper committee. By custom, the general appropriations bill is introduced in the House. A bill may be referred to more than one committee in each chamber; such a multiple referral is one way to increase the odds against a bill's passage, since the bill must then get out of more than one committee. The time limits of the legislative session means that significant opposition or delay is likely to result in the death of a bill.

The committee to which a bill is referred may or may not act on it. Ensuring that the committee gives the bill a hearing, that friendly witnesses are notified and on hand, that proper motions are made by committee members, and if possible, that the committee gives the bill a favorable recommendation are the responsibilities of the bill's sponsor. Legislators sometimes introduce bills at the request of constituents or to gain publicity, then do nothing to move the bill along. Other legislators in turn interpret such lack of action as an indication that the sponsor is not serious about getting the bill passed and ignore it themselves.

A committee can also take one of several actions on a bill. It may recommend to the legislative body a "Do Pass," a "Do Pass as Amended," a "Do Not Pass," or it may refer the bill back to the floor, "Without

Recommendation." A sponsor who fears a "Do Not Pass" recommendation will often maneuver for a "Without Recommendation" referral, since many legislators who might otherwise vote for the bill on the floor would hesitate, out of commitment to the basic committee process, to vote against a negative committee recommendation. Still even a "Do Not Pass" recommendation avoids the limbo of having the bill spend the session stuck in committee.

A committee may choose to substitute a new bill for the original one, with the substitute incorporating whatever changes the committee wishes to make. Original sponsors sometimes oppose the substitute on the floor, especially if they find it so weak that the intent of the original bill is destroyed. This has been the case with several environmental measures in recent years. A committee may also recommend referral of the bill to another committee. Or, as is quite often the case, the committee may simply do nothing and let the bill die in committee.

Committee reports are only recommendations; positive action must be taken by the full House or Senate. When a favorable committee report is adopted, or an unfavorable report overturned, the bill is placed on the calendar, which is the schedule of business the House or Senate may consider on any day. Some bills that are thought to be of a routine or noncontroversial nature and that are certain to pass without amendment or substitution are placed on a special "consent" calendar created for the purpose of expediting the business of the legislature. Such bills are given no more than ten minutes of a chamber's time before voting. The objection of five members in that chamber causes the bill to be taken off the consent calendar and to be placed on the regular calendar.

A bill on the regular calendar of either chamber is debated at its third reading (which is required by the constitution to be on a different day from its first reading, to prevent hasty action). Floor amendments may be added at this stage, or the entire bill may be substituted by another bill pertaining to the same subject. Should the House or Senate wish to hear outside testimony on a bill on the calendar, it must go into a committee of the whole, as only members of that chamber may speak on the floor during a regular session. A final vote is taken and recorded, with a majority required for passage. Bills carrying an emergency clause, a clause that makes the legislation take effect immediately upon signature of the governor, must be passed by a two-thirds vote of each chamber.

The final vote may be reconsidered the same day or the next day, in order to give the members an opportunity to change their minds. Sponsors sometimes move for immediate reconsideration, to prevent the bill from being overturned the next day, when wavering supporters may have changed their minds.

If the bill passes one chamber, it is sent with a letter of transmittal to the other house, where it will follow much the same procedure and be subject to similar tactical maneuvering. If the second chamber amends it, it is returned to the first chamber for concurrence. If concurrence is denied, the second chamber must then vote whether to recede (withdraw) from its amendment. If it refuses to recede, the bill is usually sent to a conference committee of representatives and senators familiar with the bill's details. The conference committee has only the power to consider the amendments in question. If it fails to reconcile the versions of the two chambers, a free committee may be appointed (often with the same membership as the conference committee). That committee is then charged with working out a version acceptable to both chambers. If the free committee agrees on a version of the bill, its report is submitted to the floor of each house for approval or rejection. If it is approved by both chambers, the bill is enrolled and engrossed (put into final form), signed by the presiding officers of both houses, and sent to the governor for approval or veto.

The legislature's ability to enact bills into law is subject to gubernatorial authority. The governor may veto a bill the legislature has passed, preventing it from becoming law, but he must act within three days (Sundays excepted) of receiving the bill from the legislature. Otherwise, if the legislature is still in session, it becomes law without his signature. Except for bills appropriating money, on which the executive has an item veto, the governor must veto or accept the entire bill. This requirement, of course, affects the bargaining positions of the legislature and the governor when they disagree. Sometimes the governor must accept unwanted provisions to get a desired law. The governor's veto can be overridden only by a two-thirds vote in each house.

Bills passed in the hectic last three days of the legislative session are not subject to the same gubernatorial time line as bills passed earlier in the session. Bills passed in the last three days must receive the governor's signature within twenty days of the legislature's adjournment, or they do not become law. This requirement is testimony to the fact that questionable pieces of legislation manage to get through the legislature in the closing rush. It is the responsibility of the governor and the executive staff to examine these bills thoroughly and discover any hidden defects. The legislature, as part of a complex pattern of internal maneuvering, schedules most of each session's final action on legislation for the last few days of the session. Thus, the governor's veto privilege is a very important tool for checking lawmakers.

INTERIM COMMITTEES

The legislature's work does not end at the close of the legislative session. Indeed much careful analysis of the state's problems and consideration of proposed solutions occur in the interim between legislative sessions. Like many other state legislatures that are constitutionally limited to brief sessions interrupted by lengthy interims, the New Mexico Legislature has developed interim legislative committees to enable it to perform its function as an equal branch of state government.

Interim committees are created to deal with specific problems and projects. All are joint committees, composed of both representatives and senators, with the majority and minority parties represented in proportion to their strength in each house. There are a few permanent interim committees that operate during every interim. The most prominent of these are the Legislative Council, the Legislative Finance Committee, and the Legislative Education Study Committee. Most others are temporary and go out of existence when the next legislative session convenes. Interim committees normally meet monthly, for two or three days at a time, between legislative sessions, with more frequent meetings as the legislative session approaches. Figure 3.2 lists the interim committees for the 1971–72 and 2005 sessions. While some of the committees are the same or at least consider similar subject areas, the differing interests of legislators over three and a half decades are still quite pronounced.

Some interim committees are created by statute, others by the Legislative Council. The Legislative Council appoints the chairs and members of the interim committees it creates and of some statutory interim committees as well. In other cases, the statute creating the interim committee places the power of appointment with the Speaker of the House and the Senate Committees' Committee for their chambers' respective

FIGURE 3.2
Interim Committees

1971–72	2005
Legislative Council	Legislative Council
Legislative Finance	Legislative Finance
School Study	Legislative Education Study
—	Funding Formula Study Task Force
—	Public School Capital Outlay Oversight
University Study	—
Educational Commission of the States	Educational Commission of the States
Judicial Council	Senate Rules
National Conference of Commissions on Uniform State Laws	Commission on Uniform State Laws
—	Interim Legislative Ethics
Drug Abuse Study	Tobacco Settlement Revenue Oversight
—	Courts, Corrections and Justice
Environmental Health Study	Water and Natural Resources
—	Radioactive and Hazardous Materials
—	Los Alamos National Lab Oversight
Commission on Intergovernmental Cooperation	—
—	Welfare Reform Oversight
—	Legislative Health and Human Services
—	Indian Affairs
—	Land Grant
—	Economic, Rural Development and Telecommunications
Insurance Regulation Study	Mortgage Finance Authority Act Oversight
—	New Mexico Finance Authority Oversight
—	State Permanent Fund Task Force
Examining and Licensing Study	—
—	Revenue Stabilization and Tax Policy
—	Information Technology Oversight
Legislative Reapportionment	—
—	Election Reform Task Force

*The Senate Committees' Committee also exercises the Speaker of the House's appointment powers.

Source: "State of New Mexico Forty-Seventh Legislature First Session, House Standing Committees" (Santa Fe: New Mexico Legislative Council Service, 2005); and "State of New Mexico Forty-Seventh Legislature First Session, Senate Standing Committees" (Santa Fe: New Mexico Legislative Council Service, 2005).

members. The chairs of certain standing committees normally hold key positions on related interim committees.[11]

Arguably, the most important committee is the Legislative Council, which is a sixteen-member leadership committee of the legislature consisting of eight senators and eight representatives. The Speaker of the House, President Pro Tem, and minority leaders of the House and Senate are automatically members of this committee. Its composition was changed in 1978 from a thirteen-member body (seven representatives and six senators), after a power struggle between the House and the Senate over interim committees. The immediate cause of this battle was a dispute over who would chair the interim Legislative Finance Committee; eventually other issues concerning interim committees were also raised and considered.

Next to the Legislative Council, the Legislative Finance Committee (LFC) is the most prestigious and powerful interim committee, since the LFC and its staff make budget recommendations to the legislature that carry great authority during the session. Before 1978, this committee was composed of four representatives and three senators, with the chair rotating every two years between the Senate and House members. In 1975 Representative Eddie Lopez, chair of the House Taxation and Revenue Committee, felt that he was in line to chair the LFC; but with the support of Senate members, another representative was given the chair. In 1977 Representative Lopez used the House's four-member majority to have himself declared LFC chairman instead of Senate Majority Leader C. B. Trujillo.

This break from tradition led to a major crisis in the 1978 session, when an angry Senate tied reform of the interim committee system to the "feed bill" that pays for the expenses and staff salaries of the legislature. Until a compromise was hammered out, the legislature faced increasing financial strain. Finally, the two houses reached agreement. The Legislative Council and the LFC were enlarged to sixteen and eight members, respectively, with equal representation being given to each chamber, although the House was given a six-to-four majority on the Legislative Education Study Committee. The Speaker of the House and the President Pro Tem of the Senate were designated as co-chairs of the Legislative Council, and it was specified that the chair of the LFC and LESC would rotate every two years between a senator and a representative.

While the interim-committee crisis of 1978 was precipitated by a clash over the relative power of House and Senate members, several other issues were also folded into the dispute. First was the fact that majorities on the committee could override the desires of most of the delegation from one chamber or the other, with the result that the interim committee's proposals would then have little success when they were formally introduced in that body. This problem was resolved by a prohibition against the interim committees' taking any action opposed by the majority of members from either house. Second, the powers of the minority leadership in the legislature entered into the controversy. The unhappiness of the House minority leader over the Speaker's power to appoint minority members to House and interim committees was noted in the section on legislative leaders. This Republican grievance was met by recognizing the right of minority leaders to influence the selection of their party's members to interim committees.

Interim committees do not report legislation directly to the floor of either legislative chamber for a vote, although such a procedure would be efficient. Instead, their findings and/or recommendations are introduced (if at all) by committee members and referred to the standing committees of the House and Senate in the same manner as are other bills. An interim committee may, however, draft a bill, have it introduced by members, and go on record in support of the bill. Furthermore, since many members of the standing committees of the legislature serve on interim committees of related jurisdiction, the work of the interim committees is not wasted.

A recent development with respect to interim committees has been the growing tendency of the Legislative Council to appoint advisory members. In 2005, legislators were appointed to 188 advisory memberships on twenty-two of the twenty-three interim committees. Since this is more than the total membership of the legislature, it is clear that some legislators are appointed to multiple advisory memberships. Advisory members generally sit with the regularly appointed committee members and participate in the discussion of matters pending before the committee. They are paid out of council funds (the standard per diem and mileage) but legally are not entitled to a vote. The question of advisory members voting has been a matter of controversy upon occasion because the inclusion of the votes of advisory members could overturn the majority of the statutory members. The principal argument that is raised against advisory members voting on permanent committees where the membership is fixed by statute is that it allows for the defeat of statutory intent by advisory members, when the law creating these permanent interim committees contains no provision for such members. Possibly in response to this argument, the legislature amended the statutes creating the Legislative Finance Committee to recognize and guide the temporary appointment of delegates in the event a regular member is unable to attend an LFC meeting.

The number and influence of interim committees have grown over the years since 1951. This is particularly true of the permanent interim committees. The Legislative Council (through its powers to appoint other interim committees, to name chairs and vice chairs to these committees, and to select committee members and commission studies) exercises a significant influence on the legislative workload and on the subject content of the subsequent legislative session. Frequently the work of these interim committees produces major changes in a body of law, such as an election code, a workers' compensation act, an insurance code, or a revision of the Public School Code. The Legislative Finance Committee's authority since its creation in 1957 has been expanded from studying fiscal problems of the state to acting as a watchdog on practically every activity of state government. On one occasion this included a resort to the courts to challenge line-item veto authority of the governor in the General Appropriations Act. Similarly the authority of the Legislative Education Study Committee has evolved to encompass a review of all areas and activities of public education in the state.

The Legislative Council Service

The Legislative Council Service was established by law in 1951 to provide year-round professional staff services for legislators. As its name implies, the staff is supervised by the Legislative Council. Attorneys, political scientists, researchers, legislative reference librarians, secretaries, and clerks provide many services to members of the legislature.

Bill drafting is one of the most important services provided. Before the creation of the Council Service, legislators either drafted their own legislation or turned to an attorney friend for help. Some lobbyists gained great influence by their willingness to provide bill-drafting services. That source of influence is now gone. Today the Council Service prepares well over 98 percent of the bills, memorials, and resolutions introduced in a legislative session. The bill-drafting service is provided without charge to every legislator, to interim and standing committees, and, within time limitations, to the governor, state agencies, and public institutions.

The Legislative Council Service is nonpartisan, and the staff members are prohibited from advocating or opposing legislation (although they may appear in committee on behalf of an interim committee bill). Legislators tell the Council Service staff what they wish to accomplish, and staff members draft the bills accordingly. Unless otherwise requested by the legislator, all requests to the Legislative Council Service are confidential by law.

In addition to drafting bills, the Council Service will, at the legislator's request, develop a list of arguments for and against proposed legislation, so that legislators are better prepared to debate. The Council Service also prepares research reports for legislators, maintains a comprehensive legislative reference library, and provides staff assistance to interim committees. The staff's busiest period, of course, is during a legislative session, when the immediate demands of the legislature tax their resources fully. During a session the Council Service is in charge of the legislative bill room (where anyone can purchase a copy of any bill introduced that session) and of the Bill Locator, a daily summary of the status of every bill introduced that session. The Council Service thus provides a vital service to legislators.

The wide range of services available through the Legislative Council Service, along with committee meeting rooms, semiprivate offices, and secretarial support during the session have helped the New Mexico Legislature rank high in national evaluations of state legislatures.[12] These facilities, coupled with the use of interim committees, help the legislature to obtain information on its own and exercise its collective judgment independently, instead of relying excessively on executive agencies or lobbyists for information and guidance.

PERMANENT HOUSE AND SENATE STAFF

Historically, the Legislative Council Service staff provided year-round general staff support services to the legislature. Support services ranged from dealing with constituent questions, to research, typing, or staffing interim committees. During the interim, legislators did not have individual staffs, offices, or secretarial support. In the early 1990s, some members of the House and Senate advocated the need for personal staff who could provide more individualized attention and whose loyalty would be to a particular chamber (the House or Senate) rather than to the legislature as a whole. In 1994, the legislature provided funding and enacted statutory authorization for the employment of full-time, year-round chief clerks of each house. The legislation allowed the chief clerks to each hire up to five House and Senate staff members (or their full-time equivalent) on a year-round basis. The duties of the chief clerks and their staffs are to assist the members of their respective chambers in constituent services, provide secretarial services, and assist in other legislative activities.

The push for individual staff did not end with the hiring of permanent chief clerks. In the mid-1990s, the Legislative Council Service, along with professionals from the National Conference of State Legislatures and the University of New Mexico Law School, conducted a study to assess the feasibility of hiring permanent legislative leadership staff. The feasibility study became a two-year pilot project and, eventually, the pilot became permanent. As a result, each chamber and each chamber's party leaders employ a small, permanent legislative staff to assist legislative leadership with their many institutional duties.

While the number of year-round employees remains relatively small, the ranks of temporary House and Senate employees swell substantially during a legislative session, when each member is afforded a secretary, an office, and, depending on seniority and position, a number of analysts and assistants. This session employment is only temporary, however, as most positions end with the legislative session.

THE LEGISLATORS

The qualifications for membership in the state legislature are relatively few. State representatives must be at least twenty-one years of age at the time of their election; state senators must be twenty-five. The state constitution prohibits officials of national, state, and certain local governments from serving in the legislature, but employees of the federal government, local governments, or local school districts who do not hold civil offices are eligible to serve. Legislators must be United States citizens and reside in the district they represent.

Though the qualifications for membership are relatively few, they are not without controversy. In 1988, Attorney General Hal Stratton declared that members of a school district's instructional staff could not simultaneously hold that position and the position of a state legislator (despite the fact that public school teachers had served in the legislature for many years). Stratton based his opinion on the statutory provision that prohibits any member of the legislature from receiving compensation for services performed as a state employee. Stratton reasoned that since the vast majority of school funds came from the state, schoolteachers were state employees, prohibited from service in the legislature. Stratton also raised a constitutional separation of powers argument. The attorney general's opinion had an immediate impact on several sitting members of the legislature who were schoolteachers. Rep. Barbara Perea Casey (D-Chaves) filed suit asking for a declaratory judgment by the court that Stratton was wrong. The district court and the New Mexico Court of Appeals obliged, and in a 1991 opinion the Court of Appeals held that Casey and others similarly situated were not state employees and not prohibited from serving in the legislature.[13] The state Supreme Court declined to review the question.

BENEFITS AND BURDENS OF SERVING IN THE LEGISLATURE

Unlike legislators in the majority of states, members of the New Mexico Legislature receive no salary for service. They do receive per diem during the legislative session and while attending meetings of interim committees. The amount of per diem paid is tied to the federally established Internal Revenue Service rate. They also receive reimbursement for travel costs to Santa Fe and back home once each legislative session and for mileage to each meeting of an interim committee. At best, the per diem and mileage allowance reimburse legislators' actual expenses; most legislators serve at significant financial sacrifice. Since legislators must be absent from their regular jobs for at least ninety days every two years and for several days each month because of interim committee activity, the lack of salary puts the post financially out of reach of many citizens who are salaried employees and who would otherwise make excellent legislators.

It is difficult to make precise comparisons of the total compensation of New Mexico legislators with legislators in other states because of the variety of methods of compensation employed across the country, but New Mexico's legislators are among the lowest compensated legislators in the nation. New Mexico is often used as an example of an unpaid "citizen" legislature, in contrast to a "professional" legislature such as California's, where 2004 legislative salaries of $99,000 per year were supplemented with per diem expenses, generous individual staff allowances, and compensation supplements for legislative leaders.[14] New Mexico's status as an unpaid citizen legislature is mandated by the New Mexico Constitution, which provides that legislators receive only per diem and mileage and no other compensation, perquisite, or allowance. Though the legislature has offered up numerous proposed constitutional amendments in recent years (with the hope of instituting a salary), New Mexico voters have declined to approve such a change.

Despite the constitutional restrictions on legislative compensation, the legislature has managed to provide itself with some "contingent" remuneration for service in the form of retirement pensions. In the 1970s and 1980s a few longtime legislators received a small monthly legislative retirement pension provided that they had served more than one term in the legislature and that during their term of service they had made a minimal contribution to the retirement fund. In 1987, Attorney General Hal Stratton challenged the retirement program citing the constitutional prohibition against "other compensation, perquisites or allowance." A state district court eventually upheld the constitutionality of the legislative retirement plan but the state Court of Appeals disagreed, striking down the plan in 1994. An appeal was then filed in the New Mexico Supreme Court. The Supreme Court eventually took the case and reversed the Court of Appeals decision. The Supreme Court held, *inter alia*, that the possibility of receiving retirement was "too remote and contingent" to constitute compensation under the constitution.[15] Interestingly, in 2003 the legislature decided to amend the legislative retirement program to allow a significantly more sizeable payout than that previously provided. Under the 2003 plan, for a yearly contribution of $300, a retiring legislator could receive a retirement income of over $20,000 a year (based on twenty years of service and a lifetime "contribution" of $6,000). To date, the revised plan has not been challenged.

In addition to per diem, mileage, and retirement, legislators receive other nonpecuniary privileges for service. During their attendance at the legislature and while going to and returning from sessions, members of the legislature are exempt from arrest in all cases except treason, felony, or breach of the peace. They cannot be held legally responsible for any speech, debate, or vote cast in the legislature unless bribery is proven. These privileges, which originated in the English Parliament as protection against the Crown, are important for allowing full and free debate in the legislature and are similar to protections afforded United States senators and congressmen by the speech and debate clause of the U.S. Constitution.

While legislators enjoy a number of privileges, they are also subject to certain restrictions. The state constitution provides that no member of the legislature shall, during the term for which he or she is elected, be appointed to any civil office in the state.[16] During the term for which they are elected and for a year afterward, legislators may not be appointed to any civil office that was created, or the pay of which was increased, during their term of office; nor may they have a financial interest, either direct or indirect, in any contract with the state or any municipality that was authorized during their term. Legislators are also forbidden to accept any special transportation privileges from railroads. The objective of these prohibitions, of course, is to reduce the chance of a corrupt legislature.

LEGISLATIVE APPORTIONMENT

Members of the legislature are elected from single-member geographic districts. There are forty-two Senate districts and seventy House districts. Every square foot of the state is included in one of these districts. At the time of the decennial redistricting in 2001, there were approximately twenty-six thousand people in each House district and about forty-three thousand people in every Senate district. The responsibility for drawing legislative district lines rests with the legislature. However, on several occasions for several different reasons, the court has stepped in to accomplish the task. While the process of carving the state into forty-two or seventy pieces may sound almost clerical, it is not. In fact, the legislative districting process has historically been contentious, litigious, and expensive.

It is the Constitution of New Mexico that assigns the task of drawing legislative (and congressional) districts to the legislature. Article 4

authorizes the redrawing of state Senate and House districts once following every federal decennial census. The drawing of district lines is
governed by federal and state law and has been the subject of numerous
court opinions. In fact, the United States Supreme Court's evolving interpretation of the constitutional requirements of districting has been one
of the predominant influences on the district drawing process.

New Mexico entered the Union in 1912 with a fairly well apportioned
legislature and a constitution that permitted but did not require that both
chambers be apportioned on the basis of population after every federal
decennial census. However, the legislature declined to engage in this task
after the 1920, 1930, and 1940 censuses, eventually resulting in significant
malapportionment. This situation was exacerbated by constitutional
amendments in 1949 and 1955 that gave each county one senator and
increased the size of the House to favor sparsely settled counties. Thus,
by 1960, 14 percent of the state's population could elect a Senate majority and 27 percent of the state could elect a majority in the House.
Bernalillo County had one representative in the House for every 29,133
citizens while Harding County had one representative for its 1,874 residents. New Mexico's Senate was the fourth most malapportioned state
Senate in the nation in 1960, with the House ranking eighth in comparison to other state legislatures.

Prior to 1962, an individual who wanted to challenge the disparity
in legislative districts had only one forum, the legislature itself. The United
States Supreme Court refused to consider such challenges believing that
legislative redistricting questions were political questions best left to the
legislative branch. Then in 1962, the Court reversed course, holding in
the landmark case *Baker v. Carr* that such challenges could be brought
to and considered by the Court. That decision had a momentous impact
on New Mexico, as litigants took their districting grievances to the courthouse. Lawsuits started in 1962 and were filed throughout the 1960s, 1970s,
and 1980s. Initially, litigants challenged the disparity in size of districts
(not acreage but people per district) following Supreme Court pronouncements that districts with grossly different population totals violated the Equal Protection Clause of the Fourteenth Amendment. Once
the legislature addressed the uneven population totals of districts, litigants mounted challenges alleging that the methods and the results of
the districting process were discriminatory. Such challenges were based

on the equal protection clause of the Fourteenth Amendment and protections enacted by Congress in the Voting Rights Act of 1965. Time and
again, the courts found in favor of the litigants, sometimes sending plans
back to the legislative drawing board, and sometimes choosing to draw
lines with a judicial pen.

In the 1980s, the legislature found itself before a federal three-judge
panel on several occasions. First, the court held that the process used to
approximate precinct numbers used by the legislature was discriminatory. After new numbers were obtained, the court found that the House
plan violated the federal Voting Rights Act and discriminated against language minorities. The resulting decision left the court redrawing a number of districts and placing the legislature under a "preclearance"
order—requiring future districting plans to be cleared by the three-judge
panel or the United States Department of Justice.

In the 1990s the legislature once again took up the task of redistricting. This time, with several years of prep time under its belt, the legislature had extensive geographic data from the census and the United States
Justice Department peering over its shoulder. After redrawing six Senate
districts at the request of the Justice Department, the state House and
Senate plans were approved by the Justice Department in January 1992.
In 1994, the federal three-judge panel lifted the preclearance order, allowing the legislature to proceed unencumbered in future redistricting efforts.

In 2001, the legislature again took up the task of redistricting the
state's congressional districts and the state Senate and House seats using
the 2000 federal decennial census data. This time, for the first time in
decades, the Democratic House and Senate majorities were faced with
a Republican governor. Since legislative plans are passed in the form of
a bill, such legislation ultimately requires the signature of the governor.
Political disagreements with the governor resulted in the filing of several redistricting lawsuits, and the 2001 state House and congressional
plans were ultimately drawn by the state court. The Senate eventually
passed legislation redistricting that chamber and those districts were used
to conduct elections in 2002 and 2004, respectively.

WHO SERVES IN THE LEGISLATURE

Over the last four decades, who serves in the legislature has changed
dramatically. Following national trends, legislators of the twenty-first

century tend to be more diverse, more urban, and engage in different occupations than their counterparts of decades ago.[17] Figure 3.3 compares the 1965–66, 1979–80, and the 2003–4 legislatures by occupation, region of representation, and ethnicity. The 1965 legislature represents pre-redistricted New Mexico—a time when New Mexico was one of the most malapportioned legislatures in the country. The 1979–80 legislature is post-redistricting and the 2003 legislature is two federal census gatherings and multiple redistrictings later. The occupational categories can only be approximated because many legislators draw their income from several professions. The occupation shown in Figure 3.3 is the first listed for each legislator in the official records. The four major regions of the state used are drawn from past studies of New Mexico politics.[18]

In reviewing Figure 3.3, perhaps one of the most striking observations is the urbanization of the New Mexico Legislature. In 1965, only 9 percent of state senators came from urban areas. By 2003, that number had changed to 45 percent in the Senate and 50 percent in the House. Redistricting, combined with rapid growth in Doña Ana County and the Albuquerque metro area, has resulted in a legislature where the majority of legislators live in an urban environment—an area that physically only accounts for a small portion of the state. As urban-area representation has increased, the influence of southeastern New Mexico has declined. While representation of the Hispanic north has remained steady in the House and declined in the Senate, representation of the traditional agricultural-belt counties has increased, largely as a result of the development of bedroom communities south and east of Albuquerque.

What legislators look like has also changed a lot in the last forty years. The legislature of 2003–4 is more diverse with more minorities and women winning legislative seats. The number of Hispanics serving in the legislature has increased steadily to 36 percent in the Senate and 41 percent in the House in 2003–4. In the House, the percentage roughly parallels the percentage of Hispanics residing in the state. Native Americans have also gained representation, comprising between 4 and 5 percent of the legislature. In 2003–4, two African Americans were members of the House (representing 3 percent of that body—a number that parallels the state census). No member of the New Mexico Senate was African American in 2003–4. And finally, women have steadily increased their presence in the state legislature. In 2003–4, 26 percent of the Senate and

FIGURE 3.3
Legislator Characteristics Before and After Reapportionment

	SENATE			HOUSE		
	1966 (%)	1980 (%)	2003 (%)	1966 (%)	1980 (%)	2003 (%)
OCCUPATION						
Businessman	53	48	54	56	61	38
Attorney	25	21	12	8	13	6
Farmer/Rancher	16	12	5	23	9	3
Educator/Scientist	6	14	9	10	13	21
Other*	0	5	21	3	4	31
REGION						
Urban	9	41	45	30	40	50
Agricultural Belt	47	26	24	33	26	30
Little Texas	22	19	17	23	20	13
Hispanic North	22	14	14	14	14	7
ETHNICITY						
Anglo	75	67	59	77	70	51
Hispanic	25	31	36	22	29	41
American Indian	0	2	5	1	1	4
Black	0	0	0	0	0	3

* Includes retirees in 2003

Source: "State of New Mexico Forty-Sixth Legislature First Session, Occupations" (Santa Fe: New Mexico Legislative Council Service, 2003) State of New Mexico; Thirty-Fourth Legislature Second Session, Occupations" (Santa Fe: New Mexico Legislative Council Service, 1980; "State of New Mexico Twenty-Seventh Legislature Second Session, Occupations" (Santa Fe: New Mexico Legislative Council Service, 1966); and "Enchantment: Legislative Supplement 34th Legislature 2nd Session" (Santa Fe: New Mexico Rural Electrification Cooperative, 1980).

27 percent of House members were women. Notably, the majority leader of the House, the majority whip of the Senate, and chairman of both caucuses in the Senate were women.

As the face and residence of New Mexico legislators have changed, so has their occupation. Historically, the state legislature was dominated by farmers and ranchers, lawyers, and businesspeople. Redistricting and urbanization has resulted in a dramatic decrease in the number of farmers and ranchers serving in the legislature. So too has the number of lawyers declined—a trend that has occurred across the country.[19] Finally, though the percentage of businesspeople has remained fairly steady in the Senate, the House has seen a significant decrease in the number of legislators declaring themselves as business operators. It is interesting to note that the number of educators in the legislature is significant (almost a fifth of the House membership in 2003–4) and almost a quarter of the House membership considers itself retired. Presumably the increase in interim committees and other legislative commitments makes legislative service more suitable to a retiree than an individual actively pursing a law practice or other small business.

DETERMINANTS OF LEGISLATIVE BEHAVIOR

Many factors affect the types of bills that legislators sponsor, the committee assignments they seek, and the votes they cast in committee meetings and on the floor of the House or Senate. Some of the major factors affecting legislative behavior are the legislator's age, personal background, ethnicity, political party and occupation, home region of the state, the competitiveness of the legislative district, constituents' socioeconomic status, and legislator career ambitions. The young legislator with ambition for higher office, for instance, is likely to behave differently than the young attorney who is serving a term or two just to enhance a legal practice. Both young members will behave differently, in many ways, from the retiree who is in the legislature to keep active.

Legislators' occupations and personal backgrounds affect their understanding and position on various issues, despite every effort at objectivity. Many observers argue that some legislators function as inside lobbyists, for they seem to be at least as concerned with defending the interests of their industry or profession as they are with guarding the interests of the state as a whole. The state's conflict-of-interest act attempts to limit such influence by requiring disclosures about legislators' major financial interests. Furthermore, legislative rules permit members to request that they be excused from voting on bills in which they have a pecuniary interest.

Redistricting has had a significant effect on legislative behavior, as might be expected from its previously noted impact on legislator characteristics. As is rather common in a party with a long-standing and substantial majority, the Democratic party in the House is divided between a conservative faction and a moderate to liberal faction. The House was dominated for years by the conservative members of the Democratic party,

FIGURE 3.4
Other Legislator Characteristics, 2003–4

	SENATE (%)	HOUSE (%)
PARTY		
Democrat	57	61
Republican	43	39
EDUCATION		
High School	7	7
Some College	90	93
Unknown	2	0
SEX		
Male	71	70
Female	29	30
TENURE		
Less than 4 Years	26	36
4 to 8 Years	26	24
Over 9 Years	48	40
AGE		
Under 40	2	11
41 to 50	26	17
51 to 60	50	26
Over 60	21	46

Source: "Enchantment: Legislative Supplement 46th Legislature" (Santa Fe: New Mexico Rural Electrification Cooperative, 2003).

many of them from the southern and eastern parts of the state. Redistricting has led to a slow shift in the composition of that Democratic majority as the number of legislators from southeastern New Mexico has declined. By contrast, as the legislature has become more urban, the moderate liberal faction of the Democratic party has gained strength, maintaining dominance in both chambers for most of the last two decades.

INTEREST GROUPS

As with the United States Congress, members of the New Mexico Legislature are influenced by a large number of groups and individuals

vying for legislative attention. Most active legislative lobbying is by individuals who are not legislators, although some are former legislators.
Except for employees of state agencies, lobbyists are required by law to
register with the secretary of state. They must report the source and
amount of the funds used in their lobbying and the purposes for which
they spend money while lobbying. Each session of the New Mexico
Legislature finds lobbyists representing various companies, industries,
and interest groups. Normally represented are utilities; the extractive
industries; the construction industry; the liquor industry; insurance companies; automobile dealers; banks, savings and loan associations, and
credit unions; public transportation companies; restaurant, motel, and
hotel operators; educators; local governments; environmental organizations; professional associations; organized labor; realtors; land develop-
ers; and ranchers and farmers.

Just as different lobbyists vie for attention, so too do the "hot" issues
vary from session to session. One year the major battle may be over the
formula for allocating state monies for local school districts; the next year
it may be over the appropriate level of taxation of extractive industries,
rights for domestic partners, or sex offender registration laws. Another
year battles may be waged over abortion, gambling, or the creation of
water courts.

Each interest group is ready to protect its economic or ideological
interests. Legislators' votes on many issues are determined by their basic
philosophy of government, but many legislators are also open to persua-
sion based on the merits of the arguments. A skillful lobbyist or fellow
legislator may well be able to win such members' votes. Communication
from a legislator's constituents is also sometimes effective. Some legislators, however, report that they receive almost no communication from
their constituents on many major issues.

Most legislators seemingly accept interest-group activity as a valid
part of the state's political system. F. Chris Garcia, for example, found
that in a sample of thirty-four state senators in 1977, 67 percent
believed that interest groups exercise an appropriate amount of legislative influence in New Mexico, as opposed to 29 percent who felt
it was too great. Almost 60 percent of a matched sample of their constituents, in contrast, felt that interest groups were too powerful. The
senators further reported that the strongest influence was exerted by

teachers' associations and the voters in general, with banks, labor unions, ranchers, and utilities also being fairly strong.

The difference between the way legislators and voters perceive lobbying suggests that New Mexicans are concerned with the possibility that insiders and special interests have undue influence over state politics. This suspicion of excessive elite power evidently extends to the legislators themselves. Thus Garcia's study showed that while the senators and their constituents had fairly similar positions on most subjects, most citizens felt that they had little or no influence over their representatives. The citizens and senators also clashed over whether legislators should follow the wishes of their districts or their own best judgments, with each group believing that its will should prevail.[20] In the end result, citizens are less than enamored with the performance of their legislators. The University of New Mexico's Institute for Public Policy has found in its quarterly survey of New Mexico citizens' attitudes that less than 20 percent of the respondents rate the legislature's performance as "excellent" or "good," with unresponsiveness and unethical behavior being the principal matters of public concern.

SUMMARY

New Mexico has a partisan bicameral legislature composed of a seventy-member House of Representatives and a forty-two member Senate, all elected from single-member districts. The legislature meets for sixty days in odd-numbered years and thirty days in even-numbered years, and the agenda in the thirty-day session is restricted primarily to financial affairs and topics the governor formally requests the legislature to consider. Democrats have held the majority of seats in both chambers since 1933, with the exception of the 1953–54 House and the 1985–86 Senate, but cross-party coalitions have governed each chamber in recent years. With prodding from the state and federal courts, redistricting in the past four decades has resulted in a legislature whose members now represent the various areas of the state fairly, according to population, in place of what was one of the most malapportioned legislatures in the nation.

Although ours is a part-time, non-salaried legislature, a nonprofessional legislative body by definition, it has historically received high marks in support services and representativeness. Furthermore, through intelligent utilization of its resources and the use of interim legislative committees, the New Mexico Legislature maintains substantial independence from the executive branch of government, despite the limitations resulting from the constitutionally mandated brief legislative sessions.

NOTES

1.   This chapter is based, in part, on previous chapters by Paul L. Hain, Cal Clark and Janet Clark, and Paul Hain and Richard Folmar in earlier editions of this book.

2.   Vacancies are filled by the county commission in which the district lies. If the legislative district includes residents of more than one county, the relevant county commissions each nominate a person to the governor, and the governor appoints the new legislator from among the nominees.

3.   In January 2002, the legislature convened in regular session. Though the legislature passed a proposed budget, Governor Gary Johnson refused to sign it, citing concerns about overspending. As the end of the fiscal year loomed, members of the House and Senate called themselves into extraordinary session to avert a state government shutdown on July 1, the beginning of the new fiscal year.

4.   If the petitioners obtain the signatures of 25 percent of the electors, rather than 10 percent, and file the petition with the secretary of state within ninety days after the adjournment of the legislative session at which the law was enacted, the operation of the challenged law is suspended pending the general election outcome. This 25 percent provision has never been activated.

5.   New Mexico Attorney General Opinion No. 64–137, Nov. 10, 1964, and letter to Paul Hain from Hon. Ernestine D. Evans, secretary of state, Jan. 23, 1976.

6.   Constitution of New Mexico, Article 4, Section 36.

7.   Sitting as a committee of the whole enables the House to hear witnesses and to discuss questions in a freer and more informal format. For instance, debate in a committee of the whole is not limited, and records of how members vote are not kept. Legislation, however, cannot be formally enacted by the House while sitting as a committee of the whole.

8.   The Speaker also signs all bills, resolutions, and memorials, and certifies the passage of bills over the governor's veto. This leader signs all processes ordered to be issued by the House and has the power to issue writs of arrest for any person who willfully fails or refuses to appear before the House or any committee after having been subpoenaed on order of the House. The Speaker also controls the use of House committee rooms, galleries, and offices, and supervises the work of other House employees and officers, as well as signing their payroll vouchers.

9.   The power inherent in these finance committees is well illustrated by the fact that Aubrey Dunn, who served as chairman of the Senate Finance Committee from 1973 to 1979, was called, "the second governor." Dave Steinberg, "Loss of Senator May Shift Power to House," *Albuquerque Journal*, Dec. 28, 1979, p. D-10.

10.   Engrossing is the process of incorporating into a "clean" copy of a bill all amendments to it. Normal practice in the New Mexico Legislature is to defer engrossing until the time the bill is enrolled. Amendments are merely

attached to the introduced bill. Enrolling means the preparation of the final authoritative copy of the bill as passed by both houses of the legislature. This copy incorporates all amendments adopted and agreed to by both houses and is then substituted for the original bill, signed by the presiding officers in both houses, and sent to the governor. Although not glamorous, enrolling and engrossing are important. If an error is made and not caught before the governor signs the bill into law, then the will of the legislature has been thwarted; the error can only be corrected by further legislation.

11.   The membership of each of these three major interim committees must include certain legislators: the Speaker of the House, Senate President Pro Tem, and minority leaders of the House and Senate for the Legislative Council; the chair of the State Finance Committee, the House Appropriations and Finance Committee, and House Taxation and Revenue Committee for the LFC; and one member each from the House Education Committee, the Senate Education Committee, the House Appropriations and Finance Committees, and the Senate Finance Committee for the LESC. The other minority members from the House are appointed by the Speaker from recommendations made by the minority floor leader. Although retaining the right to reject specific recommendations, the Speaker cannot appoint any minority member who is not proposed by the minority leader. In addition the Senate minority leader appoints one member of the Legislative Council whenever the minority party in the Senate is entitled to two or more positions on it.

12.   Overall the Citizens' Conference on State Legislatures ranked the New Mexico Legislature eleventh among the fifty such bodies in the United States. New Mexico ranked third on "functionality" (e.g., staff support, physical facilities, and organization and procedures); sixteenth on "accountability" (e.g., clarity of rules and procedures, internal accountability, and adequacy of information and public access to it); twenty-eighth on "information-handling capability" (e.g., adequate time in the legislative session, interim activities, and fiscal review capabilities); thirty-ninth on "independence" (e.g., expenditure control, access to information, oversight capability, conflicts of interest, and relations with lobbyists); and fourth on "representativeness" (e.g., diversity of legislators, size of legislative body, and identification of members and constituents). Recommendations for improving the New Mexico Legislature include: (1) longer legislative sessions; (2) legislative salaries of $10,000 or more a year; (3) written descriptions of committee jurisdiction and uniform committee rules; (4) formal control of minority member committee assignments by the minority party leadership; and (5) conflict-of-interest restrictions to prohibit legislators or their firms from practicing before state regulatory agencies for a fee or from doing business with the state. See Citizens' Conference on State Legislatures, *State Legislatures: An Evaluation of Their Effectiveness* (New York, Praeger Publishers, 1971).

13.   *State ex rel. Hal Stratton v. Roswell Indept. Schools,* 111 NM 495 (Ct.App. 1991).

14.   *The Book of the States* (Lexington, Ky.: Council of State Governments, 2004).

15.   *State ex. rel Udall v. Public Employees Retirement Board,* 120 NM at 793 (1995).

16.   Richard H. Folmar, *Legislative Apportionment in New Mexico: 1844–1966* (Santa Fe: New Mexico Legislative Council Service, 1966); Harry P. Stumpf and T. Phillip Wolf, "New Mexico," in E. Bushnell, ed., *Impact of*

Reapportionment on Thirteen Western States (Salt Lake City: University of Utah Press, 1970); and a previous version of this chapter, Paul L. Hain, "The Legislature," in F. Chris Garcia and Paul L. Hain, eds., *New Mexico Government* (Albuquerque: University of New Mexico Press, 1976), pp. 30–32.

17.   Alan Rosenthal, *The Decline of Representative Democracy: Process, Participation and Power in State Legislatures* (Washington, D.C.: Congressional Quarterly Press, 1997).

18.   Jack Holmes, *Politics in New Mexico* (Albuquerque: University of New Mexico Press, 1967); Harry P. Stumpf and T. Phillip Wolf, "New Mexico: The Political State," in Frank H. Jonas, ed., *Politics in the American West* (Salt Lake City: University of Utah Press, 1969); and Cal Clark and Janet Clark, "New Mexico," in B. Oliver Walter, ed., *Politics in the West: The 1978 Elections* (Laramie, Wyo.: Government Research Bureau, 1979). The four regions and the counties in them are: (1) the generally liberal Hispanic north of heavily (over 65 percent) Spanish counties (Guadalupe, Mora, Rio Arriba, Sandoval, San Miguel, Santa Fe, and Taos); (2) the Little Texas region in the southeast part of the state, which has historically displayed conservative, southern-type Democratic politics (Chaves, Curry, DeBaca, Eddy, Lea, Quay, and Roosevelt); (3) several urban counties, which contain major concentrations of the professional middle class that has been the mainstay of Republicanism in the state as well as a significant number of Hispanics (Bernalillo, Doña Ana, and Los Alamos); and (4) the remainder of the state, termed the agricultural belt, whose degree of Democratic voting varies with these counties' social composition.

19.   Rosenthal, *The Decline of Representative Democracy.*

20.   F. Chris Garcia, "Comparative Opinions of New Mexico Voters and State Senators" (Albuquerque: Division of Government Research, University of New Mexico, December 1978).

FOR FURTHER READING

The Citizens Conference on State Legislatures. *State Legislatures: An Evaluation of Their Effectiveness.* New York: Praeger Publishers, 1971. See especially pp. 256–60, "Recommendations for New Mexico."

Darcy, R., Susan Welch, and Janet Clark, *Women, Elections, and Representation.* New York: Longman, 1987.

Alan Rosenthal, *The Decline of Representative Democracy: Process, Participation and Power in State Legislatures.* Washington, D.C.: Congressional Quarterly Press, 1997.

Folmar, Richard H. *Legislative Apportionment in New Mexico: 1944–1966.* Santa Fe: New Mexico Legislative Council Service, August 1966.

Legislative Handbook, Forty-Sixth (and Forty-Seventh) New Mexico Legislature, 2003 and 2005 editions. (This handbook, published every session, contains the rules of each chamber and much other valuable current information.)

Legislative Council Service, A Citizen's Guide to Redistricting. Santa Fe: Legislative Council Service, 2001.

Chapter Four

The Fragmented Executive

I n the United States there are two main models for organizing the executive branch of a state government. One model, of which New Mexico
is an example, features numerous independently elected officers, such
as the governor, treasurer, and attorney general, along with many agencies that come under the administrative authority of a board or commission. The other type of state government has evolved from a
sustained period of reform during the past fifty years. This model, of
which New Jersey is a prime example, has only one or a few elected executives and places boards and commissions under the governor's authority. This model has the objective of placing more accountability in the
governor's office, reducing the influence of the often unpredictable politics of citizen boards, and increasing the influence of professional administrators in state agencies.

New Mexico adopted the fragmented executive system along with
the state constitution in 1912 and has doggedly maintained it through
many periods of attempted reform. Under this fragmented executive system, the governor is designated as the "supreme executive power" but is
joined by other important political figures elected to constitutionally prescribed executive offices, each with an administrative organization and
a budget of its own. Reformers have sought to amend the constitution

to reduce the number of elected executives and place those responsibilities on officials appointed by the governor. However, these efforts have
not been successful to date. In this chapter each of the constitutional executive officers, the principal independent commissions, and the executive departments under the governor will be described.

Administrative reformers have been more successful in achieving
organizational and staffing reforms in the executive departments that are
under the control of the governor. Although the reform process was initially very slow, major changes have occurred in recent decades.

In a state that employed only seventeen thousand employees, it may
seem odd that the organization of those employees and particularly
their relationship to the state chief executive was a problematic issue
for nearly thirty years. Beginning with the report of the New Mexico
State Reorganization Committee of 1952, a restructuring of state government to give the governor more authority over departmental affairs
has been a recurring theme. Other studies would follow, but it was not
until Governor Jerry Apodaca (1975–79) made executive reorganization the centerpiece of his administration that these changes finally
came about.

The problems long faced by the state are best summarized in the 1978
organization-implementation plan.

> As government grew more complex, bringing within its purview func-
> tions previously unidentified or left to resolution by the private sector,
> the most favored method of dealing with any newly acquired responsi-
> bility was to create a new agency, board or commission. Unfortunately,
> this approach was employed without the benefit of periodic, in-depth
> review of the operations of or need for these creations.... The
> inevitable by-products were expensive waste and confusion, both for
> the private citizen seeking service or mere understanding and for the
> public employee attempting to communicate, to gain information or
> to resolve problems. The situation of a government incapacitated by its
> own disorganization and the weight of its bureaucracy was not one
> unique to New Mexico. Since the mid-1960s, the states have been in the
> midst of an unprecedented push for governmental reform. While no
> uniform approach or design has emerged from this surge of activity,
> certain principles have guided the efforts of almost all states that are or

have been involved in governmental reorganization. These principles include increased accountability, increased accessibility, increased efficiency and improved intergovernmental relations.[1]

It is now almost thirty years since that reorganization plan was enacted into law. The question to be asked is whether we are closer to achieving the goals outlined above with reorganized state government. Answering this question is the implicit task of this chapter, as the functions and operations of the executive agencies of New Mexico government are examined.

THE STATE BUREAUCRACY

When examining the executive agencies in New Mexico, a number of questions arise concerning the range of work performed, the size of the workforce, the legal constraints upon hiring and promotion, and the character of the interaction between the political and policy making spheres of government and its administrative arm. This section focuses on the structural matters of size, composition, and legal environment. Subsequent discussion of the cabinet will address the question of the relation between politics and administration.

THE STRUCTURE

There are some twenty thousand state employees in New Mexico, working in twenty-two departments and well over one hundred boards and commissions. The overall organization of government has been considerably modified by the introduction of the cabinet system in 1978. However, much of that structure reflects the political heritage and philosophy of the original state constitution. Thus, for example, the state constitution mandates a fragmented executive branch, which includes both elected officials who oversee agencies functionally distinct from the governor, such as the attorney general and secretary of state, and those who oversee narrow, technical agencies that reflect the political concerns of the turn of the twentieth century, such as the Public Regulation Commission and the Public Lands Commission.

Of more direct concern to the operations of the state bureaucracy is the legacy of using boards and commissions to head state agencies. The Progressives believed that in using a board to head an agency, the

worst aspects of political influence could be prevented. Their faith in
the ability of neutral experts and citizens to manage and direct the affairs
of governmental agencies rested on a distrust of politics that remains
to this day. Thus by 1976, while thirteen agencies were headed by a single executive, there were over one hundred agencies headed by boards,
more than half of whom were composed of individuals not nominated
or appointed by the governor.[2]

The creation of the cabinet system has done little to alter this arrangement. Licensing and examining boards come under the Regulation and
Licensing Department, the head of which is a gubernatorial appointment,
but that department does not have cabinet status. The Department of
Agriculture was created by the state constitution. Appointment of the
director of the department is left to the Board of Regents of New Mexico
State University. Finally, many boards and commissions are designated
as being "administratively attached" to the various cabinet departments.
That designation effectively means that if one were to look for the budget
of those boards it would be included in the budget document for that
executive department. Policy control remains with the board, not the cabinet secretary.

The surest and best means of insulating policy from the possibly cor-
rupting influence of electoral politics is in protecting an employee from
removal (except for cause) by elected officials. Oddly, this reform, which
is so closely identified with the Progressive Era, is the one feature of government that New Mexico did not adopt upon gaining statehood.

New Mexico for most of its history has operated under the so-called
patron system, whereby regional political bosses controlled the hiring
of local and state employees. These "job brokers" dominated the hiring
process in virtually all of state government well into the 1960s. In fact,
it was not until then that a merit system was enacted. Even so, the
decades-old tradition of hiring did not disappear with the enactment
of the merit-based personnel statute. Not only were many of the then-
current employees grandfathered into their positions, but the role and
influence of the patrons remained important in a number of state agencies into the 1970s. The continuing legacy of the old ways was that to
accommodate the many people hired under the old system, the qualifications, particularly educational qualifications, for many jobs were kept
artificially low.

THE CIVIL SERVICE

The procedures and policies that govern the operation of the public service in New Mexico became law in 1961. Chapter 240 of the laws of 1961, known as the "Personnel Act," created a State Personnel Board, a State Personnel Office, and the position of personnel director. According to a 1964 attorney general's opinion, the purpose of the act was to insulate state employees from the whims and caprice of the election process, so as to provide continuity of government in a changing environment. This "merit system" was, according to that opinion, designed to replace the patronage hiring practices previously allowed with a new appointment system based on objective examination to assure that "competent" citizens are initially selected for most positions in the state public service.[3]

The coverage of this act was quite inclusive from the outset, in that it excluded relatively few categories of public employees, such as legislative, judicial, and military employees, as well as those in "policy making" positions such as department heads. The only other substantial category of employees excluded was university and public school heads (although public school employees are covered by district programs, and the universities have plans for faculty and staff). The new Personnel Office, acting through the Personnel Board, was authorized to promulgate rules to govern the full range of personnel activities. These include: (1) a classification plan, (2) a pay plan, (3) competitive entrance and promotion tests, (4) the establishment of employment lists for certification of standing, (5) hours of work, holidays, and leave, and (6) dismissal and demotion.[4]

In addition to the above duties, the Personnel Board is mandated to serve as the appeals board on employee grievances, undertake investigations and studies "necessary to the proper administration of the Personnel Act," and represent the public interest in the improvement of personnel administration in the system. In addition to the duties and responsibilities outlined above, the State Personnel Office runs extensive training programs under its Human Resource and Development Division.

After what must be regarded as a late start (the first federal civil service law was enacted in 1883 and had reached near-universal coverage by the 1930s), the state of New Mexico has created a broad-ranging personnel system that offers services and protections for the employees comparable to those found in the federal civil service or in most states. With relatively few exceptions (such as Utah and Washington), the scope of the personnel law in New Mexico compares quite favorably with those of other states. The influence of the patron system is all but gone in most state agencies, particularly in those areas where credentials were critical to credibility, such as in the Taxation and Revenue Department's need for individuals with accounting backgrounds to perform its work. Pressure points still exist in the system, but they typically are confined to policy making levels and thus senior management, rather than at lower levels of the bureaucracy.

THE EXECUTIVE OFFICERS AND DEPARTMENTS

There is no easy means of summarizing and categorizing the agencies of state government. As noted earlier, even where agencies are administratively part of a cabinet organization or are within an "independent department," direct lines of control, communication, and policy coordination do not always exist. The following account of state government is presented with this caveat: policy control does not necessarily exist over some organizational entities included as part of a given department. Where such control is relatively nominal, the locus of actual control is noted.

THE GOVERNOR

The constitutional designation of the governor as the "supreme executive power" has more formal than real meaning, because substantial powers are vested in other executive offices, boards, and commissions. The governor has the day-to-day responsibility to see that the laws are "faithfully executed" and that the financial affairs of the state are in order. The constitution gives the governor five areas of authority: appointive, legislative, budgetary, clemency, and emergency. Furthermore, a governor's informal influence through personal, political, and symbolic means is considerable; any effective governor relies heavily on these resources.

The governor's ability to appoint agency heads is a powerful means of realizing goals; the governor appoints about four hundred agency heads and other state employees who are "exempt" from the state personnel system.[5] Agency heads serve at the governor's pleasure and look to the chief executive for management direction in accordance with the governor's own style.

Executive power, however, often resides in a board, the members of which are appointed by the governor, but with whom the relationship is considerably more complicated than that of a traditional employer. The board members usually receive only per diem and mileage for their efforts and may be political supporters or leaders with a reciprocal power base of their own. In some cases board members may make all policy for the department and even appoint the agency head. Powerful boards with substantial authority include the Museum Board of Regents, the Transportation Commission, the Water Quality Control Commission, the Interstate Stream Commission, the Personnel Board, the Racing Commission, the Investment Council, and the Game Commission.

Achieving a governor's goals through the medium of a board represents one of the most taxing challenges of the office. The governor can simply tell a board what is wanted, except where the board is carrying out administrative responsibilities in areas such as rule making and adjudicatory decision making. Even communication in appropriate instances can have a political cost because of a public perception that a governor should not interfere with the operation of a board. Governors are not infrequently confronted by boards that disregard their wishes, producing a test of political skills.

The governor's constitutional authority to change the composition of a board at will (unless a statute explicitly denies that power) has been confirmed by judicial decision. Nevertheless, the political costs of exercising that power, either with holdover appointees or the incumbent's own appointees, may be unacceptably high. In the delicate area of personnel appointments, governors have on occasion removed entire boards to effect their wishes, but when they do so they run the risk of harsh media and public judgment. However, Governor Bill Richardson requested the resignation of all officials who had been appointed by his predecessor, Gary Johnson, including university regents. Further, he required his appointees to provide him with signed but undated letters of resignation to make the task of dismissing them potentially less messy. (Some of the regents refused to resign and relied on the constitutional protections that preclude their removal by the governor.)

On the other hand, governors may not simply view boards as a hindrance to their authority. Board members may bring expertise to their task that is not otherwise present within state government. Their real or apparent isolation from the governor can shield the governor from the political consequences of every disgruntled person who has been affected by a board's decision. A board can also provide an issue with the sort of hearing that a governor might like to give to it, but for which the time cannot be found. Thus governors often create advisory boards to provide these functions, increasing the very fragmentation of government bemoaned on other occasions.

The governor has considerable power to initiate legislative issues in the governor's call of the legislature into session, in messages to the legislature (such as the State of the State address at the beginning of a session), or in bills submitted by sponsors on behalf of the governor. Through control of executive agency personnel, the governor is also able to affect the sources of information available to the legislature and influence its perception of much legislation.

New Mexico governors have strong veto power. They can veto any bill passed by the legislature, including particular items in an appropriations bill, but must act within three days (Sundays excepted) of receiving the bill from the legislature. The legislature can override a veto by a vote of two-thirds of each house, except for bills that reach the governor within the last three days of a session. Since the legislature tends to postpone final actions on important measures, including the state budget, until late in the session, very important decisions often occur during the final three-day period. The governor has twenty days to consider bills passed during those last three days; such bills must receive the governor's signature if they are to become law.

The budget has increasingly become the main preoccupation of the legislative session and has shaped the public perception of the governor's power relative to that of the legislature. Executive agencies submit budget requests to the Legislative Finance Committee in the late summer, with the executive and legislative branches holding parallel budget hearings throughout the fall. In January, the newly convened legislature is presented with an executive recommendation, reflecting the governor's own decisions on the budget, as well as separate budget recommendations made by the interim Legislative Finance Committee. (See the appropriation process description in chapter 6.)

The governor's other important constitutional duties include granting pardons and reducing or suspending sentences, except in cases of impeachment or treason. A serious point of contention arose at the end of Governor Toney Anaya's term regarding the use of the governor's power to commute a death sentence to a term of life in prison.

The governor is also the commander of the New Mexico National Guard, except when the president calls it into federal service. The National Guard is an essential part of the reserve armed forces of the United States, trained, equipped, and managed under guidelines from the U.S. government. The governor appoints the general officer commanding the Guard, which can play an important role in the state when called into action by the governor. Its duties include putting down insurrection or riot, keeping the peace, defending the state against invasion, and helping in emergencies such as floods or blizzards. It should be recognized as well that the National Guard has units in many towns in the state and provides important supplemental income and status to its part-time volunteers. In some small communities, the Guard is the most important unit of the state government. Its management and political tone are important considerations for the governor and the executive staff.

The governor can often employ executive orders to set public policy, in the absence of legislation to the contrary. In recent years executive orders have been used to regulate working conditions, set personnel policy in certain areas, and make symbolic political statements on controversial issues. The executive order is also a mechanism through which the governor can respond to national or state crises. For example, in 2003 Governor Richardson issued an executive order establishing the Office of the Homeland Security Advisor in response to heightened security concerns following the attacks on the World Trade Center and the Pentagon on September 11, 2001 (Executive Order 2003–007). Activist governors can change some important conditions through executive order, provided they are willing to suffer the possible controversy and political reaction.

The governor's tenure can have significant policy implications. While the turnover of political appointees with the change of gubernatorial administrations disrupts the implementation of policies, the possibility of two consecutive four-year terms makes it harder for the legislature, other officials, and the agencies to avoid a governor's initiatives and policies.

THE LIEUTENANT GOVERNOR

The most recognized role for a lieutenant governor is to preside over the state Senate when it is in session and to vote in case of a tie. This is the constitutional provision for the office in New Mexico. The political importance of the office in many states has led the lieutenant governor into the governor's office, Congress, or another major office. Historically in New Mexico, however, the lieutenant governor has not been viewed as a major political figure able to command the lead in a race for higher office. Until the mid-1970s the office was viewed as a part-time position. The legislature changed that by statute, making it potentially a full-time position with a salary, if the incumbent so chose. The office was also given added responsibility for troubleshooting with executive agencies on behalf of citizens; this advocacy role can magnify the limited visibility of the lieutenant governor and lead to increased political importance of the office. The lieutenant governor can impose a personal interpretation on the role of advocate. Some occupants of the office have maintained their professional activities while serving as part-time lieutenant governor and have assigned most ombudsman duties to staff members. Others have concentrated a great deal of effort on the personal representation of citizens before state agencies.

The lieutenant governor succeeds to the governorship if the office becomes vacant. The lieutenant governor is also designated as acting governor when the governor is disabled or out of the state, making the lieutenant governor's visibility and potential for political ascendancy very much dependent on the governor's behavior.

The candidates for lieutenant governor are nominated separately in political party primaries, but run on party slates with the candidates for governor. Cooperation between the two top officials in the campaign is desirable, but political and personal differences can cause conflict that may carry over into the administration and, in an extreme case, into the next election.

THE EXECUTIVE CABINET

The culmination of nearly thirty years of study and analysis, the executive reorganization sponsored by Governor Apodaca was effected in 1978. The legislature established fourteen departments of which twelve were designated as cabinet departments. With the passage of time the number of departments directly answerable to the governor has grown and the composition of the cabinet has changed. The greatest growth and change occurred in the Richardson administration when five new departments were added to the cabinet, bringing the total number of

departments to twenty-three, of which twenty were designated as cabinet departments. What has not changed is the mandate of the cabinet.
According to Section 9–1–3 of New Mexico Statutes Annotated (1978),
the cabinet still:

1. advises the governor on problems of state government;
2. establishes liaison and provides communication between the
   executive departments and state elected officials;
3. investigates problems of public policy;
4. studies government performance and recommends methods
   of interagency cooperation;
5. reviews policy problems and recommends solutions;
6. strives to minimize and eliminate overlapping jurisdictions
   and conflicts within the executive branch; and
7. assists the governor in defining policies and programs to make
   the government responsive to the needs of the people.

The cabinet departments vary considerably in size, scope of
responsibility, and policy orientation. The Transportation
Department, for example, consumes major portions of the budget and
employs personnel throughout the state; on the other hand, its principal function is primarily technical—it provides the necessary
analysis for effective and timely decisions on new highway construction and needed repairs to existing thoroughfares and planning a
statewide multimodel transportation network. In contrast, the
Department of Economic Development is quite small in terms of number of employees, but has a politically important policy responsibility—the economic expansion of the state. For those in the
Transportation Department, the process of policy review is quite
straightforward; there remains a major need for more state roads
throughout New Mexico. The major difficulty is persuading legislators to support the department's list of priorities rather than adopt
a set of highway priorities more to the liking of certain powerful legislators. In the Department of Economic Development, the "problem"
of economic growth is both difficult to define and subject to so many
influences beyond state boundaries that the task is to stay out in front
of problems, not to adopt a single "solution."

CABINET AND PUBLIC POLICY

The cabinet was conceived as a means of better coordinating the policy making and policy-implementation activities of state government. Although the process has varied from administration to administration, it has worked reasonably well throughout. The coordination has operated at three levels: first, through the formal convening of the entire executive cabinet with the governor; second, through the use of cabinet councils (in effect, subcommittees) to address policy issues that cut across several cabinet departments; third, through the informal interaction among cabinet secretaries (and with public officials not part of the cabinet).

The policy role of the cabinet has been enhanced further by the practice of Governor Carruthers (1987–91) to push policy analysis down to the cabinet officers rather than to retain it as a function of gubernatorial staff. Successive governors have continued this practice. The anomaly in this choice is that this strengthens the role of the cabinet officers as an advocate of the department and lessens their role as representatives for gubernatorial policy to the agencies. For those who believe in the "theory of capture"[6] by bureaucracies, this upward, rather than downward, flow of communication is a detriment to the proper implementation of gubernatorial policy. In contrast, those who promote the use of this practice would argue that better knowledge of organizational norms and procedures is a critical first step in permitting the cabinet, as a collective body, to devise and execute multi-agency policies and programs. If the cabinet were merely a ceremonial or symbolic body with little true interaction, departmental advocacy would produce much of the same fragmentation that exists without the cabinet. Because the cabinet is designed as a policy making body, the better knowledge of departmental capabilities (which can be shared with other cabinet officers) implied by this system permits more accurate assessments of policy-implementation strategies. This constant interaction overcomes the tendency toward fragmentation and differentiation of viewpoints that is common to the departments (most of whom are responsible for a narrow range of policy). Clearly this is the view held by the state's most recent governors.

The other aspect of the cabinet's policy role concerns its relationship to the legislature. While the primary concerns of the legislature are both broader (through the budget) and narrower (oversight of the implementation of specific programs) than those of the cabinet officers, the members of the cabinet are in the best position to explain overall programmatic goals and objectives that cut across specific implementation efforts. A general description of the cabinet departments is provided below.

AGING AND LONG-TERM CARE

In 2003 Governor Richardson signaled his intent to elevate the State Agency on Aging to cabinet-level status when he signed Executive Order No. 2003–022. The legislature obliged, passing legislation to transform the State Agency on Aging into the new Aging and Long-Term Services Department in 2004. The department serves as the primary advocate and provider of services for eligible persons age sixty and older in the state. It provides transportation, outreach programs, information and referral assistance, senior center activities, long-term ombudsman oversight, employment assistance, and volunteer opportunities. The department contracts with many regional and local agencies to provide services and administer capital outlay contracts for the construction, maintenance, and equipping of facilities.

AGRICULTURE

The Department of Agriculture is unique in a number of respects; first in that its administrative headquarters is in Las Cruces, on the campus of New Mexico State University, and second because appointment power for the secretary rests with the Board of Regents of New Mexico State University, rather than with the governor.[7] At the same time, the secretary of the department is a member of the executive cabinet. The basic responsibility of the department is the promotion of the state's agricultural, ranching, and farming interests. Central to this duty is the operation, in cooperation with the federal government and county governments, of the Agricultural Extension Service. Other duties relate to pest, disease, and weed control; seeds and fertilizer; and agricultural marketing and processing.

CHILDREN, YOUTH AND FAMILIES

The Children, Youth and Families Department was created in 1992 by statute responding to a request from Governor Bruce King. At the time it represented the most significant reallocation of responsibilities among agencies since the original creation of the cabinet. It was constructed with pieces of the Departments of Human Services, Health and Corrections plus the noncabinet level Youth Authority. The department serves and supports children and families, supervises youth, "in a responsive community-based system of care that is client-centered, family focused and culturally aware."[8] It does so through four programs: Juvenile Justice; Adult and Child Protective Services; Prevention and Intervention and Program Support.

CORRECTIONS

The Corrections Department is charged with providing a balanced system of correction from incarceration to community-based supervision for offenders who are sentenced to prison or probation and offenders who serve a portion of their sentence on parole. In recent years the department has had some eighteen thousand offenders under its jurisdiction, six thousand in prison and twelve thousand on probation and parole. Although the department has been subject to frequent reorganization, it has consistently had divisions that deal with adult prisons, probation and parole, corrections industries, training of corrections officers, and administrative services.

CULTURAL AFFAIRS

In 2003 the legislature by statute raised the Office of Cultural Affairs to cabinet-level status as the Department of Cultural Affairs. The department's mission is to "lead in the preservation, development, promotion, and access to New Mexico's cultural resources—arts, history, science, and information services—for the use, education, and enjoyment of present and future generations."[9] It pursues its mission through four programs: Museum Services; Preservation, Arts, and Library Services; Education and Outreach and Leadership, Management and Administration.

ECONOMIC DEVELOPMENT

Originally created in 1983 as the Department of Economic Development and Tourism, this department has been the locus for the state government's efforts to ensure the state's long-term economic viability. However, in 1991 the legislature approved the governor's request to separate economic development and tourism functions into two cabinet departments. The specific legislative mandate to the Economic Development Department is to achieve economic diversity in the state, "to protect against dramatic changes in the state's economy and to increase revenues to help state government finance the various services it provides to the state's communities and citizens."[10] The range of activities assigned to this department includes: the promotion of the export of New Mexico products, the attraction of new industry to the state, the coordination of the preparation and analysis of the state census, and facilitating the commercialization of new technologies. The department is another one that gets reorganized with each change of gubernatorial administration, but it has consistently had divisions concerned with community economic development, business recruitment, the film industry, science and technology, and international trade.

ENERGY, MINERALS AND NATURAL RESOURCES DEPARTMENT

Created in 1987, this department is the result of the consolidation of the Energy and Minerals Department and the Natural Resources Department.[11] Organized into six divisions, much of the activity of this department is technical and associated with regulatory enforcement. Nevertheless, the department can be categorized as policy focused rather than functional, because its duties also involve direct land management, park management, and scientific research. The divisions included within the department are responsible for (1) administrative services, (2) state parks and recreation, (3) forestry, (4) energy conservation and management, (5) mining and minerals, and (6) oil conservation. The department's mission is to provide leadership in the protection, conservation, management, and responsible use of New Mexico's natural resources.

ENVIRONMENT DEPARTMENT

The Department of Environment was created by the same act in 1991 that created the Health Department to "administer the laws and exercise the functions relating to the environment department."[12] The principal responsibility of the department is to protect the health of all citizens from the environmental hazards of toxic waste, water pollution, and air pollution. The New Mexico Environment Department essentially is the state equivalent of the United States Environmental Protection Agency. Like its federal counterpart, the Environment Department, as the enforcer of environmental standards, is often at odds with the business community. Two ongoing issues that are likely to remain controversial are the need to comply with solid waste disposal standards for municipalities and counties and the ongoing effort to "clean up" sites where illegal and hazardous dumping has occurred.

DEPARTMENT OF FINANCE AND ADMINISTRATION

Originally created by the legislature in 1957, the Department of Finance and Administration (DFA) has become, in effect, the state's central accounting office, exercising overall supervision and providing uniform accounting procedures and standard accounting classifications for all units and agencies of state government. The agencies and programs that comprise the DFA include (1) the Board of Finance, (2) the Financial Control Division, (3) the Local Government Division, (4) the State Budget Division, and (5) Administrative Services.

Governmental agencies in New Mexico must have their budgets, tax plans, and expenditures approved by various divisions of the DFA. This includes not only agencies of the executive branch of state government, but also units of local government as well: cities, counties, special districts, and all others. These units of government are prohibited from issuing general obligation bonds, transferring funds from one purpose to another, or from increasing their annual or monthly budgets without the prior approval of the local government division of the DFA. Not all the functions of the department imply a review or oversight function, however. The Local Government Division is responsible for assisting other levels of government in obtaining outside grants and other funding and for providing planning and funding assistance for improving their operations. The director of this division also has the responsibility for recommending to the secretary of the DFA the suspension of a delinquent county treasurer.

The DFA secretary is one of the most influential figures in New Mexico state government, because of the central role the department plays in the preparation of the executive budget. This budget is the central policy document of state government. In helping the governor shape and reshape departmental budget requests to reflect gubernatorial priorities, the DFA, and particularly the department secretary, become more closely identified with the policy and political preferences of the governor than do the other cabinet members.

GENERAL SERVICES DEPARTMENT

Created in 1983, the General Services Department was the first cabinet post created after 1978. The department includes six divisions, responsible for (1) administrative services, (2) building services, (3) information services, (4) property control, (5) purchasing, and (6) risk management. In addition, the Information Systems Council is administratively attached to the department.

As is evident from the above list, this department's role and responsibilities are those associated with "housekeeping" and administration. Furthermore, the department's actions are undertaken on behalf of all state government. Decisions as diverse as buying paper clips, dealing with insurance claims, and renting office space in Las Cruces are assigned to the General Services Department.

HEALTH DEPARTMENT

The Department of Health Act of 1991 created the Department of Health as a cabinet department with responsibility for all public health, behavioral health, and scientific laboratory functions that had been performed by the previous Health and Environmental Department.[13] The department operates health-care facilities for the chronically ill and mentally retarded, provides preventive health-care services, and engages in technical research. The department plays a major role in providing loans to local governments for water treatment facilities and other water-related infrastructure.

HUMAN SERVICES

This department is responsible for the income-support and social-service programs of the state. The second largest agency of the state government budgetarily, much of the funding of this agency (approximately 50 percent) comes from the U.S. Department of Health and Human Services. The range of functions assigned to this department is somewhat obscured by the separation of the department into only two divisions: income support and social services. Income support programs are available to the needy, the elderly, and the disabled, as well as to children. The social services programs require both regulatory actions, such as the licensing of foster homes and adoption agencies, and the direct provision of services to needy and aging adults. Like the Environment Department, the Human Services Department is often at the center of controversy. Even though the federal government supplies 50 to 75 percent of the money for programs such as Temporary Assistance to Needy Families and Medicaid, the sheer size and growth of these programs make them a major focus of attention.

INDIAN AFFAIRS

The Indian Affairs Department serves as the coordinating body between state government and tribal government for the twenty-two New Mexico Indian tribes on a wide range of issues including taxation, water, tourism, health, and business development. (See chapter 7 on Indian Tribal Governments.)

LABOR

The Labor Department's duties range from administering the unemployment compensation fund to providing job training for the unemployed and underprivileged. The divisions of the department are responsible for (1) employment security, (2) labor and industrial issues, (3) human rights, (4) job training, and (5) administrative services.

PUBLIC EDUCATION

In 2003 New Mexico voters approved an amendment to Article 12, Section 6, of the Constitution of New Mexico that radically altered the governance of the state public education system.

According to the amendment, the powers of the Superintendent of Public Instruction, who was previously a State Board of Education appointee, were transferred to the governor-appointed Secretary of Public Education who has cabinet status. The governor is directed to fill the new executive post with a "qualified, experienced educator" whose appointment, like that of all cabinet secretary nominees, is subject to senate confirmation (Article XII, Sec. 6-A).

In addition to this change in the leadership of the department, the constitutional amendment also called for changes in the Education

Department's policy making board. Under the amendment, the State Board of Education was replaced by a Public Education Commission that has only advisory authority. In addition to losing its powers of appointment and policy making, the commission was scaled down to ten elected members. The department has policy and fiscal control over the full range of educational issues for children from kindergarten through grade twelve.

This change in the structure and status of the Public Education Department represents a significant change in the state's executive-power relationships. The governor now has decidedly more power to influence education policy than he did under the prior system.

As head of the department, the secretary is endowed with administrative and regulatory powers and duties, including all functions relating to financial accounting and the distribution of school funds to local school districts (and thus the largest budget in state government). The department's policy responsibilities include the establishment of minimum educational standards, the certification of teachers and school administrators, and deciding what textbooks can be purchased with state funds. It also oversees the operation of state-run schools for the blind and deaf and for an Indian education services program. The department also oversees the Division of Vocational Rehabilitation.

PUBLIC SAFETY

The Department of Public Safety was created as a cabinet department by statute in 1987. The purpose of the department, in the language of the statute, is:

> to establish a single, unified department to consolidate state law enforcement and safety functions in order to provide better management, real coordination and more effective use of state resources and manpower in responding to New Mexico's public safety needs and problems and to improve professionalism of the state's law enforcement and investigative functions and personnel.[14]

The department evolved organizationally over the years through the combining of related functions of the State Police Division, Motor Transportation Division, Special Investigation Division, the Law

Enforcement Academy, the Crime Laboratory, and the Emergency Management Operations.

TAXATION AND REVENUE DEPARTMENT

The Taxation and Revenue Department is the state's principal tax agency and has been one of the departments to undergo significant reorganization since its creation in 1978. In an effort to consolidate the tax and revenue-administration functions of the state, two major reorganizations, in 1986 and 1987, were authorized. The department now processes over $4 billion annually in revenue from the general public. Its current organization has five divisions: Audit and Compliance, Motor Vehicle, Property Tax, Revenue Processing, and Administrative Services.

TOURISM DEPARTMENT

The Tourism Department was created to coordinate the promotion of tourism and the hospitality industry in New Mexico. It has two divisions: Travel and Marketing and *New Mexico Magazine*. The logic in separating this department from the Economic Development Department had more to do with administration and function than policy. While the two departments both have responsibilities for creating jobs, they go about that effort quite differently. Furthermore, the split gave the tourism industry visibility appropriate to its importance in the overall economy.

TRANSPORTATION

In 2003 the Department of Highways and Transportation became simply the Department of Transportation to more accurately reflect its mission of developing and maintaining a high-quality state transportation network. Highways, railroads, public transportation, and aviation are all identified as unique but complementary components of the state transportation network. However, the primary focus of this executive cabinet department remains the maintenance, repair, reconstruction, and construction of state roads and highways. The annual decisions on where to begin new construction and what roads to rebuild or repair are of vital interest to legislators, highway commissioners, and city and county officials. The result is that this agency witnesses an interesting and often volatile blend of politics and technocracy. Although the cabinet secretary who heads the department is appointed by the governor and serves at his/her pleasure, the constitutionally established Transportation Commission is empowered to make transportation policy. The secretary must work within this divided governance.

VETERANS' SERVICES

The Department of Veterans' Services provides information and assistance to veterans and their eligible dependents so that they may obtain all of the benefits to which they are entitled. The department is responsible for some thirty separate programs ranging from veterans' tax exemption and scholarship programs to administration of the Fort Stanton State Cemetery.

THE FUTURE OF THE CABINET

After several decades of use by five different governors, it is apparent that the cabinet system is well entrenched and has proven to be an effective way to organize the executive departments. Many observers view the increased size of the cabinet with mixed feelings. But there is no agreement among public administration scholars on the optimum size of a cabinet. As the cabinet grows, it is likely that the use of the cabinet councils will necessarily grow to facilitate coordination of increasingly fragmented policy initiatives. Given the stress placed on the need for communication among cabinet secretaries to share both policy and management concerns, the size of the cabinet is critical only when communication is jeopardized.

The personality and management style of each governor plays a major role in shaping the use of the cabinet. One thing that is sure to change is the placement of policy staffs at the cabinet level rather than the prior practice of using personal staff by the governor. What does the future hold? It is possible that policy staffs will function at both levels in the future, one to support the gubernatorial agenda and one to provide backup for the work of the cabinet councils and other cabinet-initiated endeavors.

Now we turn to the other independently elected executive officers.

THE ATTORNEY GENERAL

The attorney general's role has expanded in recent years to include increasingly important policy responsibilities. The attorney general is not only the state's head prosecutor, but is also the legal advisor to the governor and other top officials. The constitutional and statutory provisions establishing the attorney general's office require representation by the attorney general in a wide range of cases where the state, its officers and employees, or its board or commission members are parties. Attorneys general are also called upon to issue legal opinions when requested to do so by state officials, legislators, and local officials who need guidance in the exercise of their official duties.

Because of the broad nature of the statutory authority establishing the office, attorneys general have often exercised individual judgments about what the priorities of the office should be. Several recent occupants of the office have established a strong presence in consumer protection and representation of the public in utility-rate cases. The office has also increased its role in subdivision regulation, environmental protection, conflicts between the state and Indian tribes over jurisdictional issues, and in the prosecution of white-collar and financial crimes.

As the office's authority has grown, so have its visibility and usefulness as a political launching pad. The attorney general is readily perceived as upholding "the law" against those who would disobey it, whether outside government, or more recently, within it. The ambiguities that are present in most substantive legal questions are rarely understood by the news media or the public. The prospect of an attorney general disagreeing with either the governor or an agency he/she represents makes for ready media interest, and the political careers of those holding the office have been advanced greatly.

Forty-two states elect their attorneys general, rather than following the federal model in which the president, as chief executive, appoints a loyal supporter to the attorney general's position. Most executives would prefer to select their own attorneys and require of them the highest degree of confidentiality and loyalty. Presidents who have elevated personal loyalty in this selection, however, have felt the criticism of the public. Most citizens probably view the office as a "watchdog" over government, for the protection of the public. In New Mexico, where this model has become established during the terms of recent attorneys general, the continuing tension between the governor and the attorney general may be viewed as serving the public interest. On the other hand, carried to an extreme, it may be viewed as primarily serving the attorney general's political ambitions.

THE SECRETARY OF STATE

The office of secretary of state has gained important responsibilities as a result of increased public awareness of the conduct of elections. The 1960s brought redistricting to many offices, from school boards to the U.S. House of Representatives, to implement the one-person, one-vote imperatives of court decisions. New requirements for bilingual ballots in areas with substantial populations speaking a language other than English also increased the focus on election administration. The secretary of state is fundamentally responsible for the conduct of elections.

Probably the most important and challenging duty of the office is administering the election process in New Mexico. A unit in the office, the Bureau of Elections, supervises the use of voting machines, trains county officials in election law and election administration, assists counties and cities during elections, and prepares manuals on the administration of election laws. Difficulties in voting often occur, and the Bureau of Elections maintains a constant effort to improve the system. It is the primary responsibility of the secretary of state today to assure every voter that a vote can be cast in a reasonable amount of time, without undue effort, with the assurance of secrecy, and with a guarantee of equality with every other voter.

The secretary of state administers an office with an assortment of real and ceremonial powers. When the governor and lieutenant governor are unable to perform the duties of the governor's office, the secretary of state assumes that authority. The secretary of state also presides over the state House of Representatives when it is organizing and until the Speaker is elected.

Other routine functions include keeping the Great Seal of the State of New Mexico, certifying the governor's signature on important documents, and affixing the state seal. Trademarks and trade names must be registered with the secretary of state's office, and notaries public receive their commissions from the office.

An increasingly important responsibility is keeping a register of lobbyists at the legislative sessions, to provide a public record of which lobbyists represent which organized interests. With the passage of the 1993 Governmental Conduct Act, the office assumed the role of state government ethics regulator. Besides regulating lobbyist activity, this job oversees the reporting of campaign finances by candidates for public office and political action committees, as well as financial disclosure by candidates and state officials. In addition, under the Governmental Conduct Act, each elected statewide executive branch public officer and the Legislative Council are required to file a general code of conduct for the employees under their supervision.

THE STATE TREASURER

The treasurer is charged with receiving and keeping all of the state's funds (except when special arrangements are made by law), with disbursing funds when called upon by law (such as in the budget appropriations), and with keeping an accurate account of the state's money.

The treasurer is also connected with a complex of agencies in which the treasurer's role might be more important than is commonly perceived. The treasurer is a member of the nine-member Investment Council. This body controls the state's two permanent funds: the Permanent Fund (comprised of funds from lands under the direction, control, care, and disposition of the Commissioner of Public Lands) and the Severance Tax Permanent Fund (comprised of funds from taxes levied on natural resources severed and saved from the land). These now total over $10 billion. Prudent and competent guidance on these investments may substantially increase earnings for state revenue.

The expert management of the state's large cash balances is a demanding, but promising, function of the treasurer's office. Investment income from these funds can provide additional budget support, keep taxes somewhat lower, and/or provide more budget options to the legislature and governor. The treasurer also sits as a member of the boards that control the Public Employees' Retirement System, the Education Retirement Fund, the Retiree Healthcare Authority, and the state's Mortgage Finance Authority, which provides money for home mortgages to low- and moderate-income purchasers.

The treasurer is a member of the State Board of Finance and works closely with the governor's Department of Finance and Administration (DFA), which is the central budget office of the state. The treasurer supports the flow of appropriations to the operating agencies by disbursing funds when presented with the proper warrant (authorization for payment) and by supplying the DFA with timely information on the state's accounts. The treasurer is also in a prime position to point out areas for improvement in the state's financial management and in the operation of the state agencies. It is a position that can contribute substantially to the efficient and effective management of state government. It is also a position of great power and one that has been marked by abuses of that power in recent years.

THE STATE AUDITOR

An office with the potential to be very controversial is that of state auditor. The function of the office is to issue financial reports on the operations of state and other governmental agencies. The reports are useful to both the executive and legislative branches, and as public records, provide evidence that can be used to enforce laws against fraud and other financial crimes. The auditor is not required to be a certified or registered public accountant. Although they are listed in the constitution, the state auditor's powers and duties are vague, resulting in changing fortunes through legislative action. A few times in the past, proposals have emanated from the legislature to abolish the position of state auditor through constitutional amendment.

Many states employ a legislative auditor in one form or another. This proposal has been considered in the New Mexico Legislature (for example, Senate Bill 198 in 1989). A legislative auditor could oppose excessive spending or carelessness, identify waste and fraud in the executive branch and independent agencies, and ensure that legislative intent is followed in the spending of appropriations. The audit staff of the Legislative Finance Committee (LFC) currently fulfills many of these tasks, serving as an informal counterpart to the state auditor.

In recent years the auditor has been able to contribute substantially to management improvements through post-audits of programs with financial problems. The responsibility for pre-audits, which occur before the end of a fiscal year and usually before the expenditure of a particular amount, is now vested in the Department of Finance and Administration. Increasingly, however, the auditor is involved in the oversight of financial practices in many different agencies and may make negative reports either before or after the end of a fiscal year.

The political environment of the office can be affected by the auditor's decisions regarding contracting audits to professional firms; if a large number of contracts are issued to private firms, various political issues arise. Favoritism, political manipulation, and conflicts of interest are all inherent possibilities. On the other hand, it may be difficult to sustain the sizable staff to do all of the audits called for within the auditor's own organization.

THE COMMISSIONER OF PUBLIC LANDS

When New Mexico gained statehood in 1912, Congress transferred 13 million acres of public lands to state control. The constitution established the State Land Office to manage these huge expanses of land for the benefit of the future citizens of New Mexico. The Commissioner of Public Lands controls, manages, and disposes of the state's public lands. More than 9 million acres remain under the commissioner's jurisdiction. The management of these lands is probably much more important than most New Mexicans realize. Some parcels located in urbanizing areas will be extremely important in city planning and local economies. Others are crucial in the state's important industries of agriculture and minerals extraction.

The commissioner sits on the Land Commission with the governor, who is chair, and the attorney general, who provides legal guidance. The commission holds the public lands in trust for the benefit of specific institutions, such as the public schools and the universities. The income amounts to about 10 percent of the state's annual revenue. The commissioner, with the consent of his associates on the Land Commission, administers all programs for the care, lease, sale, and maintenance of the land.

The commissioner is naturally at the focus of powerful political conflicts. Agriculture, mining, real estate, industrial, environmental, conservation, wildlife, hunting, and public-advocacy groups all enter the fray.

The trust obligations vested in the commissioner require that the lands be managed for the benefit of the public, but the public interest is not often easy to determine. Increasing revenues from the land is an attractive policy, since such revenues support education as well as such state institutions as the state prison and the New Mexico State Hospital and can also hold taxes down. However, an equally worthy objective is to care for and conserve the land for the future.

Very important powers of the commissioner center on the conditions and terms put on such land uses as grazing and mineral leases. New Mexico commissioners have not developed the comprehensive land-management systems used on the federal government's land in the state. This has occasionally led to efforts to transfer additional federal lands to state control, so that economic interests can deal with the commissioner rather than with federal agencies. Nevertheless, the commissioner does cooperate closely with important federal agencies, such as the Bureau of Land Management and the Environmental Protection Agency on public-lands matters. Furthermore, within state government, the Energy, Minerals, and Natural Resources Department, the Environment Department, and the Department of Agriculture might also be involved in planning and managing the vast expanses under the commissioner's control.

THE PUBLIC REGULATION COMMISSION

The preceding constitutional offices are all single, elected executive positions, established by Article V of the state constitution. The Public Regulation Commission (PRC) is a five-member body established by constitutional amendment in 1996, which consolidated the authority of the State Corporation Commission and the Public Utility Commission into a single body. Thus, the PRC's constitutional authority is drawn from an amendment to Article XI of the constitution and it differs substantially from the other offices in the fragmented executive system. The commissioners serve staggered four-year terms, at least two being elected at each general election. They can be reelected for one successive term. After two terms they are ineligible to serve as a commissioner until one full term has intervened. The commission elects a chair who presides over all aspects of the commission's operations.

The PRC has three simultaneous identities. Its constitutional identity is as the Public Regulation Commission. By statute the legislature, in order to prevent further proliferation of executive offices, has also made the commission the State Insurance Board and the State Fire Board. In each of these three capacities, the commission oversees directors of the separate functions and other administrative employees.

As the Public Regulation Commission, the commission regulates major sectors of the New Mexico economy, especially those that have "natural monopolies," the public utilities. The commission is charged by the legislature with regulating public utilities (electricity, natural gas, water, and waste water), telecommunications companies, and insurance companies to the extent necessary to provide just and reasonable rates and to assure reasonable, adequate, and efficient service for the public. In addition, the commission is charged with the duties of assuring pipeline and fire safety and with the registration of corporations.

Individuals or corporations wishing to offer intrastate (entirely within New Mexico) transportation services to the public, such as bus or air-passenger service, air or ground-freight hauling for hire, or those wanting to operate a wrecker service for automobiles, must first persuade the PRC to issue a certificate of public convenience and necessity. Operating such a business without a commission certificate is illegal. A public hearing is held before such a certificate is issued, and normally those firms already offering the service persuade the commission that there is no necessity for additional service (or competition).

In its role as State Insurance Board, the commission appoints the state insurance superintendent and has control of state insurance reserves. It sets financial requirements for the insurance industry and standards for the treatment of policyholders. A company in financial difficulty can be ordered out of business by the commission. The predecessor State Corporation Commission also carried out a comprehensive revision of the Insurance Code in 1984, which the legislature enacted into law. Some of the changes require prior approval of insurance rate increases, the review of actuarial experience in setting rates, and a sixty-day period before rate increases can go into effect.

The state's activities in the fire prevention and fire insurance areas also fall under the authority of the PRC. It monitors the training, operations, prevention, and equipment activities of the county and rural fire departments. The firefighter academy has been strengthened recently and has trained thousands of emergency responders. The state Fire Marshall's Office is directly under the commission's authority and has had a strong positive influence on the quality of fire services in the state.

All of the PRC regulatory and rate decisions may be appealed to the New Mexico Supreme Court, and many are appealed. The Court hears such appeals directly from the commission.

The question exists as to whether the PRC has sufficient staff and budget to handle the complex and diverse duties thrust upon it by the constitution and legislature. Its regulatory powers reach some of the most basic public services and should be supported by a good, solid research and legal staff and the highest quality administration. On occasion, the legislature has been critical of the commissioners' personal staff and expenditures.

CONCLUSIONS

The state bureaucracy in New Mexico has changed immensely in the last four decades. With the introduction of a merit system and a vigorous state Personnel Office, New Mexico state employees have achieved a level of competence that was impossible under a system where "rotation of office" was the norm. While some aspects of the personnel system can be improved, particularly with regard to the overall level of training and education of employees, the impetus for and expectation of change exists. Furthermore, the cabinet system has proven to provide better coordination of policy than was achieved under the previous fragmented system of organization. Because of these two factors, the state is better able to manage programs and to integrate new personnel with new responsibilities than it could have done in decades past.

The fragmentation of executive authority and responsibility created by the independently elected executive officers continues to be a matter of critical concern to political observers and administrative experts alike. However, there is no serious movement to amend the constitution to eliminate any of the elected executives.

NOTES

Special recognition and thanks are extended to Denise Fort, Alan Reed, and Raymond Cox for their contributions to this chapter that appeared in earlier editions.

1.   Jerry Apodaca, *Responsive Government 1978* (Santa Fe: State of New Mexico, 1978).
2.   Figures compiled by Professor Raymond L. Cox in 1992.
3.   New Mexico Attorney General Opinion No. 64–3, 1964.
4.   Section 10–9–13, N.M.S.A. 1978.
5.   Section 10–9–4 (6), N.M.S.A. 1978.
6.   Many academics have posited the theory that over time political appointees become co-opted by the agencies they direct and become advocates for rather than skeptics of agency programs.
7.   Article XV, Constitution of New Mexico.
8.   *Executive Budget Recommendation, Fiscal Year 2005*, p. 607.
9.   Ibid, p. 356.
10.   Section 9–15–2, N.M.S.A. 1978.

11.   Section 9–5A–1, *et. seq.*, N.M.S.A. 1978.
12.   Section 9–7–1, *et. seq.*, N.M.S.A. 1978.
13.   Ibid.
14.   Section 9–19–3, N.M.S.A. 1978.

Chapter Five

Law and the Courts

by Peter Kierst

Government exists in society to achieve and maintain both order and liberty. Individuals must be protected from those who wrong them, and the community must be protected from those who violate its norms. Organized systems are needed for this purpose. Without such systems individuals who are wronged are without recourse, unless they are bigger and stronger than those who have injured them. In a society where individuals must literally rely on their strength to secure their persons and property, the strong may prey upon the weak, the organized on the unassimilated, the majority on the minority.

In a civil society designed to prevent such abuses, courts have a central and critical role to play. If someone is injured, a court provides a regular mechanism for compensating the injury. If someone engages in behavior that threatens the peace of the whole society, a court provides a forum in which society accuses and punishes the transgressor but also where the accused is protected from unjust charges. The decisions of the court, either compensating an injury or condemning the criminal, constitute the collective judgment of society, and have the weight of society behind them for enforcement. This chapter will attempt to show how New Mexico's courts are organized to achieve these ends.

"It is emphatically the province and duty of the judicial department," said John Marshall, Chief Justice of the United States, "to say what the law is."[1] While Chief Justice Marshall was speaking of fundamental legal precepts, it is important to understand that the "judicial department" also regularly says "what the law is" on questions great and small. We traditionally think of the legislature as making the law and of courts as merely interpreting it. This is true and useful only up to a point. For example, the legislature may write a law that a second driving-while-intoxicated (DWI) offense is punishable by up to 365 days in jail. However, in your community, the court's uniform practice may be to sentence those convicted of a second DWI to two days in jail. Which is the law? The statute written by the legislature is certainly the law, and the court obeys it. But if you are the accused, the law you want your attorney to know and advise you about is what the court is going to do in your case. There are a host of questions that come before courts every day to which the court's answer can be accurately predicted. These predictions tell us what the law is in an important way, as important as any legislatively enacted statute. When political scientists say "courts make policy," that is part of what they mean.

Courts also make policy in ways that go beyond the individual case that may be decided. For example, one of the most common kinds of cases decided by courts is a negligence case. A plaintiff is injured and alleges that the injury was due to the negligence of another, the defendant. The law in New Mexico used to be that if the defendant could prove that the plaintiff's own negligence contributed in any way to the injuries, then the defendant was relieved of all responsibility for those injuries. This doctrine, called "contributory negligence," came under criticism in legal circles as unduly harsh. Some scholars, lawyers, and judges argued that it would be fairer in cases where plaintiffs were injured by their own and the defendant's negligence to determine the proportion of blame each had, and require the defendant to pay for that share of the damage caused by his or her negligence. This doctrine is called "comparative negligence." In 1981 the New Mexico Supreme Court, exercising its power to say what the law is, adopted comparative negligence and rejected contributory negligence.[2] This was a fundamental change in how disputes between individuals in New Mexico are resolved. It was accomplished not through a popular vote, nor legislative enactment, but through judicial decision.

There are limits on this power, but it is important to keep in mind the policy making function of our courts.

Almost all readers have heard the statement that "we have a government of laws, not of men." This is generally taken to mean that we govern ourselves by uniform laws, uniformly enforced. The individual opinions or passions of the judge enforcing the law should have no role in the judicial process. In this view the judicial process is a mechanical one, in which judges are like automatons, unaffected by their own beliefs and experience.

We know this view is incorrect. Judges remain human when they put on their judicial robes. They have beliefs and passions just like the rest of us. However, it is also inaccurate to assume that judges regularly impose their personal opinions on the law and those who appear before them. For one thing judges are invariably the products of a legal culture that indoctrinated them as law students and lawyers with the view that they ought to leave their personal opinions out of their work. Most judges believe as much as the rest of us in the idea that justice should be dispensed impartially. This provides a powerful curb on judicial behavior. But it is important to remember that although this may be a government of laws, the laws are made, interpreted, and enforced by human beings, not machines.

THE STRUCTURE OF THE LAW

Fundamentally, the law can be seen as having two parts: civil and criminal. Civil law concerns the resolution of disputes between individuals. As in the negligence case discussed above, if a plaintiff thinks a defendant has harmed her or him, the plaintiff can sue the defendant in the appropriate court and ask the court for compensation. The defendant can appear and explain what she or he did and why, disputing the plaintiff's claim of negligence. The court will hear all the evidence and make a decision. The verdict will ordinarily be for the plaintiff if that person has the preponderance, or greater weight, of the evidence. Sometimes the decision will be made by a jury called for that purpose. The court will also provide a mechanism for its decisions to be enforced. Thus the court is a forum in which the plaintiff and the defendant can obtain an authoritative resolution of a problem they could not resolve themselves.

Civil cases are usually matters of contract or tort. A contract is any promise between two people that the court will enforce, generally written. There must have been an offer, which was accepted, and something of value for the promise must have been exchanged. If one party thinks the other did not keep all of the terms of the promise, then the court may decide the issue.

Tort is an overarching term for a wrong done by one person to another. If the defendant walks up to the plaintiff and hits her or him, the plaintiff may sue the defendant for medical bills, lost time from work, and so on. A tort may be intentional or negligent, as when the defendant fails to notice the plaintiff while swinging a fist and hits her or him accidentally. The plaintiff may sue the defendant for the same bills and losses, alleging the defendant was negligent.

In civil cases the court is usually limited to awarding money to the injured party as compensation for actual past and future damages. In particularly egregious cases, the court can award damages intended merely to punish the wrongdoer. In some cases the court can also order changes in the party's future behavior. In the tort cases described above, the court could issue an injunction to the defendant to stay away from the plaintiff in the future. In a contract case, the court could issue an order to the defendant to keep the promise to the plaintiff. This is possible only when there are not adequate money damages the defendant can pay the plaintiff.

The fundamental difference between civil and criminal cases is that in a criminal case it is society itself that has been harmed and is seeking redress. No individual can charge another with a crime. Although we sometimes speak of someone "filing" or "dropping" charges, only the state can make that decision.

A crime is behavior that endangers society, not just an individual. Crimes are defined exclusively by the legislature, which also sets the parameters of their punishment. Traditionally, crimes are of two types: *malum prohibitum* and *malum in se.* These are Latin terms that convey something important about the nature of crime. *Malum in se* means acts that are crimes because in their very nature they are immoral or wrong. Murder is a crime because it is inherently evil, and society punishes murder because to preserve a decent society, such evil cannot go unpunished. *Malum probitium* means an act that is a crime because it is prohibited.

For example, there is nothing necessarily less moral about driving sixty-five miles per hour on the freeway as opposed to driving fifty-five miles per hour. For a time, though, driving sixty-five miles per hour on the freeway was a crime. It was a crime because the legislature adopted the lower speed as the limit of lawful behavior, in the hope that the highways would be safer and to avoid losing federal highway funds.

Crimes are also categorized by their seriousness. Less serious crimes are called misdemeanors and carry less serious punishments. In New Mexico a misdemeanor is a crime punishable by imprisonment up to one year and a fine of no more than one thousand dollars. More serious crimes are called felonies. Felonies themselves have several levels of punishment, called "degrees," from eighteen months and a five-thousand-dollar fine to life imprisonment or death.

In a criminal trial, the state must prove beyond a reasonable doubt that the accused committed the crime. This is significantly more stringent than the "preponderance" burden of proof in civil cases. The difference in burden stems from the grave consequences of a guilty verdict in a criminal case. Only people found guilty beyond a reasonable doubt can be imprisoned.

New Mexico's court system has much in common with those of the other forty-nine states. There are *trial courts*, which decide controversies between parties, and *appellate courts*, which review the decisions of the trial courts. The lowest level of trial court, and the one that has the most contact with the people, is that of the *courts of limited jurisdiction*. These are magistrate, municipal, metropolitan, and probate courts.

TRIAL COURTS

MAGISTRATE COURT[3]

The purpose of the magistrate courts is to hear smaller civil and criminal cases. These are called courts of limited jurisdiction because their legal authority, or jurisdiction, extends over a limited, tightly defined group of cases and territory. The magistrate court has jurisdiction to hear civil cases where the amount in dispute or being sought as damages is no more than ten thousand dollars. The magistrate court can try all misdemeanor cases. The geographic extent of the magistrate court's jurisdiction is the county in which it sits.

Each county in New Mexico (except Bernalillo County) constitutes one magistrate court district. Depending on the population of the county, the legislature can create as many magistrate court divisions in the county as necessary. Each division has its own judge.

Except in counties with a population over two hundred thousand people, magistrate court judges do not have to be lawyers. The magistrate judge must have a high school education, be a registered voter, and be a resident of his or her district. All magistrates are required to complete a yearly training program. These seemingly minimal requirements were born of historical necessity. In many less populous counties there simply were not (and in some cases there still are not) a sufficient number of lawyers to fill all of the positions, especially at the pay usually available.

Magistrate courts are not courts of record. That is, no transcript of their proceedings is made. A party who loses in magistrate court can appeal to the next highest court, the district court. There, the appeal will be heard *de novo*. That is, the district court will retry the matter as if the trial in the magistrate court never occurred. Since the district court has authority originally to hear any case the magistrate court can hear, some people wonder why anyone would bring their case to the magistrate court at all. There are a variety of reasons. For one thing, de novo appeal means a party has two equal opportunities to win the case. For another, magistrate courts are usually faster and less formal than district courts. People often represent themselves without attorneys and save considerable time and expense. These savings mean that cases that might otherwise not be brought at all can be brought and expeditiously heard.

MUNICIPAL COURTS[4]

The legislature has also established municipal courts in all New Mexico cities, except in those with less than twenty-five hundred people or those with more than five thousand people in counties of over two hundred thousand people. This seemingly complicated arrangement is designed basically to ensure that there is no municipal court where there is also a metropolitan court. The purpose of the municipal courts is to enforce the municipality's criminal ordinances. By law these ordinances carry a maximum sentence of ninety days in jail or up to a five-hundred-dollar fine, although municipal courts may impose up to one thousand dollars in fines for driving-while-intoxicated cases.

The municipality is allowed to set the qualifications and pay for municipal judges. The judges are elected at the regular municipal elections and are required to undergo annual training.

METROPOLITAN COURT[5]

In 1980 the legislature combined the magistrate and municipal courts into one metropolitan court for all counties with a population over two hundred thousand people. This means that Bernalillo County has the only metropolitan court in the state. Combining the two court systems in Bernalillo County allowed for the elimination of confusion and overlap in their functions; it also created the busiest court in New Mexico. As of January 1, 2003, the metropolitan court has sixteen judges. This is more than any magistrate, municipal, or district court in the state, except for the Second Judicial District Court, which is also in Bernalillo County.

Metropolitan court inherited the combined jurisdiction of the magistrate and municipal courts. Unlike them the metropolitan court is a court of record in civil cases. This means that there is no de novo appeal in civil cases from metropolitan court to district court. The district court hears metropolitan civil appeals on the basis of a transcript of proceedings and arguments made by the lawyers. Civil trials in the metropolitan court are accordingly somewhat more formal than those in the magistrate courts.

The qualifications for metropolitan court judges are also more stringent than for magistrate courts. The metropolitan judges must be attorneys and must have practiced for three years before assuming their positions.

PROBATE COURT[6]

The probate judge is elected in each county at every general election. Probate courts have limited original jurisdiction to handle informal probate proceedings: those in which no controversy arises, such as challenges to the validity of wills, for example. The primary concern of the probate court is the settlement of estates, determining the authenticity of last wills and testaments, determining heirship, and the appointment and removal of guardians of minors. Most estates will be probated informally. If controversy arises, however, formal probate proceedings are brought in district court, which has exclusive original jurisdiction over formal probate proceedings. Informal probate orders can also be set aside by a request for formal probate proceedings. In addition the district court may appoint a person to serve in place of the probate judge if the probate judge is absent or disqualified.

DISTRICT COURT[7]

New Mexico, like other states, has a trial-level court of general jurisdiction. Unlike some states, which create some general trial courts as criminal courts and others as civil courts, New Mexico's courts of general jurisdiction hear both types of cases. Some of the districts, however, split themselves into criminal and civil divisions so as to move cases more effectively. In New Mexico these courts are all called district courts.

New Mexico is divided into thirteen judicial districts. Each of the thirty-three counties is in one of these districts; the Second and Third Judicial Districts cover one county each (Bernalillo and Doña Ana, respectively). The other twelve district courts have at least two counties in them. The district courts have as many judgeships as the legislature sees fit to create.

The district courts have the most wide-ranging jurisdiction of any trial court. Any matter that a magistrate, municipal, or metropolitan court can hear can be heard by the district court. In addition, all other civil and criminal cases that cannot be heard by those lower courts can be heard in the district court.

District courts generally hear the most serious civil and criminal cases. They also can issue injunctions, decide election disputes, resolve controversies over title to and use of land, adjudicate juvenile matters, grant divorces, and hear suits against the state, in contrast to the limited-jurisdiction court.

As previously noted, district courts hear appeals from courts of limited jurisdiction in their districts; they also have general supervisory authority over those courts. They can issue writs (orders) of superintending control, directing the lower court to amend its practice to conform to the law.

District courts also hear appeals from a wide variety of administrative proceedings. These include workers' compensation matters and decisions of agencies such as the State Fire Board, the State Bank Examiner, and the various boards of county commissioners. District court judges must be lawyers and must have been in practice for at least six years before going on the bench. Each district court elects one of the judges as presiding judge, to oversee the administration of the court.

APPELLATE COURTS

The appellate court process is radically different from the trial process. Trial consists of parties presenting the evidence through witnesses and documents, and then a judge or jury deciding what the facts are and how the law applies to those facts. On appeal the appellate court assumes that the trial court's findings are correct. The party that lost at trial then has the burden of proving to the appellate court that an error of law or procedure was committed by the trial court. The losing party cannot appeal merely because it lost, nor will the appellate court retry the case or reevaluate the evidence. The appellate court reviews the transcripts of the trial and reads briefs (written legal arguments) by the attorneys for each side. On the basis of those arguments, it determines if any error was made in the trial and whether the error affected the result of the trial. The most common remedy for such an error is a new trial or perhaps a modification of the judgment of the trial court. It is a common misconception, for example, that a convicted criminal who wins a reversal of his conviction is set free. Usually such a reversal only means that the trial will be conducted again, without the error that occurred in the first trial.

In reaching their decisions, appellate courts are bound by precedent. That is, if a similar issue has been decided in the state by the appellate courts, the court will make its ruling in the new case consistent with the old ruling. If there is no New Mexico case on the point, lawyers will often use out-of-state cases as authority for their arguments. However, these cases are not binding on New Mexico's courts. By this use of precedent, there is regularity and predictability of appellate outcomes. This also means that the law evolves slowly. It takes a special case to convince the appellate court that the prior line of decisions was incorrect and that the law needs to be modified.

This use of precedent limits the power of the appellate courts to change the law as the judges might want to. Another limit on appellate power is that the court cannot reach out to correct some problem or mistake it may perceive; an appellate court must wait to have cases brought to it before it can rule on any question.

Court of Appeals[8]

The Court of Appeals was created in 1965 to serve as an intermediate appellate court between the district courts and the Supreme Court. It decides both civil and criminal appeals. Most appeals must first go to the Court of Appeals before possibly going on to the Supreme Court. This was intended to relieve some of the burden on the Supreme Court that existed at the time and to ensure that it decided only the most important cases. As a consequence, the Court of Appeals has a wider-ranging case load than the Supreme Court and is somewhat busier.

The Court of Appeals consists of ten judges who work in panels of three to decide the cases before the court. The court generally decides its cases exclusively on the basis of the briefs submitted by the parties and rarely hears oral argument from the lawyers. The court has offices in Santa Fe and Albuquerque.

Court of Appeals judges must be at least thirty-five years old, have been practicing attorneys for ten years, and be New Mexico residents for the three years prior to taking office.

The Supreme Court[9]

The Supreme Court is the final court of appeal in New Mexico. This court has mandatory jurisdiction over: criminal matters in which the sentence imposed is life in prison or the death penalty, appeals from the Public Regulation Commission, appeals from the granting of writs of habeas corpus, appeals in actions challenging nominations, and in the removal of public officers. Furthermore, the Court has discretionary jurisdiction over all cases decided by the Court of Appeals. These latter cases come to the Supreme Court by a writ of certiorari; this is the procedural device by which the party that lost the appeal at the Court of Appeals can ask the Supreme Court to review it. Unlike the Court of Appeals, which must by law review the cases that come to it, the Supreme Court can pick the cases it wishes to decide.

In choosing a case, the Supreme Court looks for significant legal or public policy issues, cases where there seems to be a conflict among its previous opinions, or cases where it believes the Court of Appeals may have incorrectly applied a former case.

The Supreme Court also has supervisory control over all the courts of New Mexico. It exercises this power by issuing writs to the lower courts when a complaining party argues that the lower courts have improperly exercised their authority. The Supreme Court has also been more active in recent years in working through the Administrative Office of the Courts to monitor and shape the administrative practices of the lower courts. This activism has been criticized by some as overreaching, but the Supreme Court has defended its constitutional prerogative in this area.

Under the constitution, the Supreme Court also has extensive rule-making authority. Working with the advice of various committees of lawyers, it promulgates the rules of evidence and procedure for all New Mexico courts. This is a significant power, in that evidentiary and procedural questions are often the keys to victory in court.

The Supreme Court consists of five justices who elect a chief justice from their number. The qualifications of the justices are the same as those for the judges of the Court of Appeals.

JUDICIAL SELECTION[10]

In 1988 New Mexico voters adopted a constitutional amendment that radically changed the manner of judicial selection in the state. Since statehood New Mexico judges had been elected by partisan elections, just like legislators and other elected officials. Judicial vacancies were filled by appointment by the governor.

In practice this meant that most judges obtained office by appointment, and few incumbents were ever defeated in elections. This led to the criticism that the closed nature of the appointment process meant that judges were not always appropriately qualified. Some people also believed that judges should not have to run in partisan elections, because this subjected them to improper and undignified political pressure.

To accommodate these concerns, the legislature drafted a unique hybrid of judicial selection by appointment and election. The procedure, adopted as a constitutional amendment, calls for judicial nominating commissions for the appellate courts, the thirteen district courts, and the metropolitan court. The magistrate, municipal, and probate courts were not affected.

Various members of the commissions are appointed by the governor, the Speaker of the House of Representatives, the President Pro Tem of the Senate, and the president of the New Mexico State Bar Association. Each commission always includes three sitting judges/justices. The appointments are structured so that the commissions are balanced between the Republican and Democratic parties. The dean of the New Mexico School of Law acts as chair of each commission. When a vacancy occurs in one of the courts, the appropriate commission announces the vacancy and solicits applications and nominations. Within thirty days of the vacancy, all applicants must be interviewed regarding their interests and qualifications. The commission then sends to the governor a list of individuals deemed qualified by a majority of the commission. The governor must make an appointment from those names within thirty days or ask for additional names. Within thirty days of receiving such names, the governor must make the appointment from the names submitted. If no appointment is made at that time, it is made by the chief justice of the Supreme Court.

The newly appointed judge must stand for election in a partisan contest at the next general election. This means, of course, that the judge must first obtain the nomination of his or her political party. The judge elected in this partisan election must subsequently stand for a retention election after serving the full term. Appellate judges must stand for retention every eight years, district court judges every six years, and metropolitan judges every four years. At a retention election, the name of the judge appears on the ballot; the voters are then asked whether that judge should be retained in office. The judge must be affirmed by at least 57 percent of those voting in the retention election or his or her term expires on January 1 following that election. The position is then vacant, and the appointment process begins again.

JUDICIAL PERFORMANCE EVALUATION COMMISSION[11]

The Judicial Performance Evaluation Commission (JPEC) was created by order of the New Mexico Supreme Court in 1997 to accomplish two tasks: 1) the improvement of New Mexico's judges, and 2) to provide useful and credible information to the voters of New Mexico on all judges standing for retention elections. The JPEC is made up of fifteen members, eight laypersons and seven lawyers, appointed by the Supreme Court for staggered terms. The commission members are selected from nominees by the governor, the chief justice of the Supreme Court, the Speaker of the New Mexico House of Representatives, the President Pro-Tempore of the New Mexico

Senate, the House and Senate minority leaders, and the president of the New Mexico State Bar Association.

The JPEC evaluates judges in four substantive areas: 1) fairness, 2) legal stability, 3) communication skills, and 4) preparation, attentiveness, temperament, and control over proceedings. The evaluation process involves gathering and assessing hundreds of confidential written surveys from lawyers, jurors, court staff, resource personnel (which include law enforcement representatives, psychologists, social workers, etc), law professors, other judges, as well as others who may be familiar with the judges' performance. The process includes a written self-assessment by the judge and a face-to-face interview of the judge by the commission. The JPEC conducts evaluations of judges on two occasions during each term in office. The first comes midway through the judge's term and is for the purpose of improving the judge's performance. The second comes before a retention election. The midterm evaluations are not publicly released, but the retention evaluations and recommendations are made available to the public. The JPEC does not evaluate judges running in a partisan election, nor are evaluations conducted until they have been on the bench for at least two years.

JUDICIAL STANDARDS COMMISSION[12]

The Judicial Standards Commission is the vehicle created to investigate allegations and complaints about the judicial performance of specific judges. "Complaints come mainly from litigants. Few come from lawyers."[13] The commission consists of nine members: five laypeople appointed by the governor for staggered five-year terms; two lawyers appointed by the Board of Commissioners of the State Bar; and two judges or justices from the Supreme Court, district court, or Court of Appeals, appointed by the Supreme Court. The lawyers and judges serve four-year terms.

If the commission finds cause for action, a majority of its members recommend appropriate action to the Supreme Court. The Supreme Court may choose to accept and act on the recommendation, gather additional evidence, or reject the recommendation. The significance of this process is that additional safeguards are provided to protect the public and to preserve the integrity of the judicial branch of the government.

OTHER PARTICIPANTS IN THE SYSTEM

JURIES

There are trial juries, sometimes called petit juries, and grand juries. The trial jury exists to decide what the true facts of a given case are, based on the evidence introduced at trial, and then to apply the law to the facts. The court instructs the jury in what the law is, and the lawyers argue the effect and importance of the evidence.

In a criminal case the district court uses a jury of twelve people. Magistrate and metropolitan courts use either six or twelve. In criminal cases the jury's decision must be unanimous. Civil juries can reach their decision with one or two dissenting votes.[14]

Grand juries are called to consider whether a person ought to be accused of a crime. The district attorney presents evidence, and the grand jury determines if *probable cause* exists to believe that the suspected individual committed the crime. If so, they pass an indictment against the individual and the case goes on to trial. Grand juries can also be convened to investigate accusations of official wrongdoing or malfeasance.[15]

The grand jury developed as a way to protect individuals against the unbridled authority of the state to charge people with a crime. The grand jury in theory filters out cases with insufficient evidence and ensures that only those about whom there is probable cause will be brought into court. In practice the grand jury almost invariably indicts the cases brought before it by the district attorney. But the act of preparing the case for indictment forces the district attorney to weigh the evidence and affords the accused parties the opportunity to discover the nature of the evidence against them.

LAWYERS

Lawyers are trained to advocate their clients' interest in court and in other legal matters. Lawyers work for individual clients, for corporate or group clients, for the public and various state agencies, and for public interest organizations.

To become a lawyer in New Mexico, a person must be twenty-one years old, a graduate from an accredited law school, complete the required application, and pass an examination that lasts two and one-half days.

All successful applicants are then granted licenses to practice law by the New Mexico Supreme Court.[16]

Most lawyers rarely go to court, but spend most of their time handling a variety of their clients' legal concerns. In doing all their work, lawyers are ethically obliged to zealously prepare and represent their clients' interests. In so doing, however, they are not permitted total latitude, but are limited to those techniques and practices the law allows.

Lawyers are subject to various criticisms, including unscrupulous conduct and an unwillingness to reform the system to make it more just. It is true that most lawyers choose to focus on getting the result their client needs from the system, rather than on repairing the system's defects. Likewise, however, those reform movements that do exist are aided by the lawyers and judges who participate in them.

Complaints of unethical or improper conduct by lawyers are investigated by the Disciplinary Board, an agency of the Supreme Court. The board's lawyers make recommendations to the Supreme Court as to whether the attorney involved should be disciplined. This discipline can consist of anything from an informal reprimand to a public reprimand to disbarment (permanent revocation of a lawyer's license).[17]

A variety of publicly employed lawyers have special roles in the judicial system.

ATTORNEY GENERAL[18]

The attorney general is the chief law-enforcement official of the state, although not in charge of the state police. Elected in statewide, partisan elections, the attorney general has an independent power base. This creates relative independence from the governor regarding the office's performance. For the most part, the attorney general directs the attention of the staff of assistant attorneys general and investigators to those affairs deemed to be of the greatest interest and concern to the public. Often these include consumer protection, organized crime, or corruption in government. The decisions of the attorney general to act directly in important political matters and policy may cause the governor to feel slighted or piqued. This is a limitation inherent in the fact that they are both independently elected officials.

The power of the attorney general is prescribed entirely by statute. It consists of acting on behalf of the state in cases in which it is a party or has an interest; giving opinions on questions of law when requested to do so by various public officials; representing other state and local officials involved in the judicial process; representing the state in all criminal appeals beyond the district court; and preparing drafts for contracts, bonds, and other documents required for the use of the state.

The attorney general is elected to a four-year term and, like the governor, may be reelected once. The constitution requires that the attorney general be a citizen of the United States, be at least thirty years of age, be a resident of New Mexico continuously for five years immediately before election, and be a licensed attorney of the Supreme Court of New Mexico in good standing.

DISTRICT ATTORNEYS[19]

Under the New Mexico Constitution, the district attorney is a part of the judicial system of the state and is a quasi-judicial officer. The district attorney may act for the state and for all counties within that district in all cases in which they may be a party or may be interested. However, the district attorney's chief duty is to prosecute those accused of crimes.

If requested, the district attorney represents the county before the board of county commissioners of any county in the district in all matters before the board. The district attorney may appear, without request, before the board when it is sitting as a board of equalization. In addition, this official advises, upon request, all county and state officers and represents in the Supreme Court or Court of Appeals any county in the district in all civil cases in which the county may be concerned, except for suits brought in the name of the state.

District attorneys are elected for four-year terms on a partisan basis. They may succeed themselves indefinitely. A district attorney must be a licensed attorney, a resident of New Mexico for at least three years prior to election, and a resident of the district in which she or he is running. Neither district attorneys nor their assistants may engage in the private practice of law while in office.

PUBLIC DEFENDERS[20]

The New Mexico Public Defender Department provides for legal representation for all indigents (people too poor to hire their own lawyers) charged in any state court (except municipal courts) with a crime that carries a possible sentence of imprisonment.

Depending upon the case and its location within the state, this assistance is given in one of three ways. The public defender system consists of full-time district defender offices in nine cities: Santa Fe, Albuquerque, Clovis, Aztec, Las Cruces, Carlsbad, Roswell, Hobbs, and Alamogordo. All other areas of the state are covered by contracts with private attorneys or by single-case appointments of private attorneys. In addition the Appellate Division, located in Santa Fe, handles all appeals in the higher courts and other post-conviction remedies.

The governor appoints the chief public defender, who directs the department. The chief public defender must be an attorney licensed to practice law in the New Mexico Supreme Court, must have actively practiced law for five years immediately prior to appointment, and must have criminal law experience.

The chief appoints a district defender for each district office. The district defenders hire the necessary staff attorneys and other assistants.

Two other entities exist to aid in administering the court system.

ADMINISTRATIVE OFFICE OF THE COURTS[21]

In most states managerial tasks in most courts are performed by judges or clerks. In recent years an increased effort has been made to train court executives or administrators to perform managerial tasks for the courts. The Administrative Office of the Courts (AOC) was created to provide professional management assistance to the courts. The AOC prepares annual budgets for the various court systems and acts as the Supreme Court's administrative arm. The courts themselves continue to be the policy making bodies, under the supervision of the Supreme Court, with the AOC facilitating the performance of their judicial roles.

CONCLUSION

Like all other political institutions, New Mexico's courts are beset with controversy. Some argue that the poor have inadequate access to the system, some believe judges are too lenient in sentencing criminals, some are concerned that minorities are underrepresented in the legal profession, and others express concerns that the judicial process is too slow and cumbersome.

There have been efforts by the courts to implement alternative methods of resolving disputes, moving away from the traditional adversarial approach. The Supreme Court has also adopted rules to make the civil litigation process more efficient. The efficacy of all these steps are important, because courts allocate several things about which people care deeply: money, freedom, and justice.

NOTES

1. *Marbury v. Madison*, 1 Cr. 137 (1803).
2. *Scott v. Rizzo*, 96 NM 682, 634, P.2d 1234 (1981).
3. N.M. Const., Art. VI §26; §35–1–1 through §35–13–3 N.M.S.A., 1978; N.M.S.A., 1978.
4. §35–14–1 *et seq.*, N.M.S.A., 1978.
5. §34–8A-1 *et seq.*, N.M.S.A., 1978.
6. §34–7–1 *et seq.*, N.M.S.A., 1978.
7. N.M. Const., Art. VI, §§13–17; §34–6–1 *et seq.*, N.M.S.A., 1978.
8. N.M. Const., Art. VI, §28; §34–5–1 *et seq.*, N.M.S.A., 1978.
9. N.M. Const., Art. VI, §§1–11; §34–2–1 *et seq.*, N.M.S.A., 1978.
10. N.M. Const., Art. VI, §§33–37.
11. Supreme Court of the State of New Mexico, Order No. 02–8500.
12. N.M. Const., Art. VI, §32.
13. Informational letter (Judicial Standards Commission, Dec. 3, 1979).
14. N.M. Const., Art. II, §12 and §14; §38–5–17 N.M.S.A., 1978; Rule 1–038, S.C.R.A. (1978).
15. N.M. Const., Art. II, §14; §31–6–1 *et seq.*, N.M.S.A., 1978.
16. Rules Governing Discipline, Rule 17–101 *et seq.*, S.C.R.A.
17. Rules Governing Discipline, Rule 17–101 *et seq.*, S.C.R.A.
18. §8–5–1 *et seq.*, N.M.S.A., 1978.
19. §36–1–1 *et seq.*, N.M.S.A., 1978.
20. §31–15–1 *et seq.*, N.M.S.A., 1978.
21. §34–9–1 *et seq.*, N.M.S.A., 1978.

Chapter Six

Local Governments

by Maurilio E. Vigil

At first glance local governments may seem to be smaller versions of state government. Local governments, after all, tax and spend money, operate from a budget, and adopt laws (ordinances), just as state governments do. In reality, however, there are fundamental differences in governmental organization, legal standing, and policy orientation between state and local governments. Local governments are more complex than state government because of the daily and immediate nature of the services they provide, their proximity to the people they serve, and the constraints under which they operate.

Legally local governments can correctly be characterized as stepchildren of the American political system, since they are units of government that were not explicitly considered in the federal system provided by the United States Constitution. Local governments therefore are technically "creatures of the state," which means that the states may create (incorporate) or destroy them and may prescribe obligations, powers, privileges, and restrictions that local government must follow. Local governments in this sense can be considered an extension of state government, since in essence they perform functions and exercise powers reserved for the states by the federal Constitution.[1]

In spite of their subordinate legal status, the practical reality is that local governments have been and continue to be important and indispensable in the American governmental process. They have served as the initial political training ground for many future state and national leaders and as experimental laboratories where innovative programs have first been tested. Probably most important, local governments continue to provide the bulk of the direct government services required by American citizens. These include police and fire protection, public-health services, public utilities, sewage and sanitation facilities, street maintenance, and parks and recreation facilities.[2] The prominence of local governments on the American scene can be illustrated not only by their range of services but also by their proliferation. In 2002 the U.S. Bureau of the Census reported that there were 87,525 units of local government in the United States, including 3,043 counties, 19,429 municipalities, 16,504 townships, 13,506 school districts, and 35,052 special districts.[3]

The classification of New Mexico's local governmental units and their numbers in 2002 were: counties, 33; municipalities, 102; townships, none; school districts, 89; and special districts, 628.[4] Comparative figures in 1957 show 316 units of local government, divided between the 32 counties, 77 municipalities, 95 school districts, and 112 special districts.[5] Thus although municipalities have increased by 25, school districts have declined (reflective of consolidation) by 6 in the thirty-year period. The number of special districts is larger than in 1957, but this may be the result of accounting rather than the creation of new districts since the acequia ditch associations are now counted as special district governments.

In addition to these units of local government, which will be described more fully later, New Mexico, with its rich multicultural history and population, presents a unique mosaic of extra-local governmental units that, according to the U.S. *Census of Governments*, "have certain characteristics of governmental units but which are treated in Census statistics as subordinate agencies of the federal government, the state or other local governments or as private rather than governmental units." Among these are the Indian pueblos, which have been here for centuries and which, through tribal law, exercise many local governmental powers. Subcounty, quasi-governmental units include county parking authorities, emergency flood districts, fire districts, health districts, historic districts, noxious-weed-control districts, road districts, special-assessment districts, special-zoning districts, water districts, and wind-erosion districts. Municipal quasi-governmental units include historic districts, housing authorities, improvement districts (involving streets, sidewalks, sewers, water, parking, parks), fire safety improvement districts, and urban-renewal authorities. Still evident as remnants of the Spanish colonization of New Mexico are community acequia or water-users' associations, which are classified as special governmental districts by the state Department of Finance and Administration.[6]

Most New Mexicans (75 percent) reside in urban areas, according to the 2000 U.S. Census, so it can be assumed that most live within the jurisdiction of a city or town, a county, a school district, and one or more special districts. The fact that these units of local government provide the bulk of services to all citizens in itself justifies concern for and study of these units of government, their powers, responsibilities, structures, and organization. This chapter is designed to provide such a general overview, including the functions of major officials in local government and their relationships to each other. The descriptive style employed is designed to compile and interpret the formal, legal provisions describing the frameworks of local governments and their powers, duties, and responsibilities as contained in the New Mexico Constitution, statutes, and court decisions. It is important to note that most legal provisions referring to local government in New Mexico are contained in Article X ("County and Municipal Corporations") of the New Mexico Constitution and primarily in volume II, Chapters 3, 4, and 5, of *New Mexico Statutes Annotated* (1978), with a few provisions in other sections of the constitution (such as Article IX, "State, County, and Municipal Indebtedness"), and periodic legislative revisions to Chapters 3, 4, and 5.[7]

TYPES OF LOCAL GOVERNMENTS IN NEW MEXICO

The standard source of defining and classifying the bases for local government has been the *Census of Governments* of the U.S. Bureau of the Census. A "governmental unit," according to census, "is an organized entity which, in addition to having governmental character has sufficient discretion in the management of its own affairs to distinguish it as separate from the administrative structure of any other governmental unit."[8]

In other words, to be counted by the census as a governmental unit, an entity must possess (1) "existence as an organized entity," (2) "governmental charter," and (3) "substantial autonomy." As stated above, the local governmental units classified by the U.S. Census in New Mexico are counties, municipalities, school districts, and special districts. Each of these categories will be described separately.

COUNTY GOVERNMENTS

County governments were the first and probably most universally adopted unit of local government in the United States. Counties in the American system owe their origin to the English "shires," which along with townships were the basic units of local government in England during the American colonial period. The appearance and spread of county governments on the American scene was natural during the settlement and colonization of the frontier, because as essentially a rural form of government, they were adaptable for governing initially underpopulated areas. Their persistence as a viable form of local government in spite of urbanization is due both to their institutionalization and to expanded demands for governmental services.

County governments can be found in every state of the Union except Connecticut and Rhode Island. In Alaska counties are called "boroughs," and in Louisiana they are "parishes." The numbers of counties varies from a low of 3 in Delaware to a high of 254 in Texas.

In New Mexico county governments can trace their origins to the Spanish colonial era, since Spanish and later Mexican policy provided for *partidos*, which were compatible with the geographic and governmental jurisdiction of the American county. These partidos were administered in the more centralized Spanish/Mexican fashion by a "prefect" appointed by the regional governor. The military occupation of New Mexico by American troops under Colonel Stephen Watts Kearny introduced the Kearny Code, which transformed the old partidos into counties, governed largely by the judiciary, which exercised executive as well as judicial authority. The *alguacil mayor* under Mexican rule became the sheriff, the chief law enforcement officer who doubled as tax collector. The Kearny Code was itself superseded by the territorial government created in 1850, but the formal structure of county government in New Mexico was not formally changed until 1876, when boards of county commissioners were established as the central governing boards for each county.[9] Throughout the territorial period, however, county boundaries were continuously changed by the legislature, as more population and special-interest groups wanted to partake in the benefits of their "own" county government and of a county seat, which in addition to serving as a seat of government doubled as a social and commercial center for the county. Since statehood in 1912, seven new counties have been created.

There are today thirty-three counties in the state. The most recent was created in 1981, when Cibola County was formed by the New Mexico Legislature and formally approved by the voters; it was carved out of the western section of Valencia County. The counties in New Mexico are as diverse as any counties across the country. Their population density is highly variable. For example, Bernalillo County, the most populous with 30.6 percent of the total state population, is the second smallest (1,169 square miles) in geographic area. The largest county, Catron, with 6,879 square miles, is the second lowest in population, with 0.2 percent of the state's population. Los Alamos County is the smallest, with 108 square miles.[10]

The county in New Mexico is a creature of the state. In a more specific sense, it is a creature of the state legislature, since state constitutional provisions pertaining to counties are rather limited, meaning that the legislature is empowered to legislate the functions, authority, power, and responsibilities of counties. The only real restrictions on the state legislature's supremacy over the counties are found in Article X, Section 2, of the constitution, which provides for the election or terms of office for county officials; Section 3, which provides that no county seat can be removed unless three-fifths of the voters in the county approve the move in an election; and Article IV, Section 24, which prohibits the legislature from passing special laws that affect only one or a few counties.[11]

County governments were originally created to "aid in administration of the policies of the state." Because of the corporate status conferred on New Mexico counties in 1876, and because of increasing demands for local governmental services, New Mexico counties have grown beyond being merely administrative subdivisions of the state and have undertaken governmental initiatives of their own. An accurate description of the current New Mexico county is that it has three major roles.

The first role of every county is that officials such as the county clerk, assessor, and treasurer continue to serve as administrative officers of the state government, assisting in such activities as public record keeping (the recording of deeds, titles, and so forth), election administration, assessment of property values, and tax collection.

The second role is that county governments have and continue to provide local governmental services, especially to nonurban areas that would not be served by the development of municipal services. For example, in most New Mexico counties the sheriff is still considered a county law-enforcement officer. Even though technically a sheriff's jurisdiction also includes cities, the norm is for sheriffs to leave law enforcement in the city to the municipal law-enforcement officials and to devote their time to law enforcement for the rural parts of the county. Reflecting this rural orientation, sheriffs and their deputies often still wear the cowboy hat indicative of the frontier sheriff tradition. The importance of county officials is probably also necessitated by the large size of the state and its low population density. County officials perform many services for rural constituencies that would otherwise not be served. Also indicative of this service function of New Mexico county government is the prominence of road and bridge construction and maintenance in the priorities and concerns of the boards of county commissioners. A commonly heard story about county commissioners in New Mexico is that some people seek the office as a way of improving the county road to their *ranchito* (small ranch), and that once this is accomplished they retire from public life.[12] Except for Bernalillo County, New Mexico has not been affected by the phenomenon of the "urbanized county," where the county has had to assume many urban functions because of dense population concentrations outside city limits. This phenomenon has, however, affected Bernalillo County, which does provide many urban services, such as law enforcement.

The third role of county governments (primarily at the impetus of the boards of county commissioners) is to provide innovative leadership in new areas of concern to the county, such as economic development and land-use regulation. County governments have figured prominently in establishing regulations on the use of land through zoning, which has affected land-development enterprises. Such regulations have had important economic impacts on counties. Some county governments have been streamlined by the appointment of county managers or planners as a way of enhancing professional expertise in dealing with these kinds of problems.

Classification of Counties

New Mexico's counties are classified by the legislature, in accordance with the dictates of the state constitution, on the basis of population and assessed property valuation. This is mainly done in order to establish an equitable salary schedule for county officials and to determine county budget requirements and limitations. The classification of counties is made by the Secretary of the Department of Finance and Administration and is subject to review and revision every two years. Figure 6.1 is a summary of the classification and criteria.[13]

The classification system employed ensures a compromise between having some uniform legislative standards and allowing for flexibility to meet the variable individual needs of the counties. Los Alamos County, the only class H county, is unique in New Mexico, in that it is the only consolidated city-county government in the state. Its unique status stems from efforts, culminating in 1948, to incorporate the "atomic city" into New Mexico government.

County Officials and the Structure of County Government

The structure and organization of county government is essentially similar among New Mexico's counties, with the voters of the county electing separate county officials and county governing boards known as the boards of county commissioners.[14] These elections result in many offices listed on a "long ballot," a phenomenon that has been a recurring problem for New Mexico state and local governments.

Although the state legislature has provided that the boards of county commissioners are the governing bodies of the counties, empowered to "adopt a budget, to levy county taxes, and to enact certain ordinances," the executive powers of the commissioners are limited by the fact that they must perform these functions in cooperation with, rather than with control over, other county officials, who are elected in their own right.[15] Notwithstanding this limitation, the boards of county commissioners are vested with substantial powers.

FIGURE 6.1
Classification of New Mexico Counties

CLASS	CRITERIA	NUMBER AND COUNTIES
A	Assessed value over $750 million, population over 100,000	2 (Bernalillo, Doña Ana)
B Over	Assessed value over $300 million, population under 100,000	13 (Chaves, Curry, Eddy, Grant, Lea, Lincoln, Mora, Quay, Roosevelt, San Juan, Santa Fe, Taos, Valencia)
B Under	Assessed value between $75 and $300 million,population under 100,000	10 (Cibola, Colfax, Hidalgo, Luna, McKinley, Rio Arriba, Sandoval, San Miguel, Socorro, Torrance)
C	Assessed value between $45 and $75 million, population under 100,000	4 (Sierra, Union, Catron, Guadalupe)
1st Over	Assessed value between $27 and $45 million	1 (Harding)
1st Under	Assessed value between $14 and $27 million	2 (DeBaca, Otero)
2nd	Assessed value between $8.25 and $14 million	0
3rd	Assessed value between $6.5 and $8.5 million	0
4th	Assessed value between $4.75 and $6.25 million	0
5th	Assessed value less than $4.75 million	0
H	Land area not more than 144 sq. miles	1 (Los Alamos)

Source: New Mexico Association of Counties website, http//www.nmcounties.org/counties.html

Boards of County Commissioners. Although executive authority is divided among several elected officials in New Mexico counties, the principal governing bodies are the boards of county commissioners. The composition of these boards has undergone marked change in recent years due to constitutional revision, legislation, and federal court decrees. In the past all counties had three commissioners representing different districts but elected by all voters in the county. At present the composition, and methods of representation are varied and changing. A constitutional amendment approved in 1988 allows any county, by a simple vote of the county commission, to expand its size to five members. In 2006, sixteen counties maintained three member boards while seventeen counties have chosen to expand to five member boards in which county commissioners are elected from single member districts within the county. All elected county officails are allowed to serve two consecutive, four-year terms; having served that, all county officials are ineligible to hold any county office for two years.[16]

As in most other elective offices in the state, the only legal requirement to run for the county commission is that the person be a qualified voter. Commissioners must also be residents of the district they wish to represent.

In the case of vacancies in the office of county commissioner, the governor may appoint a commissioner to hold office until the next general election. Thus appointed commissioners can still serve two consecutive terms if elected, in addition to the period of appointment. Commissioners, like other county officials, may be removed from office upon indictment and conviction for circumstances involving a felony, failure to discharge the duties of the office, demanding or receiving illegal fees, gross incompetency or negligence, misuse of public funds, or similar activities reflective of malfeasance and mismanagement, rendering the individuals unfit for office. Similarly, any elected county official is subject to recall by the voters of the county.[17]

Commissioners as well as other county officials are required to subscribe to an oath of office and are bonded for an amount equal to 20 percent of the funds handled by the office during the fiscal year.

The salaries of commissioners and other officials are fixed by the legislature and are based on the state classification of counties. The salaries of county commissioners vary from the class A counties (Bernalillo), where commissioners receive $25,712 per year, to the first-class county annual salary of $8,625, to the $1 per year token fee received by commissioners in Los Alamos. These figures are based on 2005 salaries. All county officials are entitled to receive reimbursements for official travel-related expenses. Per diem and mileage allowances are established by the legislature.

The commissioners are required at their first meeting after election to elect one of their own as chair to preside over commission meetings and to represent the board in a ceremonial capacity. However, the chair possesses no superior or extraordinary powers over the other members; she or he is an equal and does not even possess the power to establish an agenda for commission meetings. Often, however, in a practical sense the person chosen as chair of a commission may wield influence for the same reasons that led to her or his selection.

Boards of county commissioners are required by law to meet on the first Mondays of January, April, July, and October. They may meet at any other time necessary to conduct public business and are required to maintain minutes of meetings and publish proceedings in a general-circulation newspaper within twenty days after a meeting. County commissions are subject to the "open-meetings" law of the state, requiring that all decisions of the board be made in public and that meetings involving a quorum (a majority of the members) must be open to the public and previously announced. Most commissions hold meetings at least once a month.[18]

The boards of county commissioners are given broad grants of authority by the state legislature that essentially combine legislative and executive responsibility and powers. As such, the separation of powers principle is not in operation at this level. Commissions may sue or be sued; may purchase, hold, sell, and convey real or personal property; may enter into contracts; and may exercise corporate powers consistent with state laws.

Among the legislative powers of the county commissions is the power to prepare the budget for the county, providing for payment of all county employees' salaries and for the overall financing of county administration. Commissions are empowered to levy taxes on property and to levy special taxes as authorized by law for the financing of county government. This power over fiscal and budgeting matters has yielded to the commissions the power to allocate and distribute the county's share of state and federal funds. Such fiscal power also enables the commissions to issue bonds for special purposes. They are also the zoning authorities for the counties. Therefore they may designate planning and zoning authorities, or they may themselves regulate zoning in the county, involving use and safety of county roads, parks, and recreation. The onset of the land-speculation boom since the 1960s, a proliferation in the western states of the land-development business, and the concomitant instances of land fraud have made this zoning power particularly important for county commissioners. Land-development corporations offer the prospect of economic development and progress for a county, but often hidden strings may involve obligations for services (roads, bridges, water, and energy) that are impractical or unfeasible for the county, given its financial situation.

The commissions' administrative powers are shared with the other elected officials in the counties, who are given administrative authority or responsibility in their own right, as will be discussed below. Among the commissions' own executive powers are the following: (1) to set salary schedules for all nonelected employees of the county (including the county manager and employees directly under the commissions themselves, as well as the employees of other elected officials, such as sheriff's deputies, clerks, assessor, and treasurer); (2) to care for county property, including county buildings (courthouse, jails, libraries), equipment, and supplies; (3) to perform election duties involving organizing precincts, setting polling places, obtaining and maintaining voting machines, and acting as the ex officio canvassing board in elections (that is, the body responsible for tabulating election results and certifying winners); (4) to make appointments to boards or commissions; (5) to grant licenses and regulate public dance halls, clubs, traveling excursions (carnivals, circuses), palmists, peddlers, etc., and in local-option areas to regulate liquor sales; (6) to perform financial-management duties, such as the examination and settlement of financial accounts, and accounting, in terms of receipts and expenditures; (7) to provide for county services involving joint-powers agreements; (8) to lay out, alter, or discontinue roads and bridges and provide for their maintenance; and (9) to adopt appropriate ordinances involving activities such as building codes and animal control.

The commissions may also be involved in building and operating public facilities such as libraries, hospitals, and airports.[19]

In summary, as James Grieshop has said, commissioners have both ministerial and discretionary duties; that is, they perform some duties based on legal obligation without regard to personal judgment, as part of their job (ministerial), and in other cases they are expected to use their judgment and discretion, based on their perception of the job as an elected and accountable public official. The general role of the county commission is probably best described as the power "to represent the county and have care of the county property and the management of the interest of the county in cases where no other provision is made by law."[20]

It should be noted that the outline presented here is only a brief description of the main duties of the commissioners; each of the functions may actually entail quite complex administration.

County Assessors. County assessors are publicly elected county officials who are responsible for the valuation or assessment of property in the county, for the purposes of property taxation. It is the assessors' responsibility to mail notices of tax liability to property owners. Although this is a separate county executive office, subject to state laws, the fiscal or budgetary authority of the county commissions grants the assessors power over expenses and a limited part of the budget. Therefore the situation calls for a cooperative relationship. In situations where county-employee merit systems are in effect assessors are obligated to conform to them, if they have been agreed to and established by the commissions. The duties of assessors are thus strongly ministerial, as the office is very much an administrative subdivision of state government. County assessors may be suspended by the director of the Tax Division of the state Department of Taxation and Revenue, for failure to comply with the property-tax code or division regulations.

County Clerks. The county clerks' functions and responsibilities can properly be described as dual in nature. On the one hand, the office serves as an administrative subdivision of state government; on the other hand, clerks have their responsibilities vis-à-vis the county commission. As a state administrative subdivision, the county clerk's offices are the main public record-keeping agencies in county government, recording marriages, discharges from the military, and transfers of property. The clerks are also the main county officials charged with registering voters, maintaining up-to-date voting lists, accepting declarations of candidacy for public office, and generally coordinating the conduct of elections at the county level. In these duties the county clerks are also acting as executors of the dictates of the county commissions, which designate precincts and polling places, designate county boards of voter registration, provide for absentee voters and voting machines, and act as ex officio canvassing boards.

In addition to performing these electoral duties for the commissions, county clerks are ex officio clerks of the boards of county commissioners, must attend all their sessions, maintain minutes of their proceedings, and record their votes and actions. The clerks publish the proceedings of commission meetings and issue orders or directives adopted by the boards.

County Sheriffs. County sheriffs are the principal law-enforcement officers in the counties. As stated previously, the sheriffs' jurisdictions encompass whole counties, but they often leave law enforcement within city limits to the municipal police. In Bernalillo County, where the demand for law-enforcement services is great, and where urbanization has engulfed much of the county, the sheriff's office assumes a major role as a municipal law-enforcement agency. A modus vivendi has evolved whereby the sheriff's office provides law enforcement services for parts of the Albuquerque valley area and for communities outside of Albuquerque but still within Bernalillo County. In Mora County the sheriff exercises jurisdiction over the rural areas of the county, as well as for the village of Mora, which is not incorporated. Sheriffs have also assumed duties as peace officers in court trials, as well as in serving district court subpoenas, executing warrants, transporting prisoners, and maintaining upkeep of the county jail. Sheriffs, like other county officers, are separate executive officers, entitled to hire their own deputies, but they are also subject to the budgetary power of their county commissions.

County Surveyors. Although the office of county surveyor is provided for by state statute, only seven counties actually have one, and in those it is usually a part-time job. County surveyors must be practicing and licensed surveyors. County commissions maintain sets of survey books and authorize the surveying of county land and the payment for the surveyor's services.

County Treasurers. County treasurers are responsible for the collection of taxes and for the supervision of all county monies; treasurers must

maintain accounts of all monies received and disbursed. Such books pertaining to county indebtedness must be available for inspection upon
demand by the boards of county commissioners. County treasurers may
be suspended by the secretary of the state Department of Finance and
Administration (DFA) for failure to comply with the property-tax code
or regulations and instructions from the Department of Taxation and
Revenue or the DFA.

Probate Judges. Probate judges are special county judges charged with
the responsibility of presiding over cases involving the settlement of wills
and estates and conflicts involving their settlement. A probate judge does
not have to be a licensed attorney. The office of the probate judge is
located in the county seat. State law requires the boards of county commissioners to provide the judge with office space, clerical help, and office
supplies. Often the office of probate judge has become quite bureaucra-
tized, with most estate settlements occurring through negotiations
between attorneys and, in major cases, being settled by state district court.
Probate judges, especially in rural counties, rarely hold hearings or court
to settle estate conflicts.[21]

Appointive Officials. State law also allows county commissioners to
appoint certain officials, provided they meet the relevant legal standards
to assist in the administration of county government. County commissioners in counties with populations of one thousand or more may
appoint a licensed physician to the position of county coroner and
determine the salary. In A, B, C, and first-class counties, county commissioners are empowered to employ a county purchasing agent to oversee all county purchases of equipment and supplies and to maintain
control over county property.

County commissions are also empowered to employ and establish
the salary for a county manager, who is to act as chief administrative officer supervising personnel, fiscal, and budgetary matters, as well as property and general administration for the county.

Prospects for New Mexico County Government

While it is true that county government has come under attack as outmoded, and while many reforms have been proposed and adopted by

different states and some counties in New Mexico as a way toward streamlining it, the prospects for the survival of county government in New Mexico seem very bright.

Certainly some reforms promise to revitalize and improve county governments. Some examples are providing for greater county governmental discretion through home rule, the adoption of practices conducive to intergovernmental cooperation among various units of government, the creation of metropolitan councils of government, the adoption of reforms in personnel administration, and providing for more technical administrative expertise through the creation of offices such as county manager, chief administrative officer, and purchasing agent.

In retrospect, the integrity of New Mexico counties and their continued importance are assured by the continuing and expanded demand for all kinds of governmental services. In states like New Mexico with a large area, the need to provide governmental administration to sparsely populated areas will of course continue. The difficulty and impracticability of converting to municipal administrations the many governmental services now performed by the rural county as an administrative subdivision of the state assure the continuance of the county. The essential need for a unit of government that can serve as a point of entry for political leaders in state government and the desire to keep government close to the people are two other strong reasons.

MUNICIPAL GOVERNMENTS

Although New Mexico generally is regarded as a rural state, it may be surprising to some that the overwhelming majority (62.9 percent) live within the state's one hundred and two municipalities. Municipal governments in New Mexico, like those in the nation as a whole, have come to play an increasingly important role, as the population has become more urbanized and has demanded more and better municipal services. While New Mexico cities (aside from Albuquerque) have not been affected by urban crises such as fractionalization of government, air pollution, noise, transportation problems, urban sprawl, urban decay, and crime, they have been beset by financial difficulties and by other problems unique to their locale and populations.

The U.S. Census defines a municipality as a "political subdivision within which a municipal corporation has been established to provide general local government for a specific population concentration in a defined area."[22] It can be a city, town, village, or borough (except in Alaska). Generally speaking, municipal corporations are distinguished from other local governments by their corporate status. Incorporation grants cities the right of limited self-government. Implied among the general powers coming from incorporation are the powers to purchase, hold, or sell real or personal property; to levy and collect tax revenues; to obtain and spend nontax sources of revenue (bonds, allotments from federal grants-in-aid, revenue sharing, and so forth); and to select a form of government and elect officers to administer the affairs of the community. In 2002 there were 19,429 municipalities in the United States.

Like county governments, municipalities are creatures of the state legislature, since the legislature creates municipalities and empowers them through their charters to exercise certain powers on behalf of the state. Although New Mexico law formerly provided for three classes of municipal corporations, based on population (cities—populations over 3,000; towns—populations between 1,500 and 3,000; and villages—populations with under 1,500 but not less than 150 people), such distinctions have formally been eliminated from the statutes. Municipal corporations, whether they be cities, towns, or villages, presumably exercise similar powers, depending on their charter.[23] Because of the strength of custom, however, cities, towns, and villages continue to use one of the three designations until they qualify for a higher designation, whereupon a municipal election is held to decide on the question of changing the name of the municipality from "the town of" to "the city of," and so on.

In population, economic, and social characteristics, New Mexico's municipalities are quite diverse. Albuquerque is in a league by itself as the state's largest Standard Metropolitan Statistical Area (SMSA), with a population of 534,533 as of the 2000 census. It contains not only the largest overall population, but also the largest Hispanic and African-American populations in the state, as well as ranking third in Indian population. Las Cruces became the state's second SMSA in 1979, after requesting a special census, which found its population to be above 50,000; its population in 2000 was listed as slightly over 74,267. With SMSA status, Las Cruces has qualified for additional federal revenues. Santa Fe (with a population of 62,203 as of the 2000 census) is the only other New Mexico community with SMSA status. In addition smaller cities and towns are distributed throughout the state, with villages proliferating in spite of clear tendencies toward urbanization.

Incorporation

In New Mexico any area may petition for incorporation as a municipality, provided that it has a population density of at least one person per acre, that it contains at least one hundred and fifty persons, and that it is not within the boundary of an existing municipality. The procedure for incorporation is relatively simple. First, a written petition is drawn up, stating the proposed name of the municipality and containing a description of the area to be incorporated. The petition should be signed by either two hundred qualified electors or the owners of no less than 60 percent of the proposed territory and should be accompanied by an accurate map or plat showing the proposed boundaries and money sufficient to conduct a census.

Second, the local county commission will investigate and determine if all the legal conditions have been met and complied with and will conduct a census in the proposed municipality. Within forty-five days of a positive determination by the county commission, an election will be held in the area of the question of incorporation. If a majority of the voters vote in favor of incorporation, the city is incorporated as a municipal corporation, and an election of municipal officers will follow within two weeks. Court actions to contest the process at any stage can of course delay and be affected by the incorporation. Disincorporation is also provided for by statute, in the event that municipalities wish to revert to unincorporated status. A petition bearing the signatures of one-fourth of the voters participating in the previous municipal election is enough to initiate the process, and an election supervised by the local county commission is then called. If a majority of the voters favor disincorporation, proper provisions will be made to liquidate the assets of the municipality, and all arrangements necessary will be made in order to pay community debts.[24] The relatively simple process for incorporation could be potentially troublesome for New Mexico, in the sense that it could produce a situation common to SMSAs elsewhere in the country; that is, a desperate core city ringed by separately incorporated suburbs.

Municipal Charters in New Mexico

Because New Mexico's cities have been incorporated in different periods of the state's history, some dating back to the territorial period, and because they have been incorporated under varying statutory provisions and oftentimes continue to operate under original charters, it is appropriate to give a brief and general sketch of evolutionary patterns in municipal charters. First of all, a charter may be defined as a written document similar to a constitution, which confers legitimate status on a municipal corporation. A charter outlines the basic structure of government, grants powers to officials, enumerates the duties and functions of government, and sets limitations on them.[25] The charter as such may be an instrument created by the state through general or special statutory provision, or may be developed by a municipality itself in conformance with state law. Therefore all New Mexico cities technically operate under a charter, either one provided with a standard form of government by the state or one adopted by the municipality itself.

In general American states have provided a number of alternative patterns for cities to follow in their charters, providing for one form of government or another. Probably the earliest form employed by most states was the "special act" charter, by which a city's charter was a specific or special enactment by the legislature. The fact that every city was thus created by a special act suited to its purposes and needs meant that charters could be imposed on a city, and furthermore, that there was no inherent uniformity in the charters granted to all cities. It was this latter problem that gave rise to the "general act" charter, by which a prescribed form of government was established for all cities being incorporated. This second type provided the desired uniformity, but reduced the amount of flexibility open to cities of different sizes and varying needs. Because of the inadequacy of the previous forms, "classified" charters then emerged, which provided certain classes of charters based on factors such as population size. The most recent innovation has provided for "optional" charters, by which a city might select from certain classes one of several forms of government.[26]

New Mexico's Municipal Code has essentially followed the course of the evolution and development of various kinds of charters. Until 1884 New Mexico cities were chartered by special act of the territorial legislature; some New Mexico cities chartered before that year may still operate under such special-act charters. Silver City, for example, continues to operate under a special-act charter that conferred many home-rule powers on that community. New Mexico Statutes (Sections 3–3–1 through 3–3–4 N.M.S.A., 1978) ensure the legitimacy of these special-act charters and provide procedures for a city to follow in adopting a more current charter.

Since 1884 New Mexico has provided by general act for the chartering of cities. Changes in the general municipal-charter laws after statehood tended to provide for some options in the form of government available to cities of different size populations. For example, until recently incorporated municipalities could choose between a charter with a commission form of government or one variation of the mayor-council form.[27] In addition, however, the New Mexico Legislature in 1917 passed legislation authorizing a municipality to adopt a charter of its own, and Albuquerque and other municipalities proceeded to adopt charters. This particular legislation was liberalized by the home-rule amendment to the constitution in 1970. This confusing picture of the corporate origins of New Mexico municipalities can be clarified somewhat by saying that New Mexico municipalities were created and operated either under special acts of the legislature, general legislative decree, or separate charters adopted in conformance with New Mexico statutes.

Today a New Mexico city essentially can, by adopting a new charter or by amending its charter under the provisions of Article 10, Section 6, of the New Mexico Constitution (the home-rule provision), provide for any form of government of its choice. Such a choice is not subject to the specified provisions outlined for other forms of government provided in the general charters.

Forms of Contemporary Municipal Government

The New Mexico Municipal Code, embodied primarily in Chapter 3 of the *New Mexico Statutes Annotated*, expressly provides for three types of municipal charters, two of which prescribe a specific form of government and one of which is open-ended. The forms of government currently provided for in New Mexico are the mayor-council form, the commission-manager form, and the home-rule charter. New Mexico also provides by statute for the possibility of "combined municipal organizations," that is, for the consolidation of county and municipal governments.[28] Aside from consolidated Los Alamos, Bernalillo County, and Albuquerque form the only city-county combination that has flirted with this form of government. Voters in Bernalillo County defeated consolidation efforts in 1972 and 2003. Voters also defeated a proposal to establish Bernalillo County as an "urban" county in 2001. The following section gives a brief description of the three main forms of municipal-charter government provided by the New Mexico Municipal Code, the structure of said governments, their officers, and the duties and responsibilities of the latter.

Mayor-Council Governments. The mayor-council form of government is the most popular form of municipal government in New Mexico. Some eighty-five of the ninety-eight New Mexico municipalities operate under the mayor-council form. While most of the cities with this form of government operate under the general-charter specifications of New Mexico law (Sections 3–11–1 through 3–13–4 N.M.S.A., 1978), it should be noted that some cities with the mayor-council form are not subject to the same restrictions, because they adopted it under the home rule charter provision. For this reason the following description is applicable to most but not all cities, the notable exceptions being Albuquerque, Gallup, Las Vegas, and Silver City, which operate under their own charters.[29] The case of Albuquerque will be discussed later in this chapter. A true description of the particular provisions of government for the other home rule cities can be obtained from their respective charters, although some of those provisions are similar to the ones described here.

Elected officials in the mayor-council form of government are one mayor and at least four but not more than ten council members, along with a municipal judge. This duplicates in form the separation-of-powers principle of national and state governments. The mayor is generally recognized as the chief executive officer, the council primarily exercises legislative powers, and the municipal judge is charged with judicial responsibility. (See Figure 6.2)

Mayors. Mayors are elected at large for a four-year term in a nonpartisan election; the single qualification for the office is that a candidate must be a "qualified elector." Anyone aged eighteen or over who is registered to vote is a qualified elector. Mayors are required, within ten days after their election, to take an oath of office affirming support for the United States and New Mexico Constitutions and swearing faithfully to execute the duties of their office. Mayors, acting by the authority of their office, are not personally subject to action by the courts, but the municipality may be. Mayors may be removed for misconduct in office if their councils file a complaint in district court and a hearing held ten days after notice makes a removal determination. Should a vacancy occur in the office of mayor because of death, disability, resignation, or change of residence away from the community, the council may appoint by majority vote a qualified elector to fill the unexpired term. Depending on local discretion and ordinance, the mayor may be paid a salary, but it shall not exceed the salary paid a member of the local county commission. Mayors in the New Mexico mayor-council form of government are strong. They are empowered to supervise all municipal offices and departments and are responsible for the execution of municipal ordinances and regulations. Mayors designate all appointive municipal employees, who are then subject to approval of a majority of the councils. Generally the laws provide for mayors to submit their lists of appointees to the councils by the second Monday after their election; if a person is rejected by the council, a mayor must submit another nomination by the next meeting. Mayors' power to discharge is also subject to the concurrence of a majority of the council. Between council meetings mayors may suspend an appointed city official until the next council meeting, when the council may vote on the suspension.[30]

Many of the powers of mayors stem from the "implied executive powers" vested in any executive office; thus mayors are responsible for exercising executive power on behalf of the municipality; signing commissions, licenses, and permits issued by their councils; and representing their cities in ceremonial functions. Mayors preside over council meetings and therefore enjoy the perquisites of any presiding officer, such as recognition, rulings on motions (including parliamentary procedure), steering discussions, casting tie-breaking votes, and so on. Mayors, by virtue of their position as the highest officers in city government, their close relationship to the day-by-day operation of that government, and their acquisition of more information and knowledge on city administration and problems than any individual council members possess, are in an ideal position for leadership by advising the council on appropriate courses of policy. Needless to say, a skilled person may employ these several "strands" of executive power to great advantage in influencing the conduct of city government.

The Municipal Code, however, in the spirit of the separation-of-powers principle, has provided some important checks on executives, guarding against authoritarian rule by a mayor. The restraints are quite obvious: mayors' appointments and dismissals require the concurrence of a majority of the council. Mayors have no power over municipal ordinances and regulations, except when they are able to cast a tie-breaking vote. Generally mayors are not empowered to veto council-adopted ordinances, but are bound to execute them.

Councils. Municipal councils are the legally acknowledged governing bodies for municipalities and the branch of government vested with the charter's corporate authority. As such, councils are the chief policy making branch of municipal government. Councils by majority vote pass all ordinances, resolutions, and regulations for the community, subject only to federal and state constitutional or statutory restrictions. They provide for the creation of various appointive municipal offices, such as clerk, treasurer, police officers, and attorney, and prescribe their duties, responsibilities, and salaries. Councils are empowered to block appointments or dismissals by the mayor. They are responsible for the conduct of municipal elections. Only the councils may vote to place before the voters questions involving municipal indebtedness. By formal resolution councils are responsible for announcing upcoming elections, their date, the office to be filled, the questions to be considered, and administrative aspects such as precincts, polling districts, and canvasses.

Councils determine the time and the place for holding meetings and the rules of procedure and must maintain records of the proceedings. They must conform to the provisions of the "open-meetings" law requiring prior publication of meeting times and agenda, the admission of the public, and the publishing of proceedings.

Council members acting on the authority of the municipality are not subject to personal action in the courts. In terms of possible conflicts of interest, council members, like mayors, are required to disclose any possible financial interests in any matter requiring the decision of the council and may be disqualified from voting, unless they disqualify themselves. A majority of the council constitutes a quorum, and any binding actions of the council require a majority of the members present.

Until 1985 council members were elected either at large, by council districts, or by some combination thereof. Council members were not required to live in the ward or district they represented. However, in 1985, in response to increased pressure from federal courts and minority groups challenging voting-rights violations of at-large systems, the New Mexico Legislature enacted a law requiring municipalities with populations of ten thousand or more to elect their council members from single-member districts. The law affected both the council in the mayor-council form and the commission in the commission-manager form of government. The law also allowed cities in class H counties or with populations of less than ten thousand to adopt a single-member-district system. It allows governing bodies with more than six council members to elect two councilors per ward, provided that only one is elected in a given election. This is the form that has been used in Las Vegas.

The 1985 law also requires that the council members be residents of the districts they are elected to represent. Following each decennial federal census, covered municipalities are now required to divide the municipality into districts that are compact, contiguous, and as nearly equal in population as possible.[31]

Most of the municipalities covered by the law, whether operating under the Municipal Code or their own charter, have complied with it. The application of the districting requirement to charter municipalities has been a matter of litigation in the courts, and one municipality, Gallup, has been compelled to conform to the standard.

The qualification that a person be a "qualified elector" also holds for council members; thus any person aged eighteen or over and eligible to vote is qualified to run for a council. The term of office for council members is four years, although the terms may be staggered so as to ensure continuity. Generally there is no limitation on the number of terms that council members may serve. Should vacancies occur in council seats, mayors, with the advice and consent of the council, appoint qualified electors, who serve until the next regular election.

Council members are required to take an oath of office within ten days after their election. Compensation up to the amount paid a member of the local county commission may be provided for members of the council, based on local discretion.[32]

In summary, while the Municipal Code does provide for strong mayors with important executive responsibilities and authority, councils are by no means powerless, being themselves possessed with substantial powers of advice and consent in the normal administration of municipal governments and in municipal policy making by their power to enact or alter municipal ordinances and regulations. The extent to which they assert their own prerogatives vis-à-vis the mayor may in turn influence the tempo of municipal government.

Municipal Judges. In conjunction with the separation-of-powers principle, the judicial function in the mayor-council form of government is exercised by a municipal judge, separately elected at large by the voters of the municipality. Municipal courts have jurisdiction over matters involving conflicts, complaints, and offenses arising under municipal ordinances. Normally, municipal judges are mainly involved with violations stemming from traffic regulations and from misdemeanors in criminal law, although judges may be involved in the preliminary stages of more serious criminal offenses (felonies), handled by regular trial (district) courts. Municipal judges have power to issue subpoenas and warrants in conjunction with their courts and to fine individuals for contempt. The exact relationship of these judges to mayors and councils has long been a point of debate. It is not unusual for mayors and/or councils to try to influence municipal court operations, such as the amount of money generated from fines. Legal tradition, however, would seem to favor substantial judicial independence, even at this lower level, from other branches of government. The generation of finances by the municipal court, for example, should be only a secondary consideration compared to that of providing an effective and impartial judicial process at the municipal level.

Fines and imprisonment meted out by municipal judges are generally regulated by limits imposed by the ordinance specifying the violation. Normally, the maximum fine municipal judges can impose will not exceed five hundred dollars and the maximum imprisonment will not exceed ninety days. Municipal judges are bonded and are required to maintain financial records and make monthly reports to their councils containing information as to money received, names of people paying the money, and the amount, purpose, and date of such payments.

Municipal judges are elected in municipal elections for a four-year term; like other officials, they are required to take an oath of office. They are not required to be attorneys. Normally a single judge will constitute the municipal court, but the law allows for cities with populations of thirty thousand or more to elect more than one judge if it is deemed necessary.

Appointed Officials. Clerks are appointed by mayors, subject to approval by a majority of the council, and can be discharged by the same process. Clerks are required to attend council meetings, record proceedings (including ordinances and resolutions), and maintain minutes. Clerks are responsible for the administration of municipal elections and for duties pertaining thereto. Clerks also perform such administrative and record-keeping duties as prescribed by the councils or in the charter.

Municipal attorneys are appointed by mayors and can be similarly discharged, provided the councils concur. Attorneys must be licensed to practice law in the state of New Mexico, in addition to fulfilling such other qualifications as may be provided for by the councils. The duties of the attorneys are to provide all municipal officials with legal advice. They are responsible for attending to all legal matters and suits involving the municipalities. They must also prepare or approve contracts involving the municipality. In addition, they act as prosecuting attorneys on behalf of the municipalities in cases in municipal court that require such services, or they may represent the municipalities in cases appealed to higher courts.

Police officers are responsible for keeping the peace in a municipality. Their job is to quell assaults and batteries, riots, or disturbances and apprehend individuals fleeing from justice or those suspected of violating state or municipal law, as well as ensuring that all offenders appear in court to answer the charges against them. Police officers are commissioned by the councils and are appointed by mayors, subject to the councils' approval. Police officers are empowered to carry unconcealed arms.[33]

Variations of the Mayor-Council Form. As stated above, the Municipal Code through the home-rule-charter provision empowers a municipality to adopt its own unique version of the mayor-council form or any other type of government suited to its needs. If such a municipality adopts the mayor-council form, it is not subject to the strict standards set in the general act for this type of government.

Albuquerque is the most prominent community that has revised its charter to include the home-rule provisions. The present charter, adopted originally in 1971, has gone through a series of revisions. In 1971 Albuquerque voters rejected the first modern effort to replace the commission-manager form of government with the mayor-council form, but they did adopt the charter amendment that incorporated the liberal constitutional home-rule proposition.[34]

In 1972 a new charter, calling for a consolidated city-county government with a mayor-council form, was approved by Albuquerque voters but rejected by county voters.

Encouraged by the overwhelming support of the proposed charter and mayor-council form of government in Albuquerque itself, reformers quickly went to work on new charter revisions adopting the major provisions of the consolidated government proposal without the consolidation provision. The main proposal was for a mayor-council government.

In April of 1974, Albuquerque voters approved the propositions recommended by the charter-revision commission that had been deliberating for over six months.[35] In June 1974 Albuquerque elected its first slate of city officials under the new form of government.

In the Albuquerque Municipal Charter, the mayor is a full-time paid chief executive with a salary commensurate to the office. The mayor, elected for a four-year term, is assisted as head of administration by a chief administrative officer, appointed by the mayor and confirmed by the council. The mayor is responsible for the preparation and execution of the city budget and represents the city in ceremonial functions. The nine-member council, elected by districts and serving staggered four-year terms, is an entity in itself, with its own presiding officer. Members of the council serve part time and receive salaries (one-tenth that of the mayor's) for their services. The council is essentially a legislative body, preparing ordinances, rules, and regulations for city government and proposing charter revisions. Albuquerque municipal judges must be attorneys licensed to practice law in the state of New Mexico; they are elected at large.[36] The other significant change in Albuquerque municipal government was the creation of the metropolitan court in July 1980, which replaced the separate municipal judges and county magistrates with a single "metro" court.

There are other variations of the mayor-council form in addition to that of Albuquerque. Las Vegas, for example, also operates under its own charter, adopted in 1970 after the voters in the community voted to consolidate the two separate communities of East and West Las Vegas, which had been two incorporated towns since the nineteenth century. The Las Vegas charter duplicates many of the provisions of the general charter, but adds some of its own, such as providing for a hybrid mayor-council form with a full-time paid city manager who administers the city. The eight council members are elected from four wards, with two representing each ward, but elected alternately every two years. Still other variations in the forms of government of different municipalities may result from the adoption of ordinances that institute special provisions such as an appointive manager, different personnel systems, and special planning and zoning commissions.

What all these variations indicate is that since New Mexico municipalities were created under different laws at different periods in the state's history, it is not possible to apply a standard set of legal principles to all of them. Instead, it is necessary to look first at the nature of the municipality's charter to determine from what statute it derives, and then the applicable regulations can be determined.

Commission-Manager Governments. The second form of municipal government provided for by general statute in New Mexico is the commission-manager form. The choice of the term "commission" is unhappily confusing. The three standard forms of municipal government found in the United States are the aforementioned mayor-council form, the council-manager form, and the commission form.[37] The usual council-manager form is essentially the form called "commission-manager" in New Mexico. The commission form bears little resemblance to any municipal government ever employed in New Mexico. This form provides for a plural executive and clearly divides and assigns executive responsibilities, since each elected commissioner (there are between three and seven, but usually five) heads a department such as public works, finance, or public safety. The commission acts as a deliberative body in setting policy, but as department heads, commission members also carry out policies. This form was adopted in Galveston, Texas, as a temporary measure to expedite reconstruction following tidal-wave damage to that community in 1901, and was retained because of its success. Although as many as four or five hundred cities have experimented with the form after its success in Galveston, most, including Galveston, have abandoned it. About one hundred cities with populations of over five thousand still use the form.[38]

Commission-manager was essentially the type of government used by Albuquerque until the 1974 charter revision introduced the mayor-council variety. The Municipal Code provides that only cities with populations of over three thousand may adopt this form, but it does not require that such cities adopt it. At present Alamogordo, Aztec, Clovis, Hobbs, Lovington, Raton, Truth or Consequences, and Tucumcari operate under the commission-manager form. All other major New Mexico cities have a mayor-council form of government.

Commissions. Commissions are made up of five commissioners, who are elected for four-year staggered terms in nonpartisan elections. Originally commissions were elected at large by the whole community, although each commissioner represented a separate district. The aforementioned 1985 state law requires city commissioners to be elected by single-member districts, and most cities have complied. However, at least one city, Alamogordo, has challenged the application of the law to charter municipalities. As a result of a federal district court settlement in 1987, Alamogordo now elects four commissioners by single-member districts and three commissioners at large. For the at-large vote, it uses a unique cumulative voting system that allows a voter to cast up to three votes for a single candidate.

Commissions are the sole governing bodies in this form of government. With the commissions rest the corporate authority to adopt municipal policy through ordinances, regulations, and resolutions. All officials and departments in municipal government are under their authority. Probably the single most important function of the commissions is the selection and appointment of city managers. Since these managers will be responsible for the administration of the municipalities, the choice made by the commission is crucial in determining the success of this form of municipal government.

FIGURE 6.2
Mayor-Council Form of Government

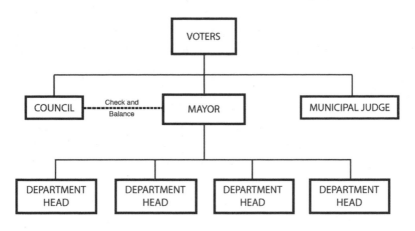

Shortly after municipal elections, commissions are required to select one of their members as "mayor." Aside from this duty to preside over commission meetings and represent the community at ceremonial functions, this official possesses no extra powers. This individual does, of course, retain all powers and duties as commissioner, such as voting on all issues before the commission.

The mayor, or chair, of each commission serves for a two-year term, and may be elected to a second two-year term (since a commissioner's term of office is four years) if the commission so desires. Mayors may be paid a salary that shall not exceed that of a county commissioner. Commissions may designate a mayor pro tem, also from their ranks, to serve in the absence of the mayor. Mayors do not have veto power; they are, like all commissioners in this form of government, subject to recall by petition of the voters in the municipality, as well as to removal for misconduct, after a proper hearing.

The qualification for candidates to the office of commissioner is that they be "qualified electors," just as under the mayor-council form. Commissioners are subject to the same kinds of rules as council members in the mayor-council form. They may receive compensation equal to that of county commissioners; they are bound to disclose all financial conflicts of interest and, if appropriate, to excuse themselves from voting on such issues. They are not personally liable in court for actions taken on the authority of their municipalities and are required to take an oath of office within ten days after election. Vacancies to commission seats are filled by the appointment of a qualified elector by the remaining commissioners.

The commission-manager charter, unlike the mayor-council form, includes provisions for initiatives and referendums, which empower citizens of the municipality to initiate proposed ordinances or regulations by petition and to reject commission-passed ordinances or regulations by petition, thereby forcing a public referendum on the issue.

City Managers. The position of city manager has become of central importance in modern municipal government. The growth of urban centers and the demand for more and better services have combined with increasing problems (often of a more complicated technical and financial nature) to underscore the need for greater versatility and expertise in dealing with a variety of problems simultaneously. Elected municipal officials, themselves lacking in experience, have turned to city managers to provide versatility and expertise in a number of fields.

The position of city manager in New Mexico, it should be noted, is not restricted to communities with a commission-manager form of government. The Municipal Code empowers any municipality to provide for the office of city manager by adopting a charter providing for one or by adopting an ordinance creating the position. It is likely that managers would function more effectively in a commission-manager form than in a mayor-council form, where there tend to be many executive administrators. The following description of the function and responsibilities of city managers thus is the most appropriate for the commission-manager municipalities, but is applicable to other municipalities to a lesser extent.

City managers are appointed by commissions for an indefinite term; thus they serve at the grace of the commissions. There are generally no residency requirements, and the salary is set by the commissions. Normally managers are picked on the basis of their education, administrative experience, and overall expertise in a variety of fields—finance, planning, civil engineering, and personnel administration.

Managers are the chief administrators, endowed by their commissions with full executive authority and responsibility. Managers are responsible not only for enforcing and carrying out all ordinances, regulations, and resolutions of the commissions and municipalities, but also for hiring and firing municipal employees (subject to personnel provisions in the municipal charter and ordinances), preparing and submitting annual budgets, seeing to their execution, overseeing the day-to-day operation of municipal government, and advising their commissions on matters of concern.

Since managers appoint all municipal employees, including department heads, they presumably have full authority to administer their municipalities. Central to managers' responsibilities is fiscal administration, which may involve managers in proposing revenue sources; establishing policy priorities by budget recommendations; allocating monies for buildings, equipment, personnel, and programs; recommending public borrowing (bonds) for special municipal projects; and preparing proposals to bring in available federal funds for allowable programs. As managers in this form of government are quite powerful and important and possess expertise that the average commissioner lacks, it is entirely possible for managers to wield substantial influence over commissioners. This can only be prevented by commissioners who make certain that their respective prerogatives as the policy makers for the municipality are respected and that managers retain their supervisory functions. Commissions may of course depend on the advice of managers, who sit as nonvoting members of the commissions; as such they can influence policy. The objective, however, is to arrive at a happy medium, where managers advise but commissions enact policy.

Other Officers. The office, powers, and duties of municipal judges in this form of government are basically the same as those of the judges in the mayor-council form described earlier. The same can be said for the appointive officers (clerks, attorneys, and police chiefs), with the exception that in the commission-manager form these officials are appointed or discharged (subject to charter merit-system provisions) by managers and are subject to their administrative jurisdiction.[39]

Home Rule and Charters

The third variation in municipal government in New Mexico stems from statutory provisions relating to home rule. A certain amount of confusion surrounds the history of charters and home rule in New Mexico. Part of this confusion stems from the very meaning and implications of the expression "home rule." Home rule confers the power of self-government to a municipality, so that it is "free" from state encroachment. In actuality, although home rule may and often does grant greater independence to a municipality in choosing its own form of government and running its own affairs, rarely does home rule, even if provided by constitutional decree, create a completely "free" city. State administrative and fiscal centralization render a city dependent long after it has adopted home rule. Home rule can better be conceived in terms of degrees of independence afforded a municipality. Thus, for example, it can be argued that New Mexico municipalities acquired a measure of home rule when the state legislature in 1917 allowed them to adopt their own charters. The Municipal Charter Act (Municipal Code Sections 3–5–1 through 3–15–16, N.M.S.A., 1978) provides that "the qualified electors of a municipality who wish to be governened pursuant to the home rule provision of the New Mexico Constitution may adopt, amend or repeal a charter."" F. D. Freedle and Edward and Dorothy Goldberg, in early editions of the *New Mexico Handbook for Mayors and Councilmen*, correctly interpreted these early charter provisions as providing for home rule. However, as Freedle also observed, this grant of independence was very limited, since home rule as interpreted by the state attorney general went only as far as allowing the city to adopt a charter, which itself was still "hemmed in" by constitutional and statutory provisions restricting chartered municipalities.[40]

The probable reason for the limited grant of municipal independence under this early home-rule provision was that it was accomplished by legislative decree, which obviously is not as forceful as a constitutional provision on the matter. It was probably this condition that prompted advocates of an expansive and liberal home-rule provision to lobby in the 1960s for the adoption of a home-rule amendment to the New Mexico Constitution. Thus a home-rule section was one of the more important and controversial revisions in local government offered by the proposed New Mexico constitution of 1969, which was rejected by the voters.[41] The advocates were not deterred, however, and in

November 1970 a home-rule amendment was approved by New Mexico's voters. The provisions of Article X, Section 6, of the New Mexico Constitution thus provide that "the purpose of this section is to provide maximum local self-government. A liberal construction shall be given to the power of municipalities."[42]

What this amendment has meant to New Mexico municipalities is that a liberal interpretation is given to the provisions of New Mexico Statutes (Sections 3–15–1 through 3–15–16, N.M.S.A., 1978), and that the voters of a municipality may decide on any form of government they want; that they are not limited to the mayor-council or commission-manager form; and that if they choose one of these forms in a separate home-rule charter, they may adopt variations that need not conform to statutory provisions for the two stated forms. Because the liberal home-rule amendment was passed only recently, its full extent remains to be seen in future developments. Albuquerque amended its charter in 1971 to encompass the new constitutional provision; it does seem that a home-rule charter has given it greater leeway in the granting of power to municipal officials, but it also seems that fiscal matters, especially those relating to imposition of taxes, are still within the purview of the state legislature. Considering the pressing financial need of New Mexico cities (and of American cities generally), the issue of financial dependence will certainly be among the most important for cities in the future. The crucial questions remain of whether the state legislature will grant greater fiscal independence to municipalities in raising revenues and in determining municipal indebtedness and expenditures, and of whether the cities can act responsibly in their fiscal administration, justifying such delegation of traditional state responsibility.

Miscellaneous Factors in Municipal Government

Municipal governments in New Mexico are given wide leeway by the state legislature in exercising the police power of the state. Thus ordinances, resolutions, and regulations are adopted by municipal officials for protecting and improving the public health, safety, welfare, morals, and comfort of its citizens. An ordinance is a municipal law adopted after presentation by one member of the council or commission and adopted by a majority of the members. Its application is local, and it is subordinate to and cannot conflict with state or federal law.

Ordinances, like laws, are enforceable and can bring fines and punishment for violations. Ordinances can be enacted on almost any conceivable subject that the city considers to be within its domain of influence under its police powers.

Municipal governing bodies may create such committees (for example, planning and zoning, or housing) as they deem necessary to carry out their functions.

Meetings of municipal governments are essentially subject to standard state requirements, including the publishing of meeting times, open meetings, agendas, quorums, appropriate parliamentary procedure, public votes, motions, resolutions, and the recording and publishing of proceedings.[43]

SPECIAL DISTRICTS

In addition to municipal and county governments, there are over one hundred special-function governmental districts provided by New Mexico law, which can be included in the broad category of local governments because they are substate governmental entities. These special districts are the most varied form of local government, performing either single or multiple functions. Their relationship to county or municipal governments is that they may exist within or overlap their jurisdictional boundaries, but they exist to perform a function or service not within the domain of either counties or the municipalities. In New Mexico the most unique and prominent of special districts are the land grants, which stem from the Spanish colonial land-tenure system, and the irrigation, water-conservancy, and flood-control districts that have evolved as a result of the dry climate of the state and the need for state-controlled use of water resources. The following summary will consider several types and variations of special districts in New Mexico. Excluded from consideration, however, will be school districts, which are described in chapter 11.[44]

Community Land Grants

New Mexico in 1992 still contained nineteen community land grants, which are also recognized as distinct governmental entities. These land grants stem from the Spanish and Mexican colonial heritage of the state, whereby grants of land were made by the Spanish and later the Mexican governments to a group of families. These grants were recognized as legitimate by the Treaty of Guadalupe Hildago (1848), following the Mexican War, and by subsequent land surveys. Such grants have continued in existence by virtue of the fact that some of the land was *ejido* (held in common) and was available for lumber, firewood, and livestock grazing by members of the village. Land grants are administered by an elected board of trustees, who are empowered to provide for the maintenance of the land, to impose charges for its use, and to provide for its lease, sale, or assessment.

Drainage Districts

Drainage districts are established by district courts upon petition by landowners or by county commissions (in the case of drainage districts within federal reclamation projects). The four that exist within New Mexico are administered either by an elected board of drainage commissioners or by a board of directors, who are empowered to levy taxes, impose benefit assessments, and issue bonds for the financing of adequate water-drainage and flood-control projects.

Flood-Control Authorities

There are two flood-control authorities in New Mexico: the Albuquerque Metropolitan Arroyo Flood Control Authority and the Las Cruces Metropolitan Flood Control Authority, both of which were established to provide for flood-control and drainage facilities. The elected boards of directors that administer these authorities derive monies from ad valorem tax levies and by bonding authority.

Irrigation and Conservancy Districts

Irrigation districts (electrical irrigation districts, irrigation districts, and irrigation districts in cooperation with federal reclamation projects), twenty of which exist in the state, are created by county commissions, upon petition. They are governed by boards of directors empowered to levy property taxes and assessments, impose fees, issue bonds, and form improvement districts in providing for water conservation, flood control, and irrigation facilities and development for each district. Conservancy districts are established by district courts upon petition by landowners after public hearings. These districts have elected boards, which are authorized to impose special assessments and charges for water sales and to issue notices of debt. Artesian conservancy districts are similarly created by district courts and governed by elected boards empowered to levy taxes and borrow money.

Natural-Resource Conservation Districts

Natural-resource conservation districts are created by the State Natural Resource Conservation Commission on petition of landowners and after hearings and a referendum. The elected boards of supervisors that administer the districts may levy assessments; require contributions from landowners who benefit, negotiate for, and accept federal aid; and levy property taxes. They may also form watershed districts as subdistricts, which in turn possess some taxing powers. There were seventy-three such districts in 1992.

Water and Sanitation Districts

There are four such districts in New Mexico, created by district courts on petition from electors and after a referendum. The elected boards of directors are empowered to levy taxes, tolls, and charges, and to issue bonds for the development and maintenance of water and sanitation facilities.

Other Special Districts

In addition to the above-mentioned special districts, there are a number of lesser units that exercise some governmental authority (health, fire, pollution, road, weed control, insect control, refuse, parking, urban renewal, and historic), as well as other districts created by either county or municipal governments. These are simply too numerous to describe in detail.

CONCLUSION

Local governments in New Mexico provide both a unique and characteristic picture of American local governance, reflecting the multifaceted picture the state presents to the nation. The organization and structure of county and municipal governments, the functions performed by local governments, and the problems (including financial problems) of the local governments in New Mexico are not drastically different from those in other states, all of which indicate that New Mexico has kept pace, for better or worse, with the rest of the country. On the other hand, the nature of some special districts, such as the land grants and water-conservancy districts, the large size of the state, and its low density of population, create a special flavor and a distinctive pattern of local government when compared to other states. Because of this mosaic, New Mexico local governments provide a provocative subject for study.

NOTES

1. Daniel C. Grant and H. C. Nixon, *State and Local Government in America* (Boston: Allyn and Bacon, 1975), pp. 59–60.
2. Ibid.
3. United States Bureau of the Census, *Census of Governments: 2002, Governmental Organization*, http://www.census.gov/prod/2003pubs/gc021x1.pdf.
4. Ibid.
5. United States Bureau of the Census, *Census of Governments: 1957, Governments in the United States*, vol. 1 (Washington, D.C.: U.S. Government Printing Office, 1957), pp. 1, 14.
6. State of New Mexico, *Special District Directory, 1991–92*, (Santa Fe: Department of Finance and Administration, 1992), p. i.
7. Most of the facts about local governments reported here are derived from statutes (primarily vol. II, chapters 3, 4, and 5, of *New Mexico Statutes Annotated, 1978, Compilation*), as well as from constitutional provisions and court decisions. However, specific references to specific statutes from which the facts derive will only occasionally be made, in the interest of brevity. When such references are given, they will be abbreviated by numerical references referring to chapter, article, and section. Thus (3–10–1) refers to Chapter 3, Article 10, Section 1, of *New Mexico Statutes Annotated, 1978 Compilation.*
8. U.S. Census, *Census of Governments: 1987*, p. 14.
9. Teresa Aragon Shepro, *Handbook for County Commissioners: New Mexico* (Albuquerque: Publication No. 75, Division of Research, Department of Political Science, University of New Mexico, 1967), pp. 4–5.
10. Sigurd Johansen, *The People of New Mexico* (Las Cruces: Bulletin 606, Agricultural Experiment Station, New Mexico State University, 1974), pp. 25, 32.
11. State of New Mexico, *The Constitution of the State of New Mexico* (Santa Fe: Secretary of State, 1974), pp. 19–20, 54.
12. These observations derive from personal experience as a lifelong citizen of the state of New Mexico.
13. Bealquin Gomez, *The New Mexico County Commission* (Las Cruces: Cooperative Extension Service, New Mexico State University, 1986), pp. 18–20.
14. It should be noted that the author has relied on the work of Shepro, *Handbook for County Commissioners*, along with that of James Grieshop, John Robey, and Bealquin Gomez, in their subsequent editions of *The New Mexico County Commission*, for the factual information that forms

the basis of this descriptive survey.

15. State of New Mexico, *New Mexico Statutes Annotated, 1978* (Chapter 3, Article 37, Section 1).

16. Article X, Sections 2 and 7, Constitution of New Mexico.

17. Article X, Section 9, Constitution of New Mexico.

18. Gomez, *New Mexico County Commission*, 1986, pp. 39–45.

19. Ibid, pp. 24–36.

20. James Grieshop, *The New Mexico County Commission* (Las Cruces: Cooperative Extension Service, New Mexico State University, 1974), p. 38. See also Gomez, *New Mexico County Commission*, pp. 45–46.

21. Gomez, *New Mexico County Commission*, pp. 12–16.

22. U.S. Census, *Census of Governments: 1987*, p. viii.

23. Edward and Dorothy Goldberg, *Handbook for New Mexico Mayors and Councilmen* (Albuquerque: Publication No. 58, Division of Research, Department of Political Science, University of New Mexico, 1960), p. 6.

24. Sections 3–2–1 through 3–2–9 and Sections 3–4–1 through 3–4–9 N.M.S.A., 1978.

25. Frank Coppler and Wilson Conover, *Handbook for New Mexico Municipal Officials* (Santa Fe: New Mexico Municipal League, 1972), p. 17.

26. See Grant and Nixon, *State and Local Government*, pp. 393–94.

27. The options are described in Goldberg and Goldberg, *Handbook*, pp. 7–11.

28. Sections 3–16–1 through 3–16–18 N.M.S.A., 1978.

29. In other words, the home-rule charter enables a municipality to adopt any form of government, including a variation of one provided by general statutes. In such cases the city is freed from having to conform to the standards set down in the general statute forms of government.

30. Coppler and Conover, *Handbook*, pp. 1–3. Frequent references hereafter made to formal provisions relative to municipal government and officials are taken from this work, as well as from J. D. Freedle, *Handbook for New Mexico Mayors and Councilmen* (Albuquerque: Publication No. 73, Division of Research, Department of Political Science, University of New Mexico, 1967). Most recent changes in the Municipal Code have also been reviewed, to ensure that the provisions are still in force and to update data in the above works.

31. New Mexico Municipal League, *Summary of 1985 Laws Affecting Municipalities* (Santa Fe: New Mexico Municipal League, 1985), p. 16.

32. Coppler and Conover, *Handbook*, pp. 3–5, and Freedle, *Handbook*, pp. 19–22.

33. Coppler and Conover, *Handbook*, pp. 5–6.

34. See Albuquerque Urban Observatory, *Charter Revision in Albuquerque: Establishment of Home Rule* (Albuquerque: 1971).

35. Paul L. Hain, F. Chris Garcia, and Judd Conway, "From Council-Manager to Mayor-Council: the Case of Albuquerque," *Nation's Cities* 13, no. 10 (October 1975), pp. 10–12.

36. City of Albuquerque, *City Charter* (March 1974).

37. Any standard textbook on state and local government uses these three designations. See, for example, Daniel R. Grant and Lloyd B. Omdahl, *State and Local Government in America* (Boston: Allyn and Bacon, 1987), pp. 378–85.

38. Ibid, pp. 397–406.

39. Coppler and Conover, *Handbook*, pp. 10–16.

40. Freedle, *Handbook*, p. 8; and Goldberg and Goldberg, *Handbook*, pp. 11–12.

41. See chapter 2, above.
42. State of New Mexico, *Constitution of the State of New Mexico*, Article 10, Section 6.
43. Coppler and Conover, *Handbook*, pp. 18–19, 22–26.
44. The main source consulted for descriptions of organization structure and function of these special districts is the *U.S. Census of Governments: 1992*.

Chapter Seven

American Indians and Tribal Governments

by Fred R. Harris and Laura Harris

American Indians, or Native Americans, are American citizens, with all the same rights and privileges of other citizens. But as early decisions of the Supreme Court established, they have a "unique relationship" with the federal government, and their tribal governments are "domestic dependent nations," units of government in our federal system.[1]

There are about 2.5 million American Indians. They are citizens of more than 550 "Indian tribes" (which may be called tribes, nations, pueblos, or native villages), many quite diverse in history, customs, traditions, and language. About half the tribes are located in Alaska, the rest in thirty-four other states. In New Mexico, there are twenty-two tribes and pueblos.

Something less than half of all American Indians live on or near their home reservations. The largest reservation is the Navajo Nation, located in the corner of New Mexico, Utah, and Arizona. Others live in various cities throughout the country, but these non-reservation Indians usually keep close ties and often maintain voting rights with their tribal governments.

United States Indian law comes from four sources: U.S. treaties, specific mention in the Commerce Clause of the U.S. Constitution, laws passed by Congress, and U.S. Supreme Court and other federal court decisions. Historically, more than three hundred treaties were entered into by the U.S. government with the various Indian tribes. The Commerce Clause of the Constitution gives Congress, not the states, the power to regulate commerce with Indian tribes. This provision has been interpreted by the courts as giving the federal government exclusive power to deal with all aspects of Indian and tribal matters, unless it delegates that power to the states—which it has rarely done.

Native Americans, then, are unlike any other ethnic group in this country, in that they have what has been called "dual citizenship" and "dual entitlement."[2]

DUAL CITIZENSHIP AND DUAL ENTITLEMENT

Dual citizenship of American Indians who are members of federally recognized tribes means that, like all American citizens, they are: (1) citizens of the United States (and, by operation of the Fourteenth Amendment to the Constitution, they are also citizens of the states where they reside); and (2) they are citizens of the tribes of which they are enrolled citizens or members. Because of treaties, constitutional provisions, acts of Congress, and decisions of the federal courts and the Supreme Court, the tribal governments of American Indians (unlike the private organizations of other ethnic groups, such as the League of United Latin American Citizens or the National Association for the Advancement of Colored People) are units of government.

Thus our American "federal system" of shared sovereignty is not just composed of federal, state, and local governments. It is made up of federal, state, local, and *tribal* governments.

Dual entitlement means that American Indians receive the same services as other citizens and are also entitled to certain additional services, such as health services. (They do not receive individual federal payments as Indians, as some people may think.)

American Indians have made considerable progress in recent times, as measured by dominant white American expectations of "progress." There are now, for example, many thousands of American Indian professionals—lawyers, doctors, accountants, engineers, and others. But as a group they are still far behind white America. The percentage of American Indians who have completed four years of college is less than half that for the total population. The poverty rate on Indian reservations is 31 percent (36.2 percent in New Mexico); the unemployment rate, 46 percent.

HISTORY OF U.S. INDIAN POLICY

The policy of the United States government (and of earlier American government) toward Native Americans and tribes has radically changed from era to era in our history.[3] The first period was one of **Conquest and Discovery**. The main key to the success of European conquest was neither the superiority of European culture nor the European possession of horses, arms, and gunpowder, but rather the invasion of European diseases.[4] American Indians, isolated on this continent, had built up no immunities to diseases like diphtheria, whooping cough, smallpox, and typhoid. These new diseases were introduced by European carriers, most of whom had, through childhood exposure, developed immunities. America's early history is replete with account after account of how massive epidemics of European diseases swept through whole Indian populations upon early contact. Added to deaths from war and brutality, these diseases killed one-half to two-thirds of entire tribes in relatively short periods of time. These catastrophes often caused overwhelming political, social, and religious disorganization. Often, tribes and cultures simply broke down. Intricate organizations, such as those required for government and irrigation, frequently collapsed. The Indian leaders who survived often disputed among themselves for authority, which frequently allowed Europeans to play one surviving group against another.

Following the conquest era came the era of **Allotments and Assimilation** (1871–1928). Federal policy sought to assimilate American Indians into the total population; that is, to have them abandon their heritage, culture, language, and religion and become "like everyone else." Some reservations were even abolished by federal law. Many Indians were settled on individual, privately owned allotments, as opposed to tribal, communally owned reservations. "Surplus" tribal land was then often sold or otherwise divided up among non-Indians. The aim of this policy was to destroy tribes as units of government and to destroy the separate identity of the individuals involved. Many Indian tribes were in fact eliminated. Many Indians were robbed of their knowledge of their own culture and language.

Next came the era of **Reorganization** (1928–45). This period began with the Meriam Report, which recommended a dramatic change in Indian policy. It was extended by the appointment of an Indian-oriented U.S. Commissioner of Indian Affairs, John Collier. The federal government declared that Indian tribes were, in effect, "here to stay," that their governments should be strengthened under the Indian Reorganization Act of 1934 (though in a kind of white man's governmental form), and that the political self-government and economic self-sufficiency of Indian tribes should be encouraged.

Soon, though, U.S. Indian policy turned back in the other direction, during the era of **Termination** (1946–61). The presidentially appointed Hoover Commission recommended the "complete integration" of American Indians into the total population—in effect, a return to the old assimilation policy. During the administration of President Dwight Eisenhower, Congress passed termination legislation to end the governmental status of a number of Indian tribes, including, for example, the Menominee tribe of Wisconsin. Several tribes disappeared as a result of this policy. There was also a related federal policy at the time of "relocation," under which individual Indians and families were encouraged to move from their reservations into cities, such as Chicago, Los Angeles, Detroit, and Cincinnati, where they were to be helped—with mixed success, as it turned out—to find jobs and housing. Congress passed Public Law 280, under which certain state governments (but not New Mexico's) were allowed to assume some jurisdiction over Indian reservations within the states' boundaries.

Beginning with the administration of President John F. Kennedy, the Indian policy pendulum began to swing back again, ushering in a new period of **Self-Determination** (1961 to the present), with policies much like those that had existed under Commissioner of Indian Affairs Collier. Indian tribes were recognized as permanent governmental units, and Indians were no longer to be forced to melt into the general population. Diversity and the right to be different were increasingly accepted as a part of the American way. President Lyndon Johnson (1963–68) caused the federal government to pay special attention to the needs of American Indians, particularly because his new anti-poverty

program found them to be the group with the lowest educational levels, the worst health, the poorest housing and employment opportunities, and the lowest family incomes. President Richard Nixon, who took
office in 1969, sent a special, separate Indian policy message to Congress,
in which he declared that American Indians have the right to "self-determination" without "termination." The Menominee tribe was restored
to the status of a federally recognized Indian tribe. Taos Pueblo
regained ownership of its forty-eight-thousand-acre sacred Blue Lake
lands from the U.S. Forest Service.

During the 1960s, encouraged by the example of the black civil rights
movement, a pan-Indian rights movement developed in the United States,
as Native Americans began to claim their rights more aggressively. There
were some extralegal actions, such as the "Trail of Broken Treaties"
takeover of the Bureau of Indian Affairs (BIA) building in Washington,
D.C., in 1972, and the occupation of the village of Wounded Knee on the
Pine Ridge Sioux Reservation in South Dakota that same year, but most
Indian efforts followed legal courses. A number of new, more aggressive
Indian organizations grew up in the 1970s, around such issues as edu-
cation, housing, and health. The Council of Energy Resource Tribes
(CERT) was formed to assist tribes with the management and control
of their own natural resources. The Native American Rights Fund (NARF)
became an aggressive advocate of Indian rights. National Indian organ-
izations, such as the National Congress of American Indians (NCAI),
Americans for Indian Opportunity (AIO), and the National Tribal
Chairman's Association (NTCA), continued their representation of Native
Americans and tribes on a broad range of Indian policy issues. As a result
of new Indian solidarity and lobbying, Congress established the
American Indian Policy Review Commission, which made specific recommendations for strengthening tribal governments and tribal
economies, included Indians as beneficiaries of new civil-rights laws, recognized tribes as sponsoring units of government for new education,
housing, and other social programs, and passed a number of important
new laws, including the Indian Self-Determination and Education
Assistance Act (1975), the Indian Child Welfare Act (1978), the American
Indian Religious Freedom Act (1979), and others.[5]

The new assertiveness of American Indians and tribes, generally
backed by the national government and the courts, caused something

of a white backlash. Groups were formed in some states to press for repeal of Indian treaties and the abolition of the power of tribal governments. These efforts gained little congressional support, although they continued to be a matter of concern to Indians.

NEW MEXICO INDIAN HISTORY

Centuries before the arrival of the first Europeans in the area that is now New Mexico, American Indians of the region had achieved highly developed cultures, political organizations, and economies. Some tribes, such as those of New Mexico's Pueblo Indians, were sedentary, or settled, while others, such as the ancestors of the present Navajo and Apache Indians, were nomadic, or wandering.[6]

In 1536, survivors of an ill-fated Spanish expedition in Florida, including Alvar Núñez Cabeza de Vaca and Estévan, a black slave from Morocco, harrowingly made their way through the present southwestern United States to Mexico. There, they related stories told them by Indians they had encountered, that rekindled an old Spanish legend about lost cities of gold—which here became the "Seven Cities of Cíbola." In 1589, a Catholic friar of the Franciscan order, Márcos de Niza, and Estévan went north under a special commission from the viceroy of Mexico to try to find the legendary cities. Estévan was killed by Indians, but Friar de Niza returned with reports that greatly increased Spanish interest in the Seven Cities of Cíbola. The following year, Francisco Vázquez de Coronado led an expedition north, accompanied by young Spanish grandees seeking fame and fortune, a contingent of friars, and a large group of Mexican Indians.

Vázquez de Coronado and his entourage, driving a goodly herd of sheep and cattle, worked their way north along the coast of the present Gulf of California, then turned east and eventually encountered Hawikuh, one of the six (although later writers called it seven) villages of present-day Zuni Pueblo. The marchers found no riches there, but they did find corn, which they needed at that moment more than gold. Zuni, apparently the basis for the reports of the Seven Cities of Cíbola, was a highly developed culture, with a complex political organization and an advanced agricultural and trading system. After a brief encounter, Coronado's party moved on east to the site of the present-day Acoma Pueblo and its Sky Village. As at Zuni, Coronado's group was not admitted into the village itself. Instead, the people of Acoma apparently encouraged Coronado to continue on eastward toward the Rio Grande, which he did. When Coronado came into the valley of the Rio Grande (between present-day Belen and Bernalillo, near today's Albuquerque), he found numerous flourishing, multistoried villages. The Pueblo peoples were living in much cleaner, more comfortable, and more prosperous circumstances than the Spanish nobles themselves had known in their home country. The complex Pueblo irrigation systems were administered by highly efficient governmental systems. People's religious beliefs and practices were intertwined with their everyday lives. Times were good for the Pueblo people who lived in these Rio Grande villages. But they were not to remain so.[7]

Near present-day Alameda, north of today's Albuquerque, one whole Pueblo village, numbering more than two hundred, moved out, or were moved out, turning over the houses and other facilities of the village to Coronado's party. From this base, Coronado sent out expeditions—west to the Grand Canyon, east to the plains of what are now Oklahoma and Kansas, and in other directions.

During their two-year stay, the Spaniards became increasingly frustrated at not finding any of the fabled, and sought-for, gold. But for the Pueblo villages, Coronado's visit was not just a source of frustration, but a disaster. European diseases likely ravaged their numbers. The Indians were subjected to overbearing and aggressive acts, as well as to prolonged food and housing freeloading. In time, the villages became less and less friendly. One Pueblo village, north of present-day Alameda, revolted. Coronado killed all of its inhabitants. The people of another village withdrew within their walls, halting all contact with the Spaniards. Coronado besieged them, and when in the dead of winter they made a rush toward the Rio Grande and its water, he killed all of them.

Finally, Coronado left and headed back to Mexico. There, his report put to rest the stories that riches similar to those that had earlier been seized in the Aztec Valley of Mexico and in the Inca highlands of Peru could also be found in North America. After Coronado's two-year expedition to the Rio Grande Valley, many villages of the area stood abandoned or devastated. Disease, warfare, and brutality had killed great numbers of the Indian people or driven them away. Ruins of one of these early villages can still be seen across the river from the town of Bernalillo. Ironically, it has been officially designated "Coronado State Monument."

Forty years after Coronado's return to Mexico, another group, a small one made up of Spanish friars and soldiers, set out for Pueblo country. When they did not return, a small rescue party was sent to get them. A larger, colonizing group came in 1590, but this one did not fare well, either. Then in 1598, the viceroy of Mexico authorized a wealthy miner, Don Juan de Oñate, to colonize the Pueblo country permanently. This time, the Spaniards came to stay. Spanish villages were established throughout present-day New Mexico, almost always immediately adjacent to, and taking over some of the best farmland, of an existing Pueblo village. The Indian villagers were required to pay taxes to the Spanish authorities and tithes to the Catholic Church. Taxes, tithes, a system of forced labor, expropriation of land, and an established church that adopted harsh measures to suppress Indian religions all eventually led to a violent revolt of the Pueblo peoples in 1680.

The Spaniards were driven south, out of their settlements and out of their capital, Santa Fe, back into Mexico. For nearly twelve years, Pueblo villages once again tried to live the old ways that had existed before the Europeans came. But in 1692, the Spaniards returned in force—again bringing with them much bloodshed, brutality, and oppression, and causing a good deal of sporadic Pueblo revolt, even into modern times in the late 1800s.

Mexico's independence from Spain in the early nineteenth century meant that New Mexico became a Mexican, rather than a Spanish, territory, but little else changed. Pueblo religious leaders made a kind of accommodation with Catholic priests and the Catholic religion. Pueblo governments worked out a regular, although sometimes difficult, relationship with local representatives of the Mexican government. Pueblo farmers tolerated the non-Indian farmers and ranchers who prospered nearby. Pueblo villagers, together with their Mexican and Spanish neighbors, sought to hold off the encroachment of nomadic Indian tribes. Mexican priests and governmental authorities attempted, with limited success, to get the Apaches and Navajos to settle down to peaceful lives in one place. At the town of Taos, near Taos Pueblo, and at Santa Fe, trappers and traders from the United States began to make increasing contacts.

The United States went to war with Mexico in 1846. Two years later, with the Treaty of Guadalupe Hidalgo, the war was ended, and a large territory, including that of the present states of New Mexico and Arizona, was soon annexed to the United States. By the Treaty of Guadalupe Hidalgo, the United States agreed to recognize the rights of the Pueblo Indians as they existed in 1848, but, in fact, it was a long time thereafter before the titles to the land the Pueblos still held onto by then were actually secure. And the United States government took up even more fiercely the attempt to subdue and settle the Navajos and Apaches.

NEW MEXICO INDIAN TRIBES

American Indians constitute around 10 percent of the population of New Mexico, one of the top four states in America in total Indian population. The reservations of the Mescalero Apaches, the Jicarilla Apaches, nineteen Pueblos, as well as parts of the Navajo reservation, are located in the state. In addition, of course, a large number of New Mexico Indians, as well as Indians from other states, live in Albuquerque and other New Mexico cities.

All of the tribal governments in New Mexico are, in a sense, "nations within a nation," or states within a state. Like all other recognized tribes in the United States, they are units of government. When New Mexico became a state in 1912, it adopted, at the urging of the federal government, a specific state constitutional provision (Article XXI, Section 2) that disclaims taxing jurisdiction and other authority on Indian reservations or lands within the state's boundaries.

With their dual citizenship, American Indians in New Mexico, as well as elsewhere in the United States, are entitled to vote, not only in any elections held by the tribes of which they are members, but also in all local, state, and national elections in the areas where they reside. But this was not always so. Even after Congress passed the Indian Citizenship Act in 1924, which made it clear that American Indians were American citizens (and therefore, under the Fourteenth Amendment, citizens of the states where they lived), five states, including New Mexico, continued, as late as the 1940s, to deny reservation Indians the right to vote in state and local elections.[8]

The denial of the right to vote in New Mexico was based on a provision—Article VII, Section 1—of the 1912 New Mexico Constitution that excluded from voting "Indians not taxed." Finally, in 1948, a three-judge federal district court ruled that an Isleta Indian could not be denied the right to register to vote because he did not pay state property taxes, with the presiding judge stating:

> The New Mexico Constitution . . . says that "Indians not taxed" may not vote, although they possess every other qualification. We are unable to escape the conclusion that, under the Fourteenth and Fifteenth Amendments, that constitutes a discrimination on the ground of race. Any other citizen, regardless of race, in the state of New Mexico who has not paid one cent of tax of any kind or character, if he possesses other qualifications, may vote. An Indian, and only an Indian, in order to meet the qualifications of a voter, must have paid a tax. How can you escape the conclusion that that makes a requirement with respect to an Indian as a qualification to exercise the elective franchise and does not make that requirement with respect to the member of any other race is beyond me. I just feel like the conclusion is inescapable.[9]

After a New Mexico Indian voting-rights law was passed in 1953, the New Mexico Supreme Court, in a 1962 decision, reiterated the right of Indians to vote in state elections, and, in a 1975 decision, affirmed the right of Indians to vote in school-bond elections, though their lands were not taxed to pay off the bonds.[10]

For many years, Indians in New Mexico were not particularly active in non-reservation politics. But this has changed. The All Indian Pueblo Council and the leadership of other New Mexico tribes encourage national, state, and local voting, as well as citizen participation generally, in addition to tribal voting and participation. Voter registration drives have greatly increased the numbers of New Mexico Indians who vote. American Indians serve in the New Mexico state Senate and state House of Representatives. Pueblos that own gambling casinos have become a significant source of campaign funds for New Mexico political candidates.

Elementary and secondary education for American Indians in New Mexico is a matter of mixed tribal, federal, state, and local responsibility. Many Pueblos and tribes operate their own state-accredited elementary schools, financed through the U.S. Bureau of Indian Affairs. Secondary education for Indian students is usually provided in public schools, either on the reservation or nearby. Zuni Pueblo, for example, is a public school district by itself. Laguna-Acoma High School is a public school. The All Indian Pueblo Council operates a secondary, BIA-financed school in Santa Fe. When New Mexico Indian young people attend a public school, the federal government makes a special contribution for this purpose to the local school district involved (similar to federal contribution for children who live on military bases and attend public schools).

Increasing numbers of American Indian young people in New Mexico attend universities, colleges, and professional schools, although the percentages of their enrollment in state colleges and universities is still below their percentage of the state's total population. The All Indian Pueblo Council, a number of individual Pueblos, the Navajo Tribe, certain private Indian organizations, and some federal programs provide financial assistance to American Indian students in institutions of higher education. The Navajo Tribe operates a community college on the reservation. At the University of New Mexico Law School, the American Indian Law Center has been especially instrumental in increasing the numbers of American Indian law graduates in New Mexico and throughout the country. These graduates have been very important in movements, programs, and court decisions that have strengthened tribal governments.

PUEBLO INDIANS

Pueblo is a Spanish word that, in this instance, means "village." Each of the nineteen New Mexico pueblos is a federally recognized Indian tribe. Their manner of living, religious practices, and culture may seem to the outsider to be all the same, but the various pueblos are often very different one from another. Their languages are often very different, too. Pueblo languages fall into three linguistic groupings: Tanoan (with three subgroups, Tiwa, Tewa, and Towa); Keres; and Zuni, a language unique to that Pueblo alone.

Present-day New Mexico Pueblos are located in six counties of the state. In the north, Taos Pueblo and Picuris Pueblo, both Tiwa-speaking, are located in Taos County; there are six Tewa-speaking pueblos (San Juan, Santa Clara, San Ildefonso, Nambé, Pojoaque, and Tesuque), all in Rio Arriba County. To the south, there are seven Pueblos in Sandoval County (the five Keres-speaking Pueblos of Cochiti, Santo Domingo,

San Felipe, Santa Ana, and Zia; Towa-speaking Jemez Pueblo; and Tiwa-speaking Sandia Pueblo). Tiwa-speaking Isleta Pueblo is located just south of Albuquerque, in Bernalillo County. To the west, in Valencia County, are the Keres-speaking Pueblos of Laguna and Acoma. Zuni Pueblo is farther west, in McKinley County.

When New Mexico was a territory of the United States, the Pueblos were not considered by federal law to be Indians, because they were said to be too settled and "civilized." Thus, for example, their lands were not protected by federal law on the same basis as the lands of other tribes, nor were the Pueblos entitled to the same services that the federal government provided to other tribes. Then, in 1913, the U.S. Supreme Court declared that the Pueblos were federally recognized Indian tribes, after all. In the case of *United States v. Sandoval*, the Court said:

> The people of the Pueblos, although sedentary rather than nomadic in
> their inclinations and disposed to peace and industry, are nevertheless
> Indians in race, customs, and domestic government, always living in
> separate and isolated communities, adhering to primitive modes of
> life, largely influenced by superstition and fetishism, and chiefly governed
> according to the crude customs inherited from their ancestors.
> They are essentially a simple, uninformed, and inferior people.[11]

Thus, in highly patronizing, even racist, words were the rights of the Pueblo Indians upheld! After that court decision, the Pueblos were entitled to the same federal protection of their remaining lands and the same federal services provided for other Indian tribes throughout the United States.[12]

Still, the *Sandoval* decision did not stop the pressure on the Pueblos to abandon their "Indianness," nor did it stop further encroachments on their land. In 1920, Senator Holm O. Bursum of New Mexico introduced a bill in the U.S. Senate that sought to favor non-Indians in the great number of pending disputes involving New Mexico Pueblo land titles. The Bursum Bill was backed by President Warren G. Harding and his secretary of the interior, Albert B. Fall (a former U.S. senator from New Mexico who later went to prison for corruption in the Teapot Dome scandal).

At about the same time that the Bursum Bill threatened the Pueblo Indians, federal efforts were also renewed to suppress their customs and religion. The commissioner of Indian affairs at the time called Pueblo Indian religions pagan and those who practiced such religions "half-animals." Alarmed, the New Mexico Pueblos reestablished the All Indian Pueblo Council. Aided by Anthony Lujan from Taos Pueblo and John Collier (later commissioner of Indian affairs under President Franklin D. Roosevelt), the council enlisted the lobbying efforts of national church and women's groups and was eventually successful in thwarting the Bursum Bill and other such attacks. In place of the Bursum Bill, a new Pueblo Land Act was passed by Congress in 1924, setting up somewhat fairer procedures for establishing their land titles. Still, non-Indians frequently wound up with title to good portions of the best irrigable Indian lands.[13]

The Indian Reorganization Act, mentioned earlier, was passed in 1934. It sought to recognize and strengthen tribal governments, attempting to mold them according to the dominant American ideas of what governments should look like. A majority of America's Indian tribes adopted written tribal constitutions under the terms of the act, establishing popularly elected tribal councils—or tribal business committees, as they were sometimes called—and a tribal chair, as chief executive. But most of the Pueblos did *not* organize under the Indian Reorganization Act. Instead, they continued their traditional governments, headed by a lifetime *cacique* (a title that the early Spaniards borrowed from the Arawak Indians of the Caribbean). But the Spaniards had also earlier required each of the Pueblos to name a governor and other secular officials, to make the Pueblo governments assume at least outside forms more familiar to the Spaniards. This dual system of government has continued ever since for a majority of the Pueblos in New Mexico. The overall, or inside, government is headed by a traditional cacique. The cacique, in consultation with tribal elders, selects the governor and other, usually one-year, secular officers, in what are described as "ages-old private ceremonies."

In 1898, because of an internal problem it could not work out in traditional ways, Santa Clara Pueblo abandoned its traditional form of government and, then, after the passage of the Indian Reorganization Act of 1934, adopted an approved written constitution and began to elect tribal officials. Today, Isleta, Laguna, and Zuni also elect their tribal officials under written constitutions. Picuris, Nambé, Pojoaque, and San Ildefonso now hold tribal elections, too. The remaining eleven Pueblos in New Mexico have continued with their traditional governments.

APACHES

Apache apparently comes from a Zuni word that means "enemy." The Spaniards adopted that overall name for the several autonomous bands of this tribe, with whom they and the Pueblos of New Mexico had an uneasy and often hostile relationship, with armed clashes. After New Mexico Territory became a part of the United States in 1848, and particularly a few years later, during the Civil War, there were increased conflicts between Apaches and U.S. soldiers. In 1863, about four hundred Apaches of the Mescalero band were forcibly taken to a concentration camp at Bosque Redondo, or Fort Sumner. Other Apaches of the Chiricahua and Warm Springs bands were sent to Fort Sill, in Oklahoma. In 1873, a reservation was established in south-central New Mexico for what was left of the Mescaleros. About two hundred members of the Chiricahua and Warm Springs bands at Fort Sill also elected to go to this reservation, and later the Lipan Apaches were brought back to the Mescalero reservation from northwestern Chihuahua, Mexico, where they had earlier been allowed to settle.

Today, under the Indian Reorganization Act, the Mescalero Apaches (including those of the Chiricahua, Warm Springs, and Lipan bands who moved there) have a written constitution that provides for an elected tribal council and a separately elected president and vice president. The tribe has been aggressive in developing a number of business enterprises, including a ski resort and lodge and a casino. They were one of the earliest tribes to assert more aggressively their governmental powers concerning taxation, the establishment of tribal courts, and licensing for hunting and fishing on the reservation, irrespective of state laws and requirements.

The Jicarilla Apaches are actually made up of two former groups, a mountain group and a plains group. Defeated by federal forces, some of them were first taken to the Mescalero reservation. But in 1887, the present Jicarilla reservation was established in north-central New Mexico (with additions in 1908), and the Jicarillas have lived there since that time. Their tribal government, set up under the Indian Reorganization Act, is based on a written constitution. There is a tribal council and an elected president and vice president. The Jicarillas have regained control over their oil, timber, land, and other natural resources from non-Indian lessees and corporations and now develop these resources more profitably for themselves.

NAVAJOS

The word *Navajo* is apparently derived from a Tewa word that signifies something like "the arroyo with a cultivated field." Related to, but somewhat different from, the Apaches, the Navajos historically clashed fiercely with the Spaniards and with the Pueblos. Like the Apaches, they engaged in bitter conflicts with federal troops during the Civil War. They were hunted down and driven out of their canyons in New Mexico and Arizona, and many of them were taken by force to Bosque Redondo, where large numbers of them died from disease and privation. Eventually in 1868, a 3.5-million-acre Navajo reservation was established, and the remaining Navajos were returned to it. In New Mexico, the Navajo Nation also has jurisdiction over the separate Ramah Navajo reservation—located in Cibola and McKinley counties, some forty miles south of the main reservation, in an area checkerboarded with mixed Navajo and non-Indian lands—as well as over the Alamo Navajo reservation, near Magdalena, New Mexico, and the Cañoncito Navajo reservation, near the New Mexico town of that name.

The Navajos are governed by a tribal council made up of delegates elected by districts and a popularly elected tribal president. The principal governing office of the tribe is located at Window Rock, Arizona. Local Navajo governmental units are called chapters and are headed by elected presidents.

In earlier times, with the encouragement and approval of the U.S. Bureau of Indian Affairs, the Navajo Nation allowed their resources to be tied up by non-Indian corporations, under poorly remunerative leases. They have since regained control of their resources and renegotiated these deals more beneficially, and they have established their own serious programs for business and agricultural development.

NEW MEXICO TRIBAL GOVERNMENTS

American Indian tribes are not "foreign nations." They cannot make treaties with foreign governments. And, since 1871, by act of Congress, the federal government no longer deals with Indian tribes through treaties. But unless the federal government has abrogated them, the treaties that were formerly entered into with Indian tribes (including, in New Mexico, treaties with the Apaches and Navajos and, for the Pueblos, the Mexican-U.S. Treaty of Guadalupe Hidalgo) are still enforceable by law. Where there is some ambiguity in Indian treaty language, the courts are supposed to interpret the language in favor of the Indians.

The federal government has "plenary," or full, power over Indian tribes, a power, strangely enough, that has been held by the U.S. Supreme Court to be based upon the international doctrine of discovery and conquest.[14] This plenary power means that the federal government can unilaterally abrogate a treaty with an Indian tribe, although if property were taken in that way, the federal government would have to pay just compensation. In most instances, the federal government has elected to honor earlier treaties, however incompletely, rather than to abolish treaty rights.

Because of the federal government's plenary power over tribes, the tribes are not in the same position in the federal system as states; states are constitutionally protected against unilateral action at the federal level to abolish them or their powers.

Neither are tribes "local governments," as are cities, counties, and school districts. That is, they are not generally subject to the jurisdiction of the governments of the states in which their reservations lie. Tribes are unique in the federal system.

Congress can delegate to states some authority over Indian reservations. One such law (Public Law 280) did delegate (or set up the procedures for delegating) to several states some authority over Indian reservations. Some states exercised all or part of this authority; some did not. Some that exercised it at first later gave up all or part of their authority to do so. But this law never applied to New Mexico. In order to have assumed such delegated authority, New Mexico would have had to eliminate from its constitution the provision disclaiming authority over Indian reservations. The state never did so. Now this delegation law has been changed by Congress so that tribal approval is required before it can be activated.

For a long time in New Mexico, state and local officials customarily took it upon themselves to exercise considerable authority, particularly enforcement authority, on some of the state's Indian reservations. But that is not true today. The Pueblos and other tribes in New Mexico have become increasingly assertive of their governmental powers, and they have moved to regain control of their land, water, and other natural resources. Some localities have made efforts to reach formal or informal agreements concerning jurisdictional disputes between the state and tribes and between local governments and tribes.

TRIBAL SOVEREIGNTY

The sovereignty, or governmental power, of tribes rests primarily on the doctrine of *inherent powers.* As one authority, based upon U.S. Supreme Court decisions, puts it:

> Today, tribal governments exercise legislative, judicial, and regulatory powers and it is clear that their authority is derived from their aboriginal sovereignty, not from the federal government.... So long as sovereign tribal rights are not voluntarily ceded by the tribes in treaties or in other negotiations approved by Congress, or they are not extinguished by Congress, they continue in existence.[15]

Tribal sovereignty, as opposed to asserted state authority, has also been upheld under the doctrine of *preemption.*[16] Primarily because of the Commerce Clause of the U.S. Constitution, which granted to the federal government the power to regulate commerce with Indian tribes, the federal government has supreme power regarding Indian tribes, as opposed to states. The courts have dismissed claims of state authority or jurisdiction in regard to Indian tribes in fields or subject matters in which Congress has legislated. Furthermore, tribal sovereignty has been upheld, as against state claims of jurisdiction or authority, under the doctrine of *infringement.*[17] Thus, states have been denied certain powers to tax or regulate activity on an Indian reservation, where such state action was found to interfere with the tribe's own essential operations. Lastly, tribal sovereignty has been upheld on the basis of *delegation,* as for example when the federal government delegated to each tribal government the authority to decide for itself whether or not alcoholic beverages might be sold within the reservation, an authority that had previously been assumed and exercised by the federal government.[18]

FEDERAL TRUST RESPONSIBILITY

The relationship of the federal government, on the one hand, and Indian tribes and individuals, on the other, is a relationship of "trust." Bolstered by federal legislation, this means that no interest in reservation or individually held Indian trust land can be sold, leased, or otherwise dealt with without the approval of the U.S. secretary of interior. But the government's trust responsibility is more than that. It is similar, as an early Supreme Court case put it, to the relationship of guardian and ward.[19]

Initially, it was thought that the trust responsibility of the federal government to Indians and Indian tribes was to be exercised solely by the Bureau of Indian Affairs. Because the programs of this agency were so poorly funded, however, federal contributions to the solution of problems of Indian education, health, housing, and other needs lagged behind federal actions in these fields for non-Indian citizens. In earlier times, too, it was assumed that the Bureau of Indian Affairs would serve as a kind of colonial, patronizing power for Indian tribes, more or less telling them what to do and running their affairs and programs for them.

Things began to change with President Lyndon Johnson's antipoverty program. The U.S. Office of Economic Opportunity (OEO) was set up at the federal level to provide services to all Americans, primarily on the basis of their socioeconomic conditions. When it was demonstrated that American Indians ranked at the bottom in virtually all socioeconomic measurements, the OEO began to serve Indians and Indian tribes directly, not through the Bureau of Indian Affairs. Today, it is acknowledged that the trust responsibility of the federal government to Indians and Indian tribes is government-wide. Thus, there is an Administration of Native Americans in the Department of Health and Human Services and similar offices or "Indian desks" in other federal agencies.

Just as it does for state and local governments, the federal government, through its various agencies and departments, now makes grants and loans to tribes and tribal programs—for example, under the Headstart and Community Action programs, the Elementary and Secondary Education Act, and the Comprehensive Older Americans Act.

The Bureau of Indian Affairs in the U.S. Department of the Interior is still, however, the principal federal agency that deals with Indians and Indian tribes, particularly with regard to land and education. The head of the bureau now ranks as an assistant secretary of interior.

The Indian Self-Determination and Education Assistance Act (1975) gave the secretary of the interior and other federal officials the power to contract with Indian tribes to turn over to them the administration of a whole range of federal programs. The purpose was to change the government's relationship with Indian tribes into that of an adviser, rather than that of an administrator. It was the announced policy of the administration of President Ronald Reagan (1981–89) to further this purpose, as when he said in a 1983 statement on Indian policy: "Our policy is to reaffirm dealing with Indian tribes on a *government-to-government* basis and to pursue the policy of self-government for Indian tribes..." Reagan's policy did, indeed, favor tribal autonomy and independence, but with an unfortunate reduction in federal aid. Later presidents have reiterated this government-to-government policy.

In New Mexico, there are separate local BIA agency offices for the Ramah Navajo, Mescalero, Jicarilla, Laguna, and Zuni reservations. There is a single BIA agency office for the eight northern pueblos and another one for the nine southern pueblos. The Department of the Interior maintains a regional office in Albuquerque.

TRIBES AND HUMAN RIGHTS

In relation to human rights, Indian tribes, again, occupy a unique position in the federal system. The provisions of the U.S. Bill of Rights were originally adopted as restraints on the federal government. The Fourteenth Amendment and its Equal Protection Clause were originally adopted primarily as restraints on state governments. Under the doctrine of incorporation, the Supreme Court later held, in a series of cases, that the major provisions of the U.S. Bill of Rights are restrictions on state governments, too. But neither the Bill of Rights nor the Equal Protection Clause is a restraint on tribal governments. To change this, at least partially, Congress enacted the Indian Civil Rights Act, in 1968.

Some people mistakenly thought at the time that this was an attempt to "give Indians their civil rights," just as a number of civil-rights laws had been passed on behalf of African Americans and other minorities. But that was not true. American Indians already had the same civil rights, in relation to the federal and state governments that all other Americans had. What the Indian Civil Rights Act did was to enact most of the provisions of the Bill of Rights and the Equal Protection Clause as restraints on *tribal* governments. New Mexico Pueblo leaders saw this as an intrusion on tribal sovereignty, but Congress overruled their objections. Thus, as a matter of federal law, not as a matter of constitutional provision, Indian tribes now are prevented from unduly restricting their own citizens' freedoms of speech and of the press, for example, and must also protect the rights of their people who are accused of crimes against self-incrimination and double jeopardy.

However, the statutory Indian Civil Rights Act is not as complete in its restraint on Indian tribal governments as the constitutional Bill of Rights and the Equal Protection Clause are on the federal and state governments. For example, the Indian Civil Rights Act does not include a prohibition against a tribal establishment of religion, although it does protect the free exercise of religion. Thus, an Indian tribe can establish a religion, of whatever kind, but it cannot prohibit the free exercise of other religions. This means, for example, that a Pueblo can prescribe that a Catholic priest will "bless the canes" (the traditional symbols of authority at each Pueblo, some originally having come from the viceroy of Mexico, others from President Abraham Lincoln) at each new inauguration, usually annually, of the governor and other secular officials of the Pueblo. Furthermore, the Equal Protection Clause, as it relates to Indian tribes under the Indian Civil Rights Act, does not require that the tribe elect its officials, if the tribe continues to choose its officials in the traditional way. Thus, a majority of New Mexico Pueblos still does not hold elections. But if a tribe changes to an election system, as eight New Mexico Pueblos have done, these elections must be fair, open, and based on "one person, one vote."

In 1979, Congress passed the Indian Religious Freedom Act, seeking to protect Indian religious sites and practices from federal and state encroachment.

TRIBES AND TAXATION

As governments, tribes may, and do, tax the earnings and activities of individuals and corporations within their reservations—non-Indian as well as Indian.[20]

States can tax off-reservation tribal activities. Individual Indians must pay state sales and income taxes on expenditures and earnings off the reservations, just as Indians must also pay federal income taxes on their earnings from wages or personal enterprises. States cannot tax reservation land or natural resources, and they cannot tax individually held Indian trust land. The federal government has elected not to tax reservation or individually held Indian trust land. States cannot tax reservation-earned Indian income, on-reservation activities of Indian businesses, or on-reservation purchases by Indians. Nor can they tax non-Indian transactions on a reservation, as this would impermissibly interfere with tribal self-government.[21]

The Indian Tribal Government Tax Status Act, passed by Congress in 1982, treats tribes in the same way as other units of government, such as cities, by exempting them from federal excise taxes and authorizing them to issue tax-exempt bonds to finance governmental functions.

Tribes, Regulation, and Gaming

Tribes have the power of regulation within the reservation, and this can include the activities and property of non-Indians as well as of Indians. Where the tribe has its own game-and-fish code and management system, for example, it can grant Indians and non-Indians the right to hunt and fish on the reservation without a state license and without obeying state game-and-fish regulations.[22]

It can generally be said that an activity that is legal under the laws of the state where the reservation is located may be permitted under license by the tribal government without state regulation or control. Specifically in regard to gambling, the U.S. Congress passed the Indian Gaming Regulatory Act in 1988. It makes lawful on an Indian reservation: Class I traditional Indian social gaming for minimal prizes, with tribal regulation alone; Class II gaming, such as bingo, with regulation by the tribe and the newly established National Indian Gaming Commission; and Class III casino, horse-racing, dog-racing, and slot-machine gaming, if such gambling is legal in the state where the reservation is located and if agreed to in a compact negotiated between the state and the tribe involved. The locations of many U.S. tribes have prevented their going into gaming, and some others have decided against such an enterprise, so that not quite 150 tribes in twenty-four states now are engaged in Class III gaming, though many more offer Class II bingo—with just eight tribes accounting for 40 percent of total Indian gaming revenues.

Where tribes have enacted zoning laws to protect the health and welfare of the tribe, these laws can be enforced in regard to non-Indian, as well as Indian, activities and land within the reservation.[23]

Tribes may license and regulate (and even, by federal delegation, prohibit) the sale of liquor on the reservation, both for Indians and non-Indians. But federal law requires that Indian liquor licensing conform with state law, including the requirement for a state license, in addition to a tribal license.[24]

Amendments that Congress adopted to the Safe Drinking Water Act and the Clean Water Act in 1986 and 1987, respectively, allowed tribes, like states, to administer federally funded water-protection programs on their reservations. Tribes also have the power to adopt air-quality standards under federal law, and when one tribe did so in conjunction with the Environmental Protection Agency, these standards were upheld in federal court, even though they affected the operations of non-Indian enterprises located outside the reservation.[25]

Tribes and Court Jurisdiction

The Indian Civil Rights Act, in addition to its other provisions, also authorized funds for the strengthening of tribal court systems, thus aiding in the rapid and rather extensive establishment and improvement of tribal courts, both in New Mexico and elsewhere.

Tribal courts have jurisdiction over reservation civil disputes, as when an Indian or non-Indian sues an Indian on the reservation.[26] Only after tribal court remedies have been exhausted can such a civil action be reviewed in federal court.[27] In New Mexico, suits by Indians against non-Indians are tried in state courts (or federal courts, depending on the circumstances), rather than tribal courts, and state courts may have concurrent jurisdiction in tribal courts when a non-Indian sues an Indian over transactions that occurred off the reservation.[28]

The Indian Child Welfare Act, passed by Congress in 1978, gives tribal courts exclusive jurisdiction over the custody or adoption of an Indian child who lives on the reservation or who is legally domiciled there but temporarily away. The act also provides that the tribe may intervene as an interested party in a state court proceeding concerning the custody or adoption of an Indian child of that tribe, who is legally domiciled off the reservation.

Tribal members who complain of a violation of their rights, such as limitation of freedom of speech or gender discrimination, under the Indian Civil Rights Act must bring this complaint to the tribal court, not to a state or federal court, unless it is a habeas corpus or similar case involving imprisonment or detention. In the latter case only, complaints may be brought to the federal courts, because only in this instance did Congress provide for a federal court remedy.[29]

In reservation criminal cases involving Indian defendants, tribal courts have jurisdiction over misdemeanors involving punishment by fines of not more than five hundred dollars or imprisonment for not more than six months. Under the federal Major Crimes Act, major crimes committed on the reservation are tried in the federal courts, if they involve offenses committed by an Indian against an Indian or non-Indian, or by a non-Indian against an Indian. A tribal court cannot try a non-Indian on a criminal charge.[30] Offenses committed on the reservation by a non-Indian against another non-Indian are tried in the state courts.

CONCLUSION

New Mexico Indians and Indian tribes contribute greatly to the cultural life and the economy of New Mexico and the communities near the reservations. For years the income from the land and natural resources of the tribes were often exploited by non-Indians. This has changed, as tribes have taken back control over their own resources. Tribes have moved into other forms of economic development, too, including gaming, to build jobs on the reservations. And these activities have contributed significantly to the state's economy.

American Indians, both reservation and non-reservation, in New Mexico and elsewhere, have reached out across tribal lines, cultures, and languages to find renewed strength in their Indianness. Tribal governments are recognized as permanent units of government within the federal system, and Indian tribes in New Mexico and throughout the nation have made important advances in political self-government and toward economic self-sufficiency.

NOTES

1.   *Cherokee Nation v. Georgia*, 30 U.S. (5 PET.) 1 (1831); and *Worcester v. Georgia*, 31 U.S. (6 PET.) 515 (1832). For a general survey and discussion of Indian law,

see Vine Deloria, Jr. and David E. Wilkins, *Tribes, Treaties, and Constitutional Tribulations* (Austin: University of Texas Press, 1999).

2.   See Fred R. Harris, Randy Roberts, and Margaret S. Elliston, *Understanding American Government* (Glenview, Ill.: Scott, Foresman/Little, Brown, 1988), pp. 133, 134; Vine Deloria, Jr., and Clifford Lytle, *The Nations Within: The Past and Future of American Indian Sovereignty* (New York: Pantheon Books, 1984); and Lynn and Kirke Kickingbird, *Indians and the U.S. Government* (Washington, D.C.: Institute for the Development of Indian Law, 1977).

3.   See Joyotpaul Chaudhuri, "American Indian Policy: An Overview," and Vine Deloria, Jr., "The Evolution of Federal Indian Policy Making," in Vine Deloria, Jr., ed., *American Indian Policy in the Twentieth Century* (Norman, Okla.: Westview Press, 1984); Deloria and Lytle, *The Nations Within*; David H. Getches and Charles F. Wilkinson, *Federal Indian Law: Cases and Materials*, 2d ed. (St. Paul, Minn.: West Publishing Company, 1986); and William C. Canby, Jr., *American Indian Law in a Nutshell*, 3d ed. (St. Paul: West Group, 1998).

4.   See William H. McNeill, *Plagues and People* (Garden City, N.Y.: Anchor Press/Doubleday, 1976); Alfred W. Crosby, *The Columbian Exchange: Biological and Cultural Consequences of 1492* (Westport, Conn.: Greenwood Press, 1972); John Duffy, *Epidemics in Colonial America* (Port Washington, N.Y.: Kennikat Press, 1972); and P. M. Ashburn, *The Ranks of Death: A Medical History of the Conquest of America* (New York: Coward-McCann, 1947).

5.   See *Prepare* (Washington, D.C.: National Impact, A Publication of the National Council of Churches, September 1977).

6.   For more information on the history and development of the Indian tribes of New Mexico, see Joe S. Sando, *The Pueblo Indians* (San Francisco: The Indian Historian Press, 1976); Raymond Friday Locke, *The Book of the Navajo* (Los Angeles: Mankind Publishing Company, 1976); Bertha P. Dutton, *Navajos and Apaches: The Athabascan Peoples* (Englewood Cliffs, N.J.: Prentice-Hall, 1976); and Philip Reno, *Taos Pueblo*, 2d ed. (Chicago: Swallow Press, 1972).

7.   In regard to the brutality of Coronado's expedition and that of Oñate at the time of the Reconquest of New Mexico, see Edward Dozier, "The Rio Grande Pueblos," unpublished paper, 1956, Coronado Room, Zimmerman Library, University of New Mexico; Herbert E. Bolton, *Coronado: Knight of Pueblos and Plains* (Albuquerque: University of New Mexico Press, 1949); and Ward Allen Minge, *Pueblo in the Sky* (Albuquerque: University of New Mexico Press, 1976), pp. 11–16.

8.   In addition to New Mexico, the other states were Idaho, Maine, Mississippi, and Washington. *Voting in the United States* (Chicago: Council of State Governments, August 1940).

9.   *Trujillo v. Garley*, U.S. Dist. Ct., Vic.A. No. 1353 (1948), cited and quoted in Daniel McCool, "Indian Voting," in Deloria, *American Indian Policy in the Twentieth Century*, pp. 111, 112.

10.   *Montoya v. Bolack*, 70 N.M. 196 (1962); *Prince v. Board of Education*, 88 N.M. 548, 543 P.2d 1176 (1975).

11.   231 U.S. 28 (1913).

12.   See Herbert O. Brayer, *Pueblo Indian Land Grants* (Albuquerque: University

of New Mexico Press, 1938), pp. 20–31.

13.   See Alvar W. Carlson, "El Rancho and Vadito: Spanish Settlements on Indian Land Grants," *El Palacio* 86, no. 1 (Spring 1979), pp. 28, 39.

14.   *Lone Wolf v. Hitchcock*, 187 U.S. 553 (1903); *Johnson v. McIntosh*, 21 U.S. (8 Wheat.) 543 (1823).

15.   David H. Getches and Charles F. Wilkinson, *Cases and Materials on Federal Indian Law*, 2d. ed. (St. Paul, Minn.: West Publishing Company, 1986), pp. xxiv, xxv.

16.   See *Warren Trading Post v. Arizona Tax Commission*, 380 U.S. 685 (1965).

17.   See *Williams v. Lee*, 358 U.S. 217 (1959).

18.   *United States v. Mazurie*, 419 U.S. 544 (1975).

19.   *Cherokee Nation v. Georgia*, 30 U.S. (5 Pet.) 1 (1831).

20.   *Morris v. Hitchcock*, 194 U.S. 384 (1904); and *Merrion v. Jicarilla Apache Tribe*, 455, U.S. 130 (1982).

21.   *White Mountain Apache Tribe v. Bracker*, 488 U.S. 136 (1980); and *Crow Tribe of Indians v. Montana*, 819 F.2d 895 (Ninth Cir. 1987), affirmed by the Supreme Court without opinion, 1988.

22.   *New Mexico v. Mescalero Apache Tribe*, 462 U.S. 324 (1983). In regard to Indian gaming, see W. Dale Mason, *Indian Gaming: Tribal Sovereignty and American Politics* (Norman: University of Oklahoma Press, 2000).

23.   *Knight v. Shoshone and Arapaho Tribes*, 670 F.2d 900 (Tenth Cir. 1982); and *Cardin v. DelaCruz*, 671 F.2d 363 (Ninth Cir. 1982), *cert. denied*, 103 S. Ct. 293 (1982).

24.   Title 18, U.S. Code, Section 1161; and *Rice v. Rehner*, No. 82–401 (U.S., July 1983).

25.   *Nance v. Environmental Protection Agency*, 645 F.2d 701 (Ninth Cir. 1981).

26.   See *Williams v. Lee*, 358 U.S. 217 (1959); and *Fisher v. District Court*, 424 U.S. 382 (1962).

27.   *National Farmers Insurance Company v. Crow Tribe of Indians*, 471 U.S. 845 (1985).

28.   *Paiz v. Hughes*, 76 N.M. 562, 417 P.2d 51 (1966); *State Securities v. Anderson*, 84 N.M. 629, 506 P.2d 786 (1973).

29.   *Santa Clara Pueblo v. Martinez*, 436 U.S. 49 (1978).

30.   *Oliphant v. Suquamish Indian Tribe*, 435 U.S. 191 (1978).

Chapter Eight

Voting, Elections, and Parties

I n November of 2004 slightly over one million (1,105,372) New
Mexicans were registered to vote. Of those registered, 63.2 percent
voted in the 2004 presidential election.[1] Compared with other states, New
Mexico has been slightly below the national average in voting participation in recent elections. But many New Mexicans follow politics with
an intensity far greater than that suggested by the turnout. This requires
some explanation.

A high level of poverty has always made state government (plus local
governments) a kind of employment agency of last resort. With good jobs
scarce in the private sector, many New Mexicans compete intensely for
jobs in state and local government, as well as for appointments and government contracts. Those who support winning candidates or parties at
the polls are more likely to succeed in obtaining these. Politics in New
Mexico, therefore, is famous for its color, personal nature, and competitive spirit, in great part because for many it is the only game in town.

This high level of interest in politics means that the rules governing the game of electoral politics are closely scrutinized, since even minor
changes and nuances can alter the calculus for success. What follows in
this chapter is a brief description of the laws governing voter registration, elections, political parties, and nominations, with a few examples
of overall party competition.

VOTER REGISTRATION AND VOTING

Voter-registration laws are enacted so that only people entitled to vote do so. Registration reduces the chances of election fraud, such as voting more than once or casting votes for dead people, acts that constitute fourth-degree felonies, but which are not unheard of in the annals of New Mexico politics. United States citizens who are residents of New Mexico and will be at least eighteen years old before election day are eligible to register to vote in New Mexico. Individuals who have been declared legally insane, however, are ineligible to register. Convicted felons were also prohibited from voting until 2001, when the restriction was lifted for those who had served their sentences. There is no minimum residency requirement, but prospective voters must register at least twenty-eight days before a given election. Citizens may register to vote, free of charge, at any registration location or at the office of the county clerk.

The federal National Voter Registration Act (the "motor voter" bill), passed in 1993, had a significant impact on the New Mexico Election Code. In general, it allowed greater access to registration and the polls and limited the restrictions that a state may place on the potential electorate. Voter registration is permanent in New Mexico unless there is a change in address, name, or party affiliation. Inactive voters may be removed from the registration roles only after missing two consecutive general elections and not responding to warnings of possible disenrollment sent out by public officials. Voters who change residence within their county should notify the county clerk to revise the address and precinct. Voters who move to a different county should register as new voters in that county and ask the county clerk to purge their registration in the former county of residence.

Each county is divided into precincts, small geographic voting territories having clearly defined boundaries and producing no more than eight hundred votes in the last general election. When more than eight hundred votes are cast in a precinct, it is split into two. All new voters are registered as members of the precinct in which they reside. Several adjoining precincts (roughly ten to twenty, depending on the size of the precincts) make up a legislative district. To avoid blatant gerrymandering (constructing legislative districts to maximize or minimize a party or ethnic group's voting strength), legislative districts are required to be made up of precincts that render a "compact and contiguous" shape, in the language of legislative apportionment. Sets of precincts are also used for other subcounty districts, such as county-commission districts or school-board districts. Only voters registered in the constituting precincts are allowed to vote for officials for a specific district or division.

New Mexico was one of the first states to permit both "no excuse needed" absentee registration and absentee voting. Before the liberalizing change in the state Election Code in 1994, this could only be done under certain conditions, including illness, disability, or temporary absence from one's home county. A "strict test" affidavit previously had been required. Military and overseas voters may vote absentee. Prisoners in any jail, detention center, or penitentiary are also eligible to vote absentee. Eligible prisoners may only vote absentee; due to abuses in the past, prisoners may no longer be taken to the polls.

An application for absentee ballots to vote in general and primary elections must be received on the proper form by the county clerk well before the election—ten to thirty days, depending on the election and the physical location of the voter. To be counted, the absentee ballot (in the proper official envelope) must arrive at the county clerk's office by 7:00 P.M. on election day. Absentee ballots may also be cast in person between 8:00 A.M. on the fortieth day preceding the election and 5:00 P.M. on the Thursday preceding the election. The absentee paper ballots are optically scanned and tabulated. If there is some kind of an administrative problem with the absentee ballot process and potential voters have not been able to cast their votes absentee, they may request an "in lieu of" ballot and vote in person. Citizens may vote absentee in municipal and school-board elections, as well as in elections to approve the issuance of indebtedness bonds. In these cases the application for an absentee ballot should be directed, respectively, to the municipal clerk or the superintendent of schools, instead of to the county clerk.[2]

Dull and routine as absentee voting laws may seem, major controversies surrounding them have appeared from time to time. In *Kiehne v. Atwood*, the election of a county clerk (Atwood) in Sierra County in 1978 was invalidated by the state district court, after it accepted arguments that some people voted absentee who were in fact present in the county on election day, and also that some people who were no longer residents of the county voted in the election. In this election exceptionally large numbers of absentee ballots were cast: 219 out of 1,407 total votes.

Excluding absentee ballots, candidate Zene Kiehne had a majority of the votes; with the absentee votes, Kiehne lost. The effect of those votes on the election was determined when the judge required those whose absentee ballots were successfully challenged to state in private to him how they had voted. When these votes were subtracted from the total, Mr. Kiehne was declared the winner and became county clerk by decree of the court. He did not seek reelection, and Mr. Atwood was elected county clerk at the next election.[3]

In another case, *State v. Naranjo*, county chairman Emilio Naranjo of Rio Arriba County was tried for unauthorized possession of blank absentee ballots in 1980. Mr. Naranjo was acquitted when the judge declared that the statute forbidding the possession of unauthorized blank absentee ballots was too vague and therefore unconstitutional. In other less formal cases, allegations sometimes arise that members of one political party have engaged in a conspiracy to encourage absentee voting by their members as a means of increasing voter turnout for that party. For example, in 1985 the Democratic party filed a suit alleging that members of the Republican party had improperly encouraged party members to make use of absentee-ballot privileges as a means of raising Republican turnout in a Doña Ana County Senate district. In the 1984 elections, Ellen L. Steele, a Republican from Doña Ana County, beat Olivia Rothschild, a Democrat, only when the effect of absentee voting in that district was taken into account. The suit was eventually dropped. These kinds of controversies have continued and most likely will until laws governing absentee-voter eligibility are clarified in the courts or by statute.

Another source of controversy has been the so-called "provisional ballots". These are to be issued if registered voters' names do not appear on the roster at their polling places or if they are first-time voters who registered by mail and they have not provided the required identification. In the 2004 general election, a major controversy took place about the requirement that voters show any sort of identification. Republicans held that all new voters who had not registered in person at the county clerk's office be required to show some kind of identification at the polls before they be allowed to vote. Democrats countered that this would unduly hamper the participation of the citizenry, particularly young people and ethnic minorities, and was an unconstitutional and unnecessary obstacle to the franchise. The conflict was heard in several courts with contradictory rulings being issued. The secretary of state and the attorney general (both Democrats) held that only first-time voters who registered by mail would have to produce some kind of identification at the polls. With election day just around the corner, both parties agreed to accept this position, at least for the time being.

Some important changes in the laws on registration and voting occurred when the Omnibus Election Reform Bill became law on July 1, 2005. Changes occurred in the areas of voter identification, provisional ballots, early ballots, ballot verification, and election official preparation. Persons wishing to cast ballots will have to provide some form of identification at the polling place. This may include a photo ID, a utility bill, bank statement, government check or paycheck, or student or tribal ID. Voters can also just provide their name, year of birth, and the last four digits of their social security number. This was a compromise between those, mainly Republicans, who had called for a certified proof of eligibility and others, mainly Democrats, who saw such requirements as too restrictive and likely to unduly exclude ethnic and racial minorities, young people, especially students, who are very mobile, and poor people. These provisions would also apply to absentee ballots. Absentee ballots can also begin to be processed five days before the election rather than waiting until election day. If identification cannot be provided at a polling place, provisional ballots can be cast. It will be counted if the individual provides an ID either to the polling officials before the polls close or to the county clerk before the election canvass starts.

The new law is also aimed at ensuring validity in the recording of votes. Beginning in 2007 or sooner, voting machines must provide a paper record of the machine vote that can be checked by the voters before their actual ballot is cast. Moreover, county clerks will then be required to conduct random audits of some voting machines and compare the results of the paper printouts with the computerized tallies. Polling officials will also receive more standardized training, including the instructions on the use of provisional ballots, and there will be more information available to voters at each polling place across the state. New Mexico was also among the first states to permit early in-person voting. Voters can start casting their ballots on the twenty-eighth day before the election and continue up until the Saturday before election day.

The initiation of early voting and much easier absentee balloting has significantly affected the electoral process in many ways. Campaigns have had to adjust their timetables to the new rhythms of the election cycle. Election administration by the state's public electoral officials has been made more complex and arduous. Perhaps most importantly, these techniques have made it much easier and more convenient for the voter. In the 2004 general election, almost half (46 percent) of the New Mexican electorate voted in other than the traditional in-person balloting at the polling place on election day, that is, either early in person or by absentee ballot. However, these electoral "reforms" do not seem to have resulted yet in an increase in electoral participation.

In 1975 Congress had amended the Voting Rights Act of 1965 to add language minorities to its coverage. The law initially had been enacted in 1965 to enable black southerners to vote despite local discrimination in voter-registration procedures. One section of the 1975 act requires bilingual voting materials and ballots wherever 5 percent or more of the population belongs to a language minority. All thirty-three counties in New Mexico fall under this category. Except for a brief period for some counties in the early 1970s, when a change in state law made bilingual ballots optional rather than mandatory, New Mexico has always printed ballots in both English and Spanish. Thus the Voting Rights Act of 1975 caused the state to renew its former rule and to print election proclamations and all voter-registration and information materials in both languages. Proposed amendments to the state constitution (by state constitutional decree) have always been on the ballot in both languages. The populations of seven counties (McKinley, Rio Arriba, Sandoval, San Juan, Otero, Taos, and Valencia) are more than 5 percent Indian in composition. But because the various Indian languages are not generally written, ballots need not be printed in these languages. Instead, oral assistance is provided at the voting places, radio announcements in various languages are made, and special voter-education programs and registration drives are conducted in the Indian communities, under the supervision of the office of the secretary of state.

New Mexico is different from other southwestern states in that Spanish-speaking citizens have had a long history of full participation and officeholding in state and local government. As author Jack Holmes points out, "in New Mexico, in short, Spanish Americans usually run their towns when they are numerous enough to do so; in Colorado, Texas, and Arizona they do not."[4] When New Mexico became a state, the Spanish-speaking citizenry did not wish to find themselves excluded from power, so Article VII, Section 3, of the state constitution stipulates: "The right of any citizen of the state to vote, hold office, or sit upon juries shall never be restricted, abridged, or impaired on account of religion, race, language or color or inability to speak, read, or write the English or Spanish languages..." Section 3 also stipulates that these provisions can be amended only by approval of at least three-fourths of the voters of the entire state and at least two-thirds of those of each county. It is justifiably referred to as an "unamendable" section of the state constitution.

ELECTIONS

As is the practice in most other states, the general election for New Mexico state and county offices is held simultaneously with the federal election, on the first Tuesday following the first Monday in November of each even-numbered year. Not all offices are filled at every election, of course, since many officials have terms in office exceeding two years.

Primary elections to choose Democratic and Republican party nominees (other than the presidential nominees) for the general election are held on the first Tuesday in June of each even-numbered year. Primaries in New Mexico are "closed," that is, only voters registered as party members are eligible to vote in a party's primary election. To compete for the party's nomination a prospective candidate must be registered as a party member by the first Monday in February preceding the primary election.

Primary elections in New Mexico involve only major political parties. Designation of this status requires that a party have received at least 5 percent of the total vote for governor in the last election. In practice this has meant that only the Democratic and Republican parties have had candidates competing in primary elections, although occasionally a "third" party, such as the Greens in the 1990s, will qualify to have a primary election.

Minor parties (those receiving less than 5 percent of the total vote for governor in the last election) may select candidates by convention or other non-primary means. State law provides that minor-party candidates must submit nominating petitions for the candidate bearing the signatures of registered voters totaling at least one-half percent of the total number of votes cast in the last general election within the constituency of the office sought. Previous law required minor parties to submit signatures totaling 3 percent of the last general-election vote, but in a 1988 case involving the Workers' World party, a federal judge placed the party on the ballot even though they had not submitted the 3 percent, declaring the law to be unconstitutional.[5] Then the signature totals were lowered to one-half percent, a figure that can mean as few as two thousand signatures.

Independent candidates (those not affiliated with a political party) who wish to be on the ballot must submit nominating petitions bearing the signatures of registered voters totaling at least 3 percent of votes cast (within the constituency of the office sought) for governor at the last general election at which a governor was elected. Candidates for statewide office must also meet certain distribution requirements. That is, they cannot obtain all of their signatures in one county.

As in all other states, the need for orderly conduct of the election has led New Mexico to require the use of voting machines in all precincts in the primary and general elections for state and county offices, as well as in municipal and school-board elections. By the 2004 general election mechanical voting machines had been replaced by electronic voting machines—touch screen, optical scan, or computerized. Whatever the type of voting device, voting machines can accommodate only a limited number of candidates for each contest. That is a major reason why the state attempts to ensure that minor parties and independent candidates wishing to be on the general-election ballot have some minimal level of support among the electorate.

Municipal elections by state law are held on the first Tuesday in March of even-numbered years, except that any municipality that has adopted a charter shall elect its municipal officers at the time provided for in the charter. Albuquerque, for instance, elects its officials on the first Tuesday after the first Monday in October of even-numbered years.

Article VII, Section 1, of the state constitution requires that school elections be held at different times from other elections, presumably to keep the administration of schools from becoming politicized by other electoral climates. Accordingly, state law provides that school-board elections are to be held in each school district on the first Tuesday in February of each odd-numbered year.

The secretary of state of New Mexico is the chief election officer of the state and is responsible for maintaining uniformity in the application, operation, and interpretation of the state's election code. This official is also responsible for the education and training of county clerks regarding elections procedures, for assisting them in the education and training of deputy registration officers and precinct boards, and for preparing and issuing instructions for the conduct of election and registration matters in accordance with state laws. The secretary of state has no jurisdiction over municipal and school-district elections.

The county clerks are the principal county election officials. They appoint and train the board for each precinct. Appointments are usually made from lists of nominees submitted by the Democratic and Republican county chairs. Precinct boards oversee the actual casting of ballots at the various polling places, count the votes cast in their precincts, and submit the tally to the county canvassing board. The composition of the precinct boards varies, depending on the number of voting machines to be used, but includes a presiding judge, two election judges of different political parties, and two to five election clerks from both parties. Also present at the polling place may be challengers and watchers appointed by county party chairs to represent the parties' interests. In primary elections any group of six candidates for county office or any group of three candidates for state or district office may appoint a watcher for each of those precincts. Precinct board members, challengers, and watchers must be registered voters in the precinct and must not be state or local law-enforcement officers.

The board of county commissioners of each county functions as the county canvassing board. This board counts the votes, as submitted by the precinct boards, and certifies the winners of contests for county offices and offices elected from districts that lie entirely within the county. The county board forwards certified vote totals in statewide contests and contests for multicounty offices to the state Canvassing Board. This board is composed of the governor, the secretary of state, and the chief justice of the New Mexico Supreme Court. The state Canvassing Board counts the votes as submitted by the counties and certifies the winner of each election for statewide office or for an office voted on by the voters of more than one county, as well as the winners of all district-attorney and district-judge elections, regardless of the number of counties in the judicial district. Votes, then, are counted and officially certified at three levels: the precinct, the county, and where applicable, the state.

Voter turnout in elections is not uniform throughout the state. In the 2000 general election, the highest rate of voter turnout among registered voters (77 percent) was found in Los Alamos County, a techno-scientific enclave, whose residents are highly educated, have high average incomes, and are 89 percent Anglo. The second highest turnout was in Union County (73 percent), which is 80 percent Anglo, followed by Harding County (72 percent). Mora County, which is one of the state's poorest and is 86 percent Hispanic, had a voter-turnout rate of 57 percent. Over the past several general elections the voter-turnout rate among New Mexico Hispanics has been about 10 percent below that of Anglos. The political behavior of Hispanic voters in New Mexico is in this respect notably different from Hispanic voting patterns in other southwestern states, where Spanish-speaking voters have turnout rates of 20 to 30 percent below those of Anglo voters.[6] Especially in urban areas, however, the percentage of the population that registers to vote and that casts ballots remains lower in working-class and mostly minority precincts than in middle-class and mostly Anglo precincts. Among New Mexico's Native American Indians, Navajos normally have much lower turnout for state and federal elections than for tribal elections.[7] This is also true for the Pueblos in the state.

As in the rest of the nation, urban voter interest and turnout in New Mexico is normally greater for general elections than for municipal and school-board elections. The latter are often decided by an electorate that is a small minority of the potential electorate. For various reasons this weights middle-class votes more heavily than those of lower classes. In rural areas of the state, however, voter interest in municipal and school-board elections is often quite high.

POLITICAL PARTIES

In October of 2004, 550, 418 New Mexicans were registered as Democrats (about 50 percent of the total, down from 65 percent in 1980), while about 359,347 were registered as Republicans (33 percent—up from 29 percent in 1980). Minor parties accounted for about 30,000 voters (3 percent), including 20,000 Greens, and around 165, 000 voters (about 15 percent of the total) who declined to state a party preference (DTS). The proportion of Republicans, minor party registrants, and "independents" (decline to state) has increased over the past twenty years. In 1990, Democrats outnumbered Republicans by a ratio of 1.68 to 1; by 2004 the ratio was closer to 1.53 to 1. Democrats were the majority in twenty-four of the state's thirty-three counties. Registered Republicans had greater numbers in Catron, Chaves, Curry, Lea, Lincoln, Los Alamos, Otero, San Juan, and Sierra counties. The highest proportions of registered Republicans were in Lincoln (56 percent) and Catron (54 percent) counties. The most heavily Democratic counties in 2004 were Guadalupe (84 percent), Rio Arriba (80 percent), and Mora (78 percent). In Bernalillo County, which contains 32 percent of all the registered voters, 46 percent are Democrats and 34 percent are Republicans—a 1.32 to 1 ratio. The largest proportion of nonparty registrants (DTS) were in the counties of Bernalillo (17 percent), Doña Ana (17 percent), and Los Alamos (18 percent).

Despite their notable advantage in voter registration, Democratic party candidates often lose New Mexico elections. For example, throughout the 1980s and 1990s and up to 2004, Republicans held two of the state's three seats in the U.S. House of Representatives and one U.S. Senate seat. Indeed, from 1977 to 1983 both U.S. senators were Republicans. The state often votes Republican for president, and in 1986 Republicans were elected governor, lieutenant governor, attorney general, and commissioner of public lands. New Mexico is thus reasonably competitive between the two parties in statewide elections. However, Democrats continue to dominate most county governments, although not as strongly as in the past. After the 1990 elections, Republicans dominated county governments in Catron, Chaves, Lincoln, Otero, and San Juan counties, were strong in Los Alamos County, and were fairly competitive with the Democrats in seven more. Thus Democrats were clearly dominant in only about one-half of the counties.

Partisan control of the New Mexico Legislature has also been less certain. As discussed in chapter 3, several recent legislative sessions have seen one or both chambers of the legislature governed by a coalition of Republicans and conservative Democrats. In part the Democrats' weakened position results from a trickling down the ballot of traditional Democrats' willingness to vote Republican, a phenomenon that began with "presidential Republicans" during the years when Eisenhower was president. Many registered Democrats now vote for Republican state legislative candidates. In 1988, for example, only five New Mexico Senate districts contained a majority of registered Republicans; but Republicans won all of those districts and eleven more. Eleven districts in the New Mexico House of Representatives had a majority of registered Republicans; but Republicans won ten of those eleven districts as well as fourteen seats where a majority of the constituents were registered Democrats. New Mexico legislative districts in which Republicans are the majority of registered voters almost always elect Republicans, whereas dominantly Democratic legislative districts need about a 30 percent Democratic registration advantage to be reasonably safe for Democratic legislative candidates.

Gradual shifts in electoral behavior have marked most of New Mexico's history. The first two decades of statehood witnessed keen competition between the parties for control of statewide elective offices. Of the first eight elections for governor, for example, each party won four, alternating in power every four years. Republicans won just over half of the first eight elections for lesser statewide elective executive posts. The parties were much less competitive, however, at the legislative level. Republicans controlled the entire legislature for fourteen of the state's first twenty years and controlled the Senate until 1933.

The Great Depression and Franklin D. Roosevelt's election as president marked the beginning of an era of Democratic dominance in New Mexico, as in many other states, but since the 1980s there has been a resurgence of competition between the two parties. Democrats have held a majority of seats in both houses of the state legislature since 1933, except for the 1953–54 House and the 1985–86 Senate, although a coalition of Republicans and conservative Democrats controlled the House from 1979 through 1982 and in 1985–86. A similar bipartisan coalition controlled the Senate for the 1988 session.

Democrats won all statewide elections from 1932 through 1948, when Republican Edwin L. Mechem was elected governor. In the fifty-four years from 1949 through 2002, Republicans held the office of governor for a total of twenty-four years, that of lieutenant governor for eighteen years (formerly that office was elected independently of the governor), attorney general for four years, commissioner of public lands for eight years, one Corporation Commission seat (of three) for six years, state auditor for four years, and state treasurer for two years. In 1980 a Republican was elected to the New Mexico Supreme Court. Numerous close elections in the 1980s and 1990s, along with the Republican victories of 1986, 1994, and 1998, attest to the increasing competitiveness of Republican candidates in statewide races.

But statewide partisan trends disguise the many variations in partisan trends in different counties and areas of the state. For instance, since statehood the six southeastern counties known as Little Texas (Chaves, Curry, De Baca, Eddy, Lea, and Roosevelt) have drifted away from overwhelming Democratic majorities toward increasingly strong support for Republican candidates. Although that trend varies by county, the region's vote for governor has shifted from 75 percent Democrat in the early years of statehood to more competitiveness in the 1970s, 1980s, and 1990s. Indeed, although Little Texas voter registration in the early 1990s was still about 1.8 to 1 Democratic, in the governor's race, the area has voted Republican in 1952 and in every election since 1974. With the exception of 1928 (when the strongly Protestant electorate of Little Texas voted against Democratic Catholic nominee Al Smith), the area consistently voted heavily Democratic for president until 1952, when it voted for General Eisenhower. Lyndon Johnson (1964) has been the only Democrat since 1952 to win the area's support for president. Despite the trend toward voting Republican at the top of the ticket, Democratic candidates for local office and the state legislature in Little Texas were favored until recently. In the 1970s only Chaves County had significant Republican challenges for control of county government. Republicans won all Chaves County offices but two in the 1998, 2000, and 2002 elections and won one or more county offices in every Little Texas county except De Baca.

In 1975 eight of the nine state senators from Little Texas were Democrats; by 1991 three of the eight Little Texas senators were Republicans; and in 2004 (Forty-sixth Legislature, Second Session) six of the eight state senators from Little Texas were Republicans. The 1975 House legislative delegation included nine Democratic Representatives and five Republican representatives. In 1991 six of the thirteen Representatives were Republicans; and in 2004, a majority, six of the eleven, were members of the GOP.

The Republican trend in Little Texas was offset for decades by movement in the opposite direction in the Hispanic counties. Newcomers have changed the population mix of some traditionally Hispanic counties, but Guadalupe, Luna, Mora, Rio Arriba, San Miguel, and Taos counties remain 55 percent or more Hispanic. These normally produce strong Democratic majorities in local, gubernatorial, and presidential elections. In 1990, for example, Democrats won all county offices in Guadalupe County and all but sheriff and one county-commission seat in Mora County. This pattern of Democratic dominance has not extended to elections for the U.S. Senate.

Because it has almost one-third of the voters in the state, Bernalillo County, which contains Albuquerque, is very important to both parties. In 1990 52 percent of the county's voters were registered Democrats, 42 percent were Republicans, and the remainder (6 percent) were minor-party members or declined to state a party preference.[8] By 2004 Democratic registrants had diminished by six points to 46 percent; Republicans lost eight points, down to 34 percent; and "independents" (DTS) had grown considerably—to 17 percent. Since some 34 percent of the state's registered Republicans live in Bernalillo County, compared to only 29 percent of the state's registered Democrats, the county figures more importantly in Republican than in Democratic affairs. Democrats frequently win statewide elective offices despite a disadvantaged outcome in Bernalillo County; Republicans have not won such an election since the Depression without carrying Bernalillo County. Republicans also hold many nominally nonpartisan city of Albuquerque posts, since much of the Democratic party's strength in the county lies outside the city limits. Republicans usually hold some Bernalillo County offices. In 1992, for example, Republicans held two of five county-commission seats, the county clerk's office, and probate judge; in 2002 one county commissioner and the county sheriff were Republicans.

Political parties are required by law in New Mexico to adopt written rules and regulations providing for their organization and government and to file these with the secretary of state. The county organizations of each party are required to adopt the state party's rules, although each county party organization may adopt supplementary rules, provided these neither conflict with their state rules nor abridge the lawful political rights of any person. County party organizations must file their state rules and regulations, along with any supplemental rules, with the county clerk. This requirement provides all members of the party with access to the rules and regulations, without which a faction within a party could be at a disadvantage. Factional party politics have in fact made this requirement necessary. Parties that do not comply with these regulations are denied a place on the ballot.

A political party's rules must provide: (1) a method for calling and conducting conventions and for selecting delegates to conventions; (2) a method for selecting state central-committee members and other officials, along with provisions for filling vacancies in such positions; and (3) a method for amending party rules and regulations. Party rules must also spell out the powers and duties of various party officials and governing bodies, as well as the structure of the state and county party organizations. They must also require that meetings to elect party officers or delegates be held at a public place during the week specified by the state party chair; they must provide that notice of such meetings be published by the officers of the county party organization in a newspaper of general circulation two weeks prior to the meeting. The notice must specify the time, date, and place of the meeting. This requirement is also the product of factional party politics in the not-so-distant past.

The Democratic and Republican parties in New Mexico are similar in organization, although important differences in internal procedure do exist. Both parties consider as members all citizens who declare themselves party members when they register to vote; only these persons may participate in party affairs. Both parties are organized at state, county, ward, and precinct levels. Each has a state party chair and other state officers, a state central committee, a state executive committee, and a small party staff. Each county party organization has a county chair and other officers and a county central committee. Ward and precinct business is conducted by officers of those local party organizations and in public meetings of all interested party members in the ward or precinct. Precinct or ward meetings elect delegates to county conventions. County conventions elect delegates to state party conventions. Party members who want to participate in party affairs need only inquire about the time and place of their precinct or ward meetings, persuade their supporters to attend the meeting with them, and seek election as delegates. In New Mexico, as in most parts of the country, the gradual decline in the influence of parties has reduced participation at the local level. Many students and newly interested voters have been astonished at the ease and speed with which they were able to exert significant influence over party affairs at the county or even state levels within each party. Both parties are receptive to serious participation in party affairs by young or inexperienced voters. Indeed each party has large numbers of officials who have been involved only for short periods of time.

Major party decisions are made at state conventions. When a state convention is not in session, however, the state central committee is the party's supreme governing body. Because of its size and the difficulty of arranging meetings, the state central committee often delegates much of its authority to the state party chair and the state executive committee for day-to-day decision making.

NOMINATIONS

New Mexico has experimented with various nominating procedures for the major parties. Until 1938 nominations were by party convention, a system that permitted each party to balance its slate of nominees to appeal to the various ethnic and geographic communities of the state. Critics of the convention system argued that it gave too much control to party leaders over policy, patronage, and the selection of nominees, and that it permitted decisions to be made by party elites in smoke-filled rooms, rather than by the party membership. Nomination by convention ended when Governor Clyde Tingley, who was engaged in a contest with the state Democratic party chair for control of the party machinery, provided the leadership behind which the legislature united to enact a law providing for a closed direct primary, beginning with the 1940 election.[9]

Nomination by primary election does not entirely negate the influence of party leaders, but it does give more influence to rank-and-file party members and to campaign technicians. It also permits maverick contenders occasionally to win nomination to major office and makes more difficult the party leaders' job of fielding a ticket balanced among the various ideological, ethnic, and geographic sectors of the party. It also reduces any obligation individual officeholders might feel to support the party platform. With campaign funding now largely handled by political action committees, it also reduces the buffer that parties used to provide between officeholders and special-interest groups.

Charles B. Judah recorded that in its first decade, the direct primary in New Mexico was marked by several additional difficulties. Many contests saw candidates "who entered the race not in order to win but to draw votes from someone else."[10] The device was especially effective in increasing tensions between Anglo and Hispanic communities, since it often was based on the acknowledged tendency of some voters to cast their ballots on the basis of ethnic identity.

Another practice reported by Judah was that of obtaining names on a nominating petition without filling in the office for which the candidate planned to run. "Thus armed the political gangster surveyed the field, not to find the office for which he wished to run but rather the one where he might be paid the most for not running. If clever he might levy tribute on more than one candidate."[11]

To eliminate these practices at the state (but not county) level, the 1949 legislature passed a law, effective with the 1950 election, to provide for pre-primary nominating conventions, followed by primary elections. Only those capturing 25 percent or more of the convention vote were eligible for ballot positions in the primary. This device gave party leaders greater influence over nominations than they had enjoyed during the first decade of direct-primary nominations, but less than had been the case prior to 1940. The debate over the relative merits of the direct primary over the pre-primary convention followed by a primary has continued, as have experiments with variants of each method.[12] A lively debate over these issues continues among political insiders.

Pre-primary conventions were required in 1950, 1952, and 1954. The state returned to the direct primary for elections from 1956 through 1962. Pre-primary elections were again required in 1964 and 1966, but then abandoned in favor of the direct primary from 1968 through 1974. During the latter period, constitutional challenges were made to the filing-fee and petition mechanisms used to limit the number of candidates. As a result, the 1972 primary election saw twenty-five Democrats and eight Republicans vying for their respective party nominations to the U.S. Senate.

In large part to restore order to the nominating process, the state returned to the pre-primary convention system in 1976, with its application only to nominations for United States representative, senator, and statewide elective offices such as governor, attorney general, and supreme court justice. Other nominations (such as for district judgeships, state legislature, or county offices) continued to be by direct-primary election without convention designation. The pre-primary convention was eliminated for the 1984 election. In 1993 the pre-primary convention was reestablished in a new and more limited form. In 2003 the state legislature passed a law enabling both major parties to use the convention method of selecting their presidential delegates; both parties have chosen to do so.

The conventions once again filtered and prioritized each party's aspirants. Candidates vie to obtain each party's endorsement and for a favorable position on the ballot. Candidates must receive a minimum of 20 percent of the convention delegates' votes to win a place on the June primary ballot. If more than one candidate receives the 20 percent, each is placed on the ballot in corresponding order to the number of votes received. Those who do not qualify by reaching the 20 percent mark at the state convention must obtain a certain number of signatures on a petition—twice as many as needed to initially be considered as a candidate by the conventions. The candidates who do well at the conventions accrue several advantages including being considered the favorite with the attendant publicity and all that it brings in the way of status and contributions.

Individuals seeking major-party nomination to state or county office must be registered to vote as a member of that party and submit nominating petitions to be put on the primary-election ballot. The nominating petition of a candidate for statewide office must be signed by a number of registered voters (members of the candidate's party) equal to at least 3 percent of all votes cast for candidates for governor in the party's last gubernatorial primary election.

Because inevitably some people who are not registered to vote sign petitions, or sign more than one, and because it is known that people who sign nominating petitions are more likely to feel an obligation to turn up to vote for the candidate, candidates obtain as many nominating petition signatures as they can muster—often two or three times the number required by law. Each voter is entitled to sign only one petition for each office, except in cases where more than one position is to be filled. The nominating petitions of candidates for county or district offices (such as U.S. representative, district judge, or state senator) must be signed by a number of voters (of the candidate's party) equal to at least 3 percent of the total vote for governor, in the appropriate county or district, in the party's last preceding gubernatorial primary.

Candidates for statewide office and for U.S. representative must file their nominating petitions with the secretary of state during business hours on the first Tuesday of March of the election year. Candidates for county offices, state legislature, and judicial district offices must file their nominating petitions during business hours on the first Tuesday of April of the election year. All district judge and district attorney candidates file their nominating petitions with the secretary of state, as do candidates for legislative districts that include precincts from more than one county. Other legislative candidates and those seeking county office file their nominating petitions with their county clerk.

If after a primary election a vacancy occurs in a party's list of nominees for the general election, the party's state or county central committee, depending on the office, has the authority to fill that vacancy by filing the name of the party nominee with the appropriate filing officer. If no one sought the nomination in the primary election, however, then no "vacancy" exists, and the party committee cannot nominate a candidate later on. An attorney general's ruling to that effect became the focus of a court suit and bitter political debate in 1980, when incumbent Democratic U.S. Representative Harold Runnels died after the primary election. No Republican had sought the congressional nomination to oppose the popular incumbent. After an unsuccessful court effort to get on the ballot, Republican Joe Skeen was forced to run as a write-in candidate. He won; it was only the second time in the twentieth century a write-in candidate had been elected to Congress.[13]

PRESIDENTIAL NOMINATIONS

From statehood through 1968, New Mexico's Democratic and Republican delegates to the national-party nominating conventions were selected by state party conventions. The delegates to the state convention, in turn, had been selected at county conventions, composed of delegates who had been elected at precinct or ward meetings of party members. The selection of national-convention delegates by state conventions gave much discretion to state and county party leaders concerning which presidential aspirant to support. Party rank and file were relatively unimportant in the selection process.

In 1972 the state experimented with national delegate–selection criteria. National-convention delegates were apportioned between the leading two presidential candidates in each party's primary. Leaders of both parties were unpleasantly surprised by the results. In the Democratic presidential primary, Senator Hubert Humphrey came in third and thus was awarded no delegates. He was nevertheless clearly the national-party nominee for president. His supporters among the Democratic leaders in New Mexico found themselves sitting at home watching the national convention on television. Republican leaders, in turn, were chagrined that the new state rules required that New Mexico send a delegate to the convention to vote for Congressman Paul McCloskey, an outspoken critic of the Nixon administration's Vietnam policies. Thus the only vote at the 1972 national Republican convention cast against Nixon came from New Mexico. Leaders of both parties agreed to return to a convention system of choosing national convention delegates in 1976, and the state legislature enacted the appropriate laws.

In 1976 the Republican leadership chose to give Ronald Reagan all the state's Republican delegates, in spite of polls that showed a slim majority of New Mexico Republicans favored Gerald Ford, and even though almost half of the state convention delegates favored Ford. In the Democratic party, Jimmy Carter and Morris Udall both received substantially larger shares of New Mexico's national-convention delegates than their support among the Democratic voters would justify. After the 1976 experiment, the state returned to proportional-representation schemes for selecting delegates to the national convention, so that New Mexico delegations would reflect the statewide primary vote in each party.

A seven-member nominating committee—composed of the chief justice of the state Supreme Court, the Speaker and minority leader of the state House of Representatives, the President Pro Tem and minority leader of the state Senate, and the chairs of the state Democratic and Republican parties—is required, by a law passed in 1980, to nominate "all those generally advocated and nationally recognized as candidates of the major political parties participating in the presidential primary for the office of president of the United States."[14] Candidates nominated by the committee have fifty days in which to ask that their names be withdrawn.

After the primary election, the secretary of state forwards to the party chair the name of each presidential candidate receiving at least 15 percent of that party's total primary-election vote. A delegate-selection convention is then held to select delegates to the party's national nominating convention. National-convention delegates must be chosen in proportion to the share of the vote received by each candidate who polled 25 percent or more of the vote cast in the party's primary election. A candidate receiving between 15 and 25 percent of the vote may receive a national-convention delegate if, after the initial designation of delegates among candidates receiving 25 percent or more of the vote, there is a residual left over. All national-convention delegates are committed to vote for their designated presidential candidate, but only on the first ballot of the national convention.

The reader may well wonder why the state legislature has devoted so much attention to presidential delegate-selection rules, especially since New Mexico is allotted only a miniscule proportion of the national-convention delegates in either party. The reasons appear to be partly philosophical and partly political. As is noted elsewhere in this book, New Mexicans tend to favor mechanisms that permit the direct expression of the will of the people. This preference is shared by much of the press, in part because of their influence over voters in primary elections. Yet presidential politics involves high stakes for many of New Mexico's political and economic elites. They are thus tempted to manipulate the delegate-selection process so as to maximize the potential rewards to be gained by siding with the winning presidential aspirant. The state's electoral laws reflect the tension between the pressure for democratization of the nominating process and the desire to maximize state political gains in the national-party system.

New Mexico held its presidential primary elections in June until 2004. However, by June virtually all other states' primary elections had already been held, and in recent elections the presidential nominee had already been determined. Since New Mexico, a very small state in population, had held its primary election on the same day as California, the most populous state, along with several other states, news media and candidate attention in presidential years in New Mexico had been all but nonexistent, even if the nomination had not already been determined. If there was any suspense left, the California returns were the only ones that were likely to receive attention. Thus New Mexico voters, in comparison with their counterparts in New Hampshire or other small states that hold their primary elections earlier, had played virtually no role at all in the selection of the nominees for president of the United States. Because of this, in 2004 the presidential primaries were moved up earlier—to February. The 2004 primaries in New Mexico consequently received significantly more attention by the press, the candidates, and the public. This was a harbinger of things to come, as New Mexico became one of the top-tier target or "battleground" states in the 2004 presidential campaign.

CONCLUSION

Citizens of New Mexico often underestimate the significance of laws governing the machinery of elections, nominations, and parties. To be sure these laws often seem painfully intricate and arcane. Current laws governing registration, elections, nominations, and political parties, however, are very much the product of political abuses committed by members of both parties in prior years. Constant awareness and understanding of the electoral codes are the best assurance against the recurrence of such abuses in the future.

Democrats have a 1.5 to 1 statewide advantage over Republicans in the number of registered voters who are party members, but this advantage has dropped significantly in the past two decades. Furthermore, Democrats seem more willing than Republicans to vote for the other party's candidates. Thus, the state is reasonably competitive between the two parties, especially for president, governor, U.S. senator, and U.S. representative. Democrats have the advantage for the less visible statewide offices, while the Republican presidential candidate has the advantage. Republicans are becoming increasingly competitive for the control of local government, but Democrats still have the upper hand in most counties.

Finally, no account of voters, elections, and parties in New Mexico would be complete without some reference to the ethnic factors that affect each of these considerations directly. To begin with, it is demonstrable that Hispanics, Indians, and Anglos tend strongly, when given a choice between candidates, to vote for persons of their own ethnic group. Since Anglos easily outnumber Hispanics and Indians, at first glance this tendency might seem to militate against these minority groups. There are two reasons why this is not necessarily so. First, since Hispanic and Indian citizens are concentrated geographically in certain counties and within many counties, there are electoral districts of all kinds where Hispanic (and, to a lesser extent, Indian) candidates are favored by sheer numbers. And for three decades federal court cases have consistently ruled against apportionment plans that seemed likely to diminish the potential voting strength of these minority populations.

Second, and of equal importance, Hispanic and Indian citizens are exceptionally concentrated within the Democratic party. Indeed, Hispanic Democrats are only slightly less numerous than Anglo Democrats. Since the Democratic party is dominant in more than half the state, especially at local levels, this has tended to help Hispanic candidates (especially in primary elections) more than would be expected if the Hispanic population were evenly dispersed between the two parties. Thus a pattern has emerged whereby Hispanics tend to be overrepresented statewide in lower offices, especially at the county level, and only slightly underrepresented in the higher offices.

Several recent trends have acted to lessen the importance of ethnicity as a partisan factor in New Mexico voter-allegiance elections. First, a generalized decline in the strength of parties has led to a slight reduction of both ethnic overrepresentation in the Democratic party and of overall Democratic party strength itself, as younger people of differing ethnic and partisan backgrounds come into the political arena. Second, the increased use of the electronic media such as the internet (and money) in campaigns has given voters more direct access to candidates. Voters have far more information today about candidates than simply their ethnicity, and it is increasingly difficult to predict outcomes based on ethnicity alone.

Nevertheless, ethnicity continues to play a major role in the New Mexico political scene. Along with party identification, it is the most important predictor of a person's voting behavior. Ethnic factors often influence the outcome of primary elections, and ethnicity deeply affects interparty competition.

NOTES

This chapter is a revision and updating of a chapter in the third edition coauthored by Paul L. Hain and Jose Z. Garcia.

1.   Secretary of State, *State of New Mexico Official Returns*, 1988a004 (Santa Fe: Office of the Secretary of State).

2.   This information, as well as other information in this chapter, is contained in the *Election Handbook of the State of New Mexico*, published periodically by the secretary of state of New Mexico.

3.   This information was provided by Mr. William Lutz, one of the principal attorneys in the case.

4.   Jack F. Holmes, *Politics in New Mexico* (Albuquerque: University of New Mexico Press, 1967), p. 20.

5.   *Albuquerque Journal*, Aug. 24, 1988, p. B-3.

6.   F. Chris Garcia and Rudolph O. de la Garza, *The Chicano Political Experience* (North Scituate, Mass.: Duxbury Press, 1977), Chapter 7.

7.   For a discussion of variations in turnout for different types of elections in New Mexico, see Holmes, *Politics in New Mexico*, pp. 125–30. Also, see Jack E. Holmes, "Navajo Voting: Disjunctions and Parallels in Tribal and White Man's Elections," paper presented at the 1976 annual meeting of the Western Political Science Association in San Francisco, California.

8.   Secretary of State, *Official Returns*, 1990.

9.   Charles B. Judah, *Aspects of the Nominating System in New Mexico* (Albuquerque: Division of Government Research, Department of Government, University of New Mexico, 1957), p. 3.

10. Ibid., p. 8.

11. Ibid.

12. The intensity with which citizens view attempts to strengthen the influence of party leaders over nominations is reflected by the fact that this issue has been involved in the only two attempts ever made to annul legislation by popular vote (see chapter 3, above, for a discussion of Article IV, Section 1). On two occasions, in 1950 and 1964, unsuccessful efforts were made to reverse legislation that changed the major-party nominating system from a direct primary to a pre-primary convention followed by a primary. Both times the vote was overwhelming for annulment of the legislation, but both times less than 40 percent of those who voted for governor voted in favor of annulment, so the legislation stood.

13. Timothy De Young and F. Chris Garcia, "Despite the Odds: How to Wage and Project a Successful Write-in Campaign," *Electoral Studies* 2, no. 3 (1983), pp. 241–52.

14. Secretary of State of New Mexico, *Election Handbook of the State of New Mexico* (Santa Fe: Office of the Secretary of State, 1979), p. 88.

Chapter Nine

Politics and the Media

by Bob M. Gassaway and Fred V. Bales

I n the country at large, 97 percent of adult Americans read a newspaper or listen to radio or watch television every weekday.[1] For most
people "the news" is a major window on the world, a key source of information about everything from local weather to world finance. Stories
about politics and government are among the most widely read in newspapers.[2] Despite many years of research, however, we are still unable to
specify exactly how the media influence their audiences through news
reports, political advertising, editorial endorsements of candidates, and
other messages. Even though the research indicates that no amount of
media bombardment can directly cause people to adopt a particular view
or to take a particular action, evidence exists that the media do exert
power over what is considered to be important. As political scientist
Bernard Cohen has said, "While the media are not very good at telling
us what to think, they are stupendously good at telling us what to think
about."[3] In fact, a researcher who has devoted much effort to understanding how news coverage influences public opinion about political affairs
has concluded: "We judge as important what the media judge as important. Media priorities become our own."[4]

In light of this important role that the media plays in politics and
government, this chapter will address a number of different questions.

FIGURE 9.1
New Mexico Media Inventory

NEW MEXICO MEDIA	MEDIA IN ALBUQUERQUE[a]	STATEWIDE TOTALS[b]
General-Circulation Newspapers		
Daily Newspapers	2	18
Twice weekly	0	6
Weekly	3	21
Total Newspapers	5	45
Television Stations		
Network Affiliates	7	14
Educational (PBS)	1	3
Independent	0	1
Religious	3	4
Total Television Stations	11	22
Radio Stations		
AM Network Affiliates	5	36
AM Independents	3	12
AM Religious[c]	2	3
AM Educational	0	1
AM Spanish-Language[d]	3	11
AM Navajo-Language[e]	0	1
Total AM stations	13	65
FM Network Affiliates	2	27
FM Independents	6	35
FM Religious[c]	2	5
FM Educational	2	10
FM Zuni-Language[e]	0	1
Total FM Stations	12	78

[a] Other media serve the Albuquerque market, including broadcast stations in nearby communities. The numbers in this column are for media organizations based in Albuquerque.

[b] Numbers in this column indicate media based in Albuquerque and media in the remainder of the state. Other broadcast stations had been licensed in several New Mexico communities, but had not gone on the air at the time of writing.

[c] These stations broadcast religious programs almost exclusively; some other stations broadcast several hours of religious programs each week.

[d] These stations broadcast Spanish-language programs almost exclusively; some other stations broadcast several hours of Spanish-language programs each week.

[e] These stations broadcast in American Indian languages almost exclusively; some other stations broadcast several hours of programs in American Indian languages each week.

First, how do the news and advertising media deal with political campaigns? How do political candidates and their parties use newspapers and broadcast media in campaigns? How do media audiences respond to information from radio, television, and newspapers? Then finally, how do the media cover politicians in office? Examining these questions will help shed light on the potentially great role that the media play in the politics of this state.

SOME DEFINITIONS

It will be useful at this point to take a moment and define some terms commonly used to discuss media involvement in politics.

Media. This word describes broadly the distribution systems of radio, television, and the print media. Radio is one *medium* of communication, television is another *medium*, and newspapers are a third. Collectively these and magazines are "the *media.*"

News. This is information that newspapers, radio stations, and television stations distribute in the form of news reports. These reports are noncommercial messages prepared by journalists employed by local news organizations or purchased from some news organizations, such as the Associated Press (AP). Although the news sources from whom journalists get information influence which stories are prepared and even how they are prepared, the end results should be the products of editorial choices made by the staffs of news organizations dispensing the information.

Advertising. This term applies to paid messages appearing on radio and television and in the print media. Although media organizations may impose certain limits of good taste, the content of *advertising* is determined by those who pay the bills.

Commercials. Broadcasters sell advertising in the form of commercials. Federal regulations grant politicians preferential rates if their pictures are seen in TV commercials or their voices are heard on radio. Broadcasters and people in the advertising industry commonly refer to commercials as *spots*, which is short for *spot announcements.*

Audience. The *audience* is the reason the whole media industry exists. Advertisers pay all the costs of commercial radio and television, and they pay about 75 percent of the cost of putting out most newspapers, in order to reach people who turn to the media for information.

MEDIA ROOTS

The modern media's interest in American political life is rooted firmly in our history. The U.S. Constitution and the Bill of Rights reflect the views of their authors that people are rational beings capable of governing themselves, and that when offered a choice between truth and falsehood, people will (in the long run) recognize the truth. A free press is considered essential in providing the information people need to govern themselves; to censor competing ideas is to risk shutting out the truth.

To protect the free flow of information from the interference of government, the First Amendment to the U.S. Constitution says:

> Congress shall make no law respecting the establishment of religion, or prohibiting the free exercise thereof; or *abridging the freedom of speech*, or *of the press*; or the right of the people peaceably to assemble, and to petition the Government for a redress of grievances. [Emphasis added]

The New Mexico Constitution contains similar language in Article II, Section 17, while reminding speakers and writers that the right of free speech can be abused:

> Every person may freely speak, write and publish his sentiments on all subjects, being responsible for the abuse of that right; and no law shall be passed to restrain or abridge the liberty of speech or of the press. In all criminal prosecutions for libels, the truth may be given in evidence to the jury; and if it shall appear to the jury that the matter charged as libelous is true and was published with good motives and for justifiable ends, the party shall be acquitted.

Of particular interest in the state constitution is the mention of libel, the branch of the law that allows victims of printed or broadcast defamatory content to bring civil suits against the media. The state constitution talks about truth as a defense, but truth can be a difficult matter to prove in a court of law. Of more practical use to journalists is the well-known federal-court decision in *New York Times v. Sullivan*. In the 9 to 0 Sullivan decision, Justice Brennan wrote that the standard for proving libel against a public official was higher than that of a private citizen. In their position as a public servant, officials cannot recover damages for libel "unless he proves that the [defamatory falsehood] was made ... with knowledge that it was false or with reckless disregard of whether it was false or not ..." This protects the ability of the press to operate as a critical body. By setting the public officials' ability to sue for libel at a higher standard, Sullivan allows the press to criticize the government without fear of being charged with libel so long as a reasonable attempt is made to find if a criticism is true.

Libel laws aside, some journalists contend that the First Amendment provides the legal basis for today's media to stand apart from government, independent and free. They infer that the broad freedoms provided in the First Amendment are intended to allow the media to function as the fourth, external part of that system of checks and balances intended by the writers of the Constitution when they created the separate legislative, executive, and judicial branches of government. Periodically public officials and others attempt to rein in the media. One of the most famous cases, *Near v. Minnesota*, involved a Minnesota law that allowed courts to stop the publication of newspapers that a single judge found to be "malicious, scandalous or defamatory." The law was used in an effort to silence J. M. Near's paper; although he had a reputation for running a scandal sheet, the move to shut the paper down did not come until it published stories about a corrupt mayor and police chief.[5] When the U.S. Supreme Court ruled in 1931 that the Minnesota law was unconstitutional, the court established a basic doctrine that has endured since. Except in the most extreme cases, such as matters of national security, the First Amendment prohibits "prior restraint," which means telling the press ahead of time what it must not publish.

Another point of constitutional interest concerning the press is the so-called reporters' privilege, in which reporters cannot be forced by a court to reveal the identities of their informants. In the 1960s and 1970s, the instances of reporters asserting this privilege increased markedly, leading to a Supreme Court case, *Branzberg v. Hayes* (408 US 665 [1972]). In this case, a reporter (Branzberg) had spent time with some drug users in Kentucky. He wrote an article about their activities, in which he changed their names to protect them. When subpoenaed by a grand jury, he refused to reveal their identities. In a very divisive 5 to 4 decision, the Court found that the reporters' privilege does not exist. In the aftermath, the media's reaction was a resounding condemnation of the Branzberg decision and there were calls for state and federal shield laws to protect this privilege. In response, twenty-six states, including New Mexico, enacted laws or judicial rules protecting this right.

WINDOW ON A DISTANT WORLD

The modern news media have become important players in our culture's political life, especially in big cities and at the state and national levels. The need for some surveillance of the world beyond the range of our own senses has grown with our own country. Because it is physically impossible for most of us to have firsthand knowledge of the actions of Congress, the New Mexico Legislature, or even our local city council and county commission, most citizens settle for news reports about the public officials who affect our lives. The linkage between the mass media and the political world has been recognizable since the media were in their infancies; as was true fifty years ago, offices and meeting rooms at all levels of government are common stopping places when today's journalists make their rounds. The authors of one of the most widely used journalism textbooks in the country cover the basics of government structure and how to read a city budget, because covering government is deemed so essential to the craft of reporting.[6]

From a journalistic perspective, the political world is seen as a public world. Most journalists assume that the public is entitled to know about the actions of public officeholders. Similarly most journalists assume that the public is entitled to know the background of people in public office and of political candidates running for office. However, politicians and government officials do not always share the journalistic view of what meetings and documents should be accessible to the public, so reporters sometimes have to dig laboriously to find the information.

Interestingly, although the U.S. Constitution and the New Mexico Constitution provide for freedom of the press, they only protect the right to publish opinions and to report information that journalists already possess. A journalist's right to gather information is constrained in important ways.

OPEN MEETINGS AND RECORDS

New Mexico, like all other states and the District of Columbia, has open meetings and open records laws.[7] Although journalists usually have led the fight to have such laws adopted and enforced, these "sunshine" laws protect a right of access for all citizens and interest groups, not just the media. The New Mexico Open Meetings Law allows citizens to attend public meetings of government entities at the local and state level, including being present for discussion and voting on matters of public interest. Local school boards are among those bodies covered by the act.

Often to the media's frustration, meetings or parts of meetings are closed under one of several exemptions written into the law. Among the leading exceptions are those meetings or parts of meetings involving certain personnel matters, such as hiring, promotion, or dismissal. Also on the list of exemptions are meetings for discussing the purchase or disposal of real estate or water rights by a public body, strategy sessions related to collective bargaining, and legislation not yet presented to either house of the state legislature. This latter provision has allowed important budget hearings to be closed to the public in the past, but in 1990 the legislative leadership announced that such meetings would be open in the future.

During the 1989 legislative session, lobbyists for New Mexico's broadcasters and publishers succeeded in strengthening the open meetings law. Specifically the law now allows county district attorneys to prosecute meeting-law abuses; in the past only the state attorney general could hear such complaints. Also the fine for violating the open meetings law was increased from $100 to $500, and public bodies were forbidden from breaking down into smaller groups in closed sessions after a quorum of the whole body has been convened.

The New Mexico Open Records Law covers all public records of the state, but exceptions prevent unrestricted access. Among the many exceptions are those records pertaining to physical or mental examinations, children, attorney disciplinary actions, crime-victim reparations, and information declared confidential by other state laws.

One particular weakness of the process, from the viewpoint of journalists trying to meet deadlines, is that no response time is specified under the state's open records law. A majority of states, in contrast, require a public official to respond to an open-records request within a set number of days or a period described as "prompt" or "reasonable."

A potentially explosive area of conflict between media practitioners and public officials arises when a journalist promises confidentiality to a source later considered indispensable to a judicial proceeding. Such a situation brings into sharp focus the conflict between a reporter's obligation to maintain media independence from government and the duty of all citizens to testify at trials and other judicial proceedings, so that justice can be served. In addition, the journalists must consider the more personal problem of standing by their promise to keep secret the identity of a news source.

By 1987, the legislatures in half of the states, including New Mexico, had adopted "shield laws" to protect journalists from testifying against their will in legal proceedings.[8] However, the New Mexico law was struck down by the state Supreme Court, on the grounds that it violated the separation-of-powers doctrine by placing in the hands of the legislature power that properly belonged to the judiciary. Subsequently, the New Mexico Supreme Court adopted a shield "law" as part of its rules of evidence (Rule 514).[9]

Placing the protection of a reporter's sources and notes in a judicial rule instead of in a legislative act makes New Mexico unusual among all the states. As a practical matter, however, any shield provision carries exceptions. In the judicial rule benefiting New Mexico journalists, for example, the protection will be denied if someone wanting to know the identity of a confidential source can convince a judge that the identity of the new source is crucial to a legal proceeding. In short, state judges have the power to decide whether information is so important to a case as to outweigh the need of the media to protect confidentiality.

SETTING AN AGENDA

Researchers can directly observe what stories journalists report, and they can identify the opinions the media express, but it is much more difficult to discover what impact the information and opinions have on people using the media. One of the most promising recent approaches to measuring media influence is called "agenda-setting," an approach originally developed to study the news coverage of presidential politics.

The basic interest of agenda-setting research is to measure whether the mass media influence the personal agendas of members of their audiences. The common approach of researchers is to observe the actual content of the news media in a local area and to identify the issues covered in news reports about political campaigns. The research must take into account differences in agendas reflected in each medium. The media agendas are then compared to what a sample of voters says are the key issues of the campaign.

Agenda-setting studies frequently have found high correlations between the agendas of the media and their audiences, but causation is more difficult to sort out. Studies employing complex statistics strongly suggest that media agendas influence members of media audiences in determining their own agendas of concern, but more research will be needed to sort out the process through which the media influence people and the degree to which the media are important in forming public opinion.

Even though researchers can demonstrate that the media are important sources of information, the media are not the only means available for learning about the political world (or anything else). The personal experiences of people and what they learn from other people are important too. All people evaluate new information in terms of their background understanding of the social and physical worlds, which allows people to put new information into some context and to develop opinions about this new knowledge and its importance.

CROSSING THE MEDIA BRIDGE

Social psychologists have demonstrated convincingly that people are defining animals.[10] They attempt to gather information about the world around them, determine how they should respond to that world, and then act out a response. Each person carries a vast storehouse of definitions previously worked out or learned from someone else. But new information and new events require people to work out new reactions and new responses, or even to replace old definitions with new ones. It is this flexibility of deciding how to respond that inspires political campaigners as they map out their plans for advertising, news releases, and public announcements intended to attract the attention and approval of voters.

Even incumbent politicians can have very little direct, personal contact with a meaningful number of their constituents. City councilors in relatively small communities experience this problem, but it becomes more pronounced for legislators and holders of state and federal offices. To combat this isolation from voters, politicians seek to use the media as what an experienced Santa Fe press officer describes as a "bridge" between their offices and the people of New Mexico. Don Caviness, deputy for public affairs under Governor Garrey Carruthers, said that he used different tactics to accomplish different goals. For example, the broad coverage that the Albuquerque media provide can sometimes be an important tool.

> We have a very nice capital media corps, but they have limited interests and if we had to totally rely on them to get out a message we want out, we couldn't be sure it would happen. You've got mining, agriculture, oil, human services and other programs throughout the state, and any number of programs and agencies that understandably are of limited interested to the capital media corps, whose primary focus is politics. Unless there is some scandal or noteworthy controversial thing happening, they may not be very interested. For example, we think it is neat that the Agriculture Department has helped export 10,000 head of cattle from New Mexico to Mexico, but that kind of thing is of absolutely no interest to the people in Santa Fe in the capital press corps.
>
> You have journalists who specialize. When I worked in the Department of Corrections [as a press officer], if I wanted to make a notification or I wanted to put out whatever, I knew who to call immediately because we interacted constantly. I find in the governor's office that you have people who specialize in mental health or human services or anything else. On a daily basis you may work with five different reporters from the same newspaper, each working on a different story.
>
> Then you also have another interesting phenomenon; for instance if the governor is going to be doing something in Albuquerque, such as giving a talk to the Rotary Club next Thursday, it is necessary to contact the city editor's office to see if they are aware of it, rather than dropping a news release in the box here for the capital reporters, because the Santa Fe people are not going to go down to Albuquerque to cover that story.[11]

Politicians and their staffs use a variety of techniques to get media space.

1. *The news conference.* This approach works best for presidents, governors, and other top officials, including mayors. It gives officials the chance to make an

announcement, but journalists usually try to ask questions also.

2. *The news release.* This is a written announcement of something that officials want journalists to report to their audiences.

3. *The photo opportunity.* This is an approach usually intended to show a high official signing a new bill into law or meeting with another high-ranking official, often one from another country. Presidents tend to garner more coverage through this approach than do any other officials.

4. *The press briefing.* Press secretaries usually conduct briefings. They commonly describe their bosses' reactions to some event or make an announcement on behalf of the boss.

Some newspapers have correspondents covering the capital all year, while others send in reporters only for the annual meeting of the New Mexico Legislature. But the state's smaller newspapers rely on the Associated Press or United Press International and syndicated columnists to provide them with information about events in Santa Fe. In addition to mass-media coverage, several specialized newsletters, some published by trade or professional associations, provide capital coverage for people with a special interest in the workings of government.

MANIPULATING THE IMAGE

One of the most direct means for politicians to convey messages to the public is paid advertising in the mass media. But the high cost of advertising, particularly for a message that a politician wants to go all over New Mexico, often is prohibitive, except during election campaigns, when donated money will pay the costs. Even though the costs are high, most politicians think advertising is vital in campaigns.

"Media determines elections," said Diana Welch, the manager of state Senator Bill Valentine's unsuccessful 1988 campaign to unseat U.S. Senator Jeff Bingaman. "If you can't get your message out to the people, you can't compete. You can only see so many people when you're

stumping, or campaigning in person. Even though you make eye contact with hundreds of people in a parade, they'll know what you look
like, but they won't necessary know what you stand for."[12]

The dominance of television advertising over newspaper advertising
in modern political campaigns was dramatically proven in the Bingaman-
Valentine campaign. Bingaman's total campaign budget was close to
$3 million, but only about $1,300 of that sum was spent on newspaper
ads. Valentine, with a more modest campaign budget, spent no money
on newspaper advertising. At one point in the campaign, Valentine cited
his advisors, who felt that undecided voters watch television rather than
read the newspapers. The latter contention is hotly contested by sources
in the newspaper industry, who cite studies to the contrary.[13]

Campaign advertising in at least one 1988 New Mexico congressional
campaign and in the U.S. presidential race were criticized for containing so many negative attacks by opposing candidates. In New Mexico's
First Congressional District, Republican Steve Schiff and Democrat Tom
Udall used a variety of media formats to attack each other. Schiff used
the help of a California consultant who had earlier worked for the Reagan-
Bush campaign, and Udall hired a New York adviser who was also working for several other Democratic congressional candidates. "Although the
majority of voters understandably don't like negative advertising, it is
proven to work, and we have an extremely tight race," Schiff said during the campaign. "I'm convinced that if he attacks me and I don't
respond, I'll lose."[14] Schiff won his race.

But Larry Calloway, an *Albuquerque Journal* columnist who has covered state government for years, says that a look at recent history in the
state suggests a counterbalancing phenomenon at work:

> Negative campaign advertising doesn't seem to work in New Mexico
> politics because we're small in population and so many voters are per-
> sonally acquainted with the candidates.
>
> When Sen. Joseph M. Montoya ridiculed astronaut Harrison
> Schmitt by comparing him in Spanish to a space monkey, people didn't
> like it, and Montoya lost. When Sen. Schmitt in the next election [1982]
> used TV ads that carelessly associated his opponent with the horror of
> the 1980 penitentiary riot, there was revulsion, and Schmitt lost.

The winner: Jeff Bingaman, gentlemanly former state attorney
general who in his political career has always appeared to be above
attack-dog politics.[15]

Negative advertisement may have played a role in the 2002 gubernatorial election. Both the outgoing Republican governor and lieutenant
governor initially withheld their endorsements from State Representative
John Sanchez, the Republican candidate, over attack ads that he had aired
against Lt. Governor Walter Bradley during the Republican primary election campaign. This party division early in the race, while rectified later
with both Johnson and Bradley lending their support, may have given
Richardson a better chance to court moderates and conservatives, both
groups with potential swing voters. The U.S. congressional races were
also heavily negative. In the Second District, Republican Steve Pearce and
Democrat John Arthur Smith traded shots very early on in a close race.
The First District, where Heather Wilson faced a strong challenge from
Democratic State Senate President Pro Tempore Richard Romero,
descended almost to the point of name-calling at one candidate debate
in Albuquerque. While strongly favored incumbent Senator Pete
Domenici stayed above the attack politics, his Democratic opponent,
Gloria Tristani, attempted to close the wide margin with ads accusing
the veteran senator of being a sellout to Washington politics. Only the
Third District, where Tom Udall ran unopposed, seemed to be immune
to negative advertising.

An *Albuquerque Journal* poll, which it reported on October 17, 2002,
showed that three-quarters of the respondents said that they were turned
off by nasty political attack ads. Why, then, do candidates use them in a
state that seems to punish attackers more than the attacked? In the same
article, Brian Sanderoff, the president of an Albuquerque polling firm,
stated simply that "sometimes they work, despite voters' disdain."

Whether candidates choose to use negative or positive advertising,
the decision on when and where to use it involves major strategic
choices. For example, when Senator Paula Hawkins, R-Florida, ran for
reelection in 1986, she used social security commercials showing her
meeting with President Reagan, a commercial obviously targeted at elderly voters. Campaign workers found that 80 percent of the people over
the age of fifty-five in the most populated areas of the state would see

a commercial if it were aired at the same time on three Miami television stations, a concept known as "roadblocking." Even people who browse among several channels are likely to get the message with such an approach.[16]

Other candidates have used computers in a "punch-and-counter-punch" strategy to provide quick reaction to an opponent's attacks.

> If a candidate makes a point, "a punch," during a speech covered by
> TV's 10 O'Clock News, an opponent can "small-sample" survey target
> voters within hours, produce an appropriate message for the next
> morning's "counter punch" in time for the wire services, morning TV
> newscasts, radio and probably the "bull dogs" of the PM newspapers.
> Depending on deadlines, some AM papers may even have a full-text
> news release with appropriate "counter punch" quotes.[17]

INJECTING OPINIONS

In New Mexico and throughout the country in the nineteenth century, newspapers commonly were aligned with political parties and run by editors with political ambitions. Newspaper content unabashedly reflected party bias, a condition perhaps exaggerated in New Mexico because of its territorial status. One researcher has concluded:

> The adventurous journalists of the pre-railway era were by nature
> opportunists, men who, because of the extreme poverty of New
> Mexico, sought through journalism the rewards of politics. As a
> necessary corollary, the political affiliations of the journalists of a
> dependency such as New Mexico changed with the changing fortunes
> of the national political parties, for national power controlled
> territorial political rewards.[18]

Today when newspapers tend to be local monopolies independent of political-party control, some observers have waxed nostalgic about the competition fostered during the party-press era. But New Mexico press historian Porter Stratton says that New Mexico's citizens were ill served in those days, because papers presented political propaganda rather than the true issues of territorial life, and because most readers subscribed only to the paper reinforcing their own prejudices.[19]

By the turn of the century, New Mexico newspapers were gaining circulation and advertising and coincidentally the independence that has been associated with the press right down to the present. Yet despite the often-heard claim that the modern news media seek to be objective providers of fact, many news organizations serve up opinions, both direct and indirect, along with their facts. Two media researchers offer this brief example:

> *Time* magazine's choice of words to describe three presidents of the United States systematically painted very different pictures of those men. Never reticent at expressing its feelings and opinions of those in the news, *Time* subtly played on the connotative meanings of words to convey its interpretations and images of Harry S. Truman, Dwight D. Eisenhower, and John F. Kennedy. The magazine's choice of adjectives, adverbs and synonyms for the verb "said" conveyed consistent connotative messages during each administration. *Time's* negative feelings about Truman were conveyed in such words and phrases as: "said curtly," "barked Harry S. Truman," "grinning slyly," and "petulant, irascible President." In contrast, Eisenhower "said with a happy grin," "chatted amiably," "said warmly," and "paused to gather thought." Finally, there was the neutral handling of Kennedy, who in the pages of *Time* for the most part simply "said," "announced," and "concluded."[20]

The media may reflect their biases in other ways. For example, the manner in which a television news story is presented may influence the way viewers respond to it.[21] And even the facial expressions of a television newscaster may sway some voters.[22] The political scientist Michael Parenti suggests that media biases have important outcomes:

> Candidates learn that if they take a stand on controversial issues, the press is less likely to get their position across to the public than to concentrate on the controversy arising from the position taken. Suddenly their judgment and suitability will be called into question. So rather than the press using its coverage to fit the campaign, candidates trim their campaigns in anticipation of coverage. In the act of reporting on political life, the media actively help shape it.[23]

Some news organizations, especially newspapers, express their opinions directly by endorsing the candidates they think are best suited for the job. In New Mexico newspapers have a long history of candidate endorsements. Research suggests that for about half of New Mexico's newspapers, the publisher (who often is the owner of the paper) makes the decision about who to endorse; another 29 percent of publishers make the choice jointly with the editor of the paper, who usually is a professional journalist and does not own stock in the paper. An editorial board makes the decision for 14 percent of papers, and the editor makes the choice alone for 7 percent.[24]

Because of its statewide circulation, the *Albuquerque Journal*'s endorsements traditionally draw attention and comment. Whether the *Journal*'s endorsements make any difference is a matter of conjecture. For example, of the four races at the top of the ballot (president, U.S. senator, governor, and U.S. representative) the *Journal* endorsed twenty-three winners and nine losers from 1966 through 1988. Yet if one looks at the governor's race alone, the paper managed to endorse only one winner (Garrey Carruthers) in the seven races during that time. If the governor's race is an indicator of a newspaper's political power in a state, then the *Albuquerque Journal* would not seem to be an important player at that level of New Mexico politics. However, the explanation may be simply that the *Journal*'s political views, at least as expressed in editorials, are more conservative than those of the majority of voters. During the twenty-two-year span in which endorsements were examined, the *Journal* backed twenty-six Republicans and only six Democrats for the top four races on the ballot, although the state has a strong Democratic tradition.

Although a study of California papers suggests that editorial endorsements in statewide races and in plebiscites in propositions may have little or no effect, two different studies in New Mexico suggest that newspaper endorsements are important in mayoral elections.[25] The race for mayor of Albuquerque attracted thirty-three candidates to a nonpartisan election in May of 1974, after voters decided to end the council-manager form of government and replace it with a mayor-council structure. Paul Hain, a University of New Mexico political scientist who said that the situation would maximize the impact of an editorial endorsement, estimated that endorsements of the same candidate by the city's two daily newspapers increased by 5 to 7 percent the number of votes the candidate received.[26]

In another study, journalism professor Sean McCleneghan found that newspaper endorsements were the most important of ten variables in deciding which candidates won fourteen mayoral races in the state. Although endorsements were the most important, McCleneghan also found that four other media-related variables ranked in the top ten: newspaper coverage was second, newspaper advertising was fifth, television advertising was eighth, and television news coverage was tenth. Other important variables included incumbency, local economic conditions, campaign spending, voter turnout, and the candidate's gender.[27]

SUMMARY

This chapter has drawn on a variety of evidence to indicate that the news media play important roles in the political process in New Mexico. They inform voters through news reports and advertising, and many voters look to the political endorsements of candidates by newspapers for guidance in voting for candidates.

In fact, information on politics and government is among the most widely read news that newspapers carry. Media coverage of election campaigns and the conduct of government officials while in office provide most people with information they would not get in any other way, because most of the everyday work of politicians is beyond the view of voters. News reports can put an issue on the public agenda and keep it there.

The Albuquerque news media, which extend coverage to much of the state, are useful tools for candidates seeking state office, because they simplify media buying decisions. But the high cost of the big-city media price the Albuquerque newspapers and broadcast stations out of many local races.

The uneasy state of codependence between politicians and the media is likely to continue into the foreseeable future. Government and political matters always have been deemed the bread and butter of the news business, covered extensively by the media and followed extensively by media audiences. For their part political figures need the media to reach the public, whether for purposes of relaying important information on governmental matters or for reaching potential voters during election campaigns. Fortunately, in recent years the conflicts arising from this arrangement have not reached the degree of animosity they did during the first quarter of the century, when renowned *Albuquerque Tribune* editor Carl Magee was provoked to shoot a political adversary, a district judge, killing a bystander in the process.[28]

Nevertheless, the government and the media are two institutions that have grown increasingly powerful in recent times; even though they often seem to reinforce one another in pursuing mutually advantageous ends, these giants frequently collide, and doubtless will continue to do so, over such conflicts as access to information, campaign coverage, and the role of media polls and advertising.

NOTES

1. Leo Bogart, *Press and Public: Who Reads What, When, Where and Why in American Newspapers*, 2d ed. (Hillsdale, N.J.: Lawrence Ehrlbaum Associates, 1989).

2. Brian S. Brooks, George Kennedy, Daryl R. Moen, and Don Ranly, *News Reporting and Writing*, 3d ed. (New York City: St. Martin's Press, 1988), pp. 454–55.

3. Bernard Cohen, *The Press and Foreign Policy* (Princeton, N.J.: Princeton University Press, 1963), p. 13.

4. Maxwell McCombs, "Agenda-Setting Research: A Bibliographic Essay," *Political Communication Review* 1, no. 3 (Summer 1976), p. 3.

5. Thomas L. Tedford, *Freedom of Speech in the United States* (New York: Random House), pp. 327–29.

6. Brooks et al., *News Reporting*, pp. 454–55.

7. *New Mexico Statutes Annotated* (1978), Sect. 10–15–1 to 10–15–4 and Sect. 14–2–1 to 14–2–3.

8. Brooks et al., *News Reporting and Writing*, pp. 454–55.

9. "*New Mexico Rules of Evidence*," Sec. 11–514, N.M.S.A. 1978, as amended.

10. George Herbert Mead, *Mind, Self and Society: From the Standpoint of a Social Behaviorist*, ed. Charles W. Morris (Chicago: University of Chicago Press, 1934); and Erving Goffman, *The Presentation of Self in Everyday Life* (Garden City, N.Y.: Anchor, 1959).

11. Telephone interview October 1988; notes in author's possession.

12. John Robertson, "Valentine Aide Thinks Poll Missed TV Campaign," *Albuquerque Journal*, Oct. 11, 1988, p. D-3.

13. *Shop Talk* (New Mexico Press Association) 57, no. 11 (November 1988), p. 2.

14. Ellen Marks, "Candidates Accentuate the Negative," *Albuquerque Journal*, Oct. 31, 1988, p. A1.

15. Larry Calloway, *Albuquerque Journal*, Oct. 11, 1988, p. A-3.

16. Clark Edwards, "The New Political Machine," *News Computing Journal* (Summer 1988), pp. 43–44.

17. Edwards, "New Political Machine," pp. 44–45.

18.   Porter A. Stratton, *The Territorial Press of New Mexico 1834–1912*
       (Albuquerque: University of New Mexico Press, 1969), p. 7.

19.   Stratton, *Territorial Press of New Mexico*, p. 201.

20.   Maxwell E. McCombs and Lee B. Becker, *Using Communication Theory*
       (Englewood Cliffs, N.J.: Prentice Hall, 1979).

21.   Larry L. Burriss, "How Anchors, Reporters and Newsmakers Affect Recall
       and Evaluation of Stories," *Journalism Quarterly* 64, nos. 2, 3
       (Summer–Autumn 1987), pp. 514–19, 532.

22.   Brian Mullen et al., "Newscasters' Facial Expressions and Voting Behavior of
       Viewers: Can a Smile Elect a President?" *Journal of Personality and Social
       Psychology* 51, no, 2 (1986), pp. 291–95.

23.   Michael Parenti, *Inventing Reality: The Politics of the Mass Media* (New York:
       St. Martin's Press, 1986).

24.   Ruth Ann Ragland, "How Mayor Candidates Seek Endorsements in New
       Mexico," *Journalism Quarterly* 64, no. 1 (Spring 1987), pp. 199–202.

25.   Kenneth Rystrom, "Apparent Impact of Endorsements by Group and
       Independent Newspapers," *Journalism Quarterly* 64, nos. 2, 3
       (Summer–Autumn 1987), pp. 449–53, 532.

26.   Paul L. Hain, "How an Endorsement Affected a Non-Partisan Mayoral Vote,"
       Journalism Quarterly 52, no. 2 (Summer 1975), pp. 337–40.

27.   J. Sean McCleneghan, "New Mexico Newspapers and Mayoral Elections,"
       Journalism Quarterly 60, no. 4 (Winter 1983), pp. 725–28.

28.   Susan Ann Roberts, "The Political Trials of Carl C. Magee," *New Mexico
       Historical Review* 50, no. 4 (October 1975), p. 306.

Chapter Ten

The Fiscal Structure

INTRODUCTION AND OVERVIEW

This chapter provides a comprehensive overview of the state's fiscal structure and pertinent issues and policies. It reviews recent revenue and expenditure data in a comparative framework and discusses the constitutional and statutory provisions that govern the state budget as well as debt issuance.[1]

The chapter begins with a section on New Mexico's tax structure including some of the issues that have arisen recently with regard to taxation as well as reforms that have been enacted. This discussion is followed by sections presenting major state government funds, state budget process, state government recurring spending, state capital spending and debt policies, and local government finance.

THE TAX STRUCTURE

Three sources provided 81 percent of total state and local taxes collected in New Mexico in fiscal year 2002: sales and gross receipts taxes (48 percent), income taxes (22 percent), and property taxes (11 percent).[2] Most states depend on these same taxes, but there are significant differences among states as to their relative importance in producing revenues. Such differences may be attributed to the various states' economic circumstances, politics, and historical tax structure. Also, unlike all but a few

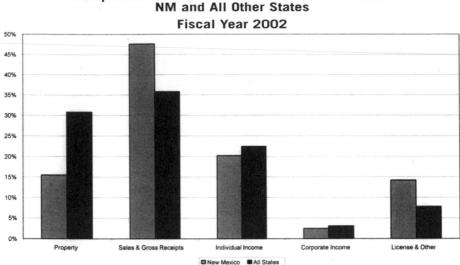

FIGURE 10.1
**Comparison of State and Local Revenues Shares:
NM and All Other States**
Fiscal Year 2002

states, New Mexico collects a significant share of revenues from taxes, rents, and royalties on mineral production. Figure 10.1 compares New Mexico's tax structure with the averages for all other states.

GROSS RECEIPTS TAX

In FY 2002 New Mexico governments raised slightly less than half (47.6 percent) of tax revenues from general sales (gross receipts) and selective excise taxes (such as those on cigarettes, gasoline, and alcohol). New Mexico relies more heavily on sales taxes than most states, ranking eighth highest in the country for the percentage of revenues from this source.[3] New Mexico is one of a handful of states that impose the sales tax on a wide range of services as well as goods. There are several benefits to imposition of sales taxes on services. Taxing services may tend to make this tax less regressive than many states' sales tax systems, since upper-income families spend relatively more on services. Furthermore, because services are a growing sector of the general economy, the New Mexico gross receipts tax is relatively elastic compared to many states' sales tax systems. New Mexico gross receipts tax revenues grow at a rate nearly proportional to overall state economic growth. Finally, gross receipts tax revenues tend to be less sensitive to the business cycle than a tax on goods alone.

Although sales taxes continue to be a key part of the tax structure, the state is somewhat less dependent on this revenue source than in the past. In recent years, several goods and services have been exempted from gross receipts taxes, contributing to the decline in importance of this revenue source. Prescription drugs were exempted in the 1990s; food and some medical services were exempted in 2004; and, in 2005, the state enacted a "back-to-school" gross receipts tax holiday for school-related items such as school supplies, clothing, shoes, and computers. The elimination of the gross receipts tax on food was accompanied by an increase in the overall gross receipts tax rate to make up foregone revenue.

A remaining, unresolved gross receipts tax policy issue is the taxation of business services. Taxing inputs results in a "pyramiding" effect that can put some businesses at a disadvantage with competitors from other states where such inputs are not taxed. While this issue is of keen interest to the business community and political leaders, an immediate fix may prove difficult because the revenue loss implied would be large. In 2005, the legislature provided a gross receipts tax credit to partially address this issue.

Property Taxes

In fiscal year 2002, the property tax accounted for only 15.5 percent of total tax revenues in New Mexico, about half the 30.8 percent share in the average state. New Mexico ranks forty-ninth among the states in the share of revenues from property taxes. In 1981, after the so-called Big Mac tax cut, the property tax in New Mexico largely became a local government revenue source, funding both general operations and capital outlay. This low utilization of the property tax is mainly due to a constitutional provision (Article 7, Section 2) that limits the property tax for operational purposes to 20 mills (one mill equals one one-thousandth of a dollar of assessed property value). The 20 mills are divided between counties (11.85), municipalities (7.65) and school districts (0.50). The constitutional provision was passed during the 1930s, at the same time that the gross receipts tax was enacted. The New Mexico Supreme Court has ruled that assessed value should be uniform throughout the state, at one-third of market value. Thus the 20 mills represent 2 percent of one-third of market value, resulting in an effective tax rate of two-thirds of 1 percent. Notably, many local governments do not impose the maximum rate.

Personal Income Taxes

Personal income tax revenues have grown rapidly during the past two decades in New Mexico. In fiscal year 2002, this tax represented 20 percent of total New Mexico taxes, up from 15 percent in 1989 and just 5 percent in FY 1978. However, New Mexico still relies less on the personal income tax than most other states (see Figure 10.1). As of 2002, New Mexico ranked thirty-fifth among the states in the percentage of revenues from state personal income taxes. In 2000, individual income taxes per capita in New Mexico were $484, ranking thirty-seventh among all states. While these rankings indicate that the state's income tax rates are competitive, some business and political leaders contend that the state's top tax rate placed the state at a competitive disadvantage in the battle for economic development. As of 2003, the state's top personal income tax rate was 8.1 percent, the eighth highest in the country. In response to these concerns and at the urging of the governor, the legislature passed legislation significantly reducing income tax rates over a five-year period in 2003. The phased-in rate reform gradually reduces the top marginal tax rate from 8.1 percent in 2003 to 4.9 percent in 2008. Once the rate reductions are fully implemented, the state's ranking can be expected to drop below the median top rate for all states, which stood at 6 percent in 2003. Historically, New Mexico's personal income tax has been very progressive and responsive to increases in income, growing faster than personal income. The newly enacted tax rate reductions will make the tax both less progressive and less elastic. Nevertheless, the income tax can be expected to continue to grow at a little faster rate than personal income.

Severance Taxes/Rents and Royalties

Another major revenue source for the state is taxes, rents, and royalties on natural resources, primarily crude oil, natural gas, and coal. These revenues constitute a significant share of state general fund revenues, and are a major source for the state's capital investment program. Energy related revenues are a blessing and a curse for state budgets. They are beneficial in that these revenues allow the state to impose relatively low

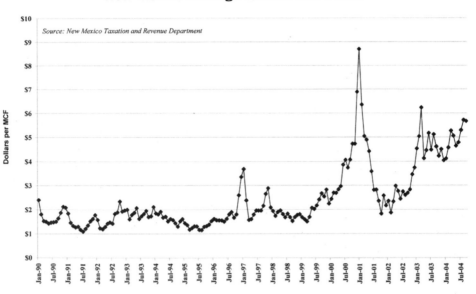

FIGURE 10.2
New Mexico Average Natural Gas Prices

Source: New Mexico Taxation and Revenue Department

tax rates on individuals, as well as to avoid the worst of the budget crises that confronted many states in recent years. They are problematic because they are volatile and difficult to forecast. The base for these revenues is the value of production less deductions for royalties and transportation costs. Sharp swings in prices affect values and thus revenues. The graph of natural gas prices shown in Figure 10.2 illustrates historical volatility.

In fiscal year 1982 energy related revenues brought $993 million to New Mexico; by 1990 these had declined to $424 million. Recent increases in energy prices have led to large revenue increases in the past couple years. In fiscal year 2004, energy related revenues to state and local governments totaled $1.3 billion. The varying shares of state general fund revenues from these revenues again illustrate their volatile nature. In fiscal year 1999, energy related revenues distributed to the general fund totaled $280 million or 8.8 percent of total revenues. Two years later, these revenues contributed $769 million to the general fund, or 19.1 percent total revenue. Figure 10.3 summarizes the state's general fund revenue sources.

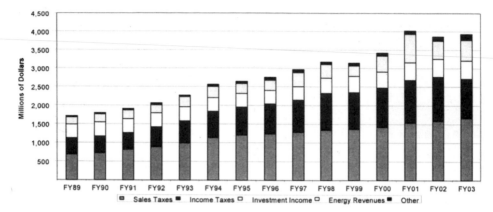

FIGURE 10.3
State General Fund Revenues by Major Source

FUND STRUCTURE OF STATE GOVERNMENT

Article IV, Section 30, of the New Mexico Constitution provides that "money shall be paid out of the treasury only upon appropriations made by the legislature." Appropriations are made and accounted by fund. There are approximately one thousand funds in the state treasury, many authorized by statute, others established by the Department of Finance and Administration. Figure 10.4 presents the most important state funds.

The general fund is the state's principal operating fund. It receives most state tax revenue, investment income from the two permanent funds and shared federal mineral royalties and provides funding for most state agencies and universities and public schools. For fiscal year 2004 general fund appropriations for recurring operations were $4.127 billion. The second biggest operating fund is the Road Fund with fiscal year 2004 appropriations of $635 million, which receives gasoline and diesel taxes, weight distance taxes, and vehicle registration fees. Road fund revenues are dedicated to maintenance and construction of roads. Other state funds accounted for approximately $1.5 billion of fiscal year 2004 appropriations for such purposes as game protection, risk management, boards and commissions, and water resources management. In addition in fiscal year 2004, the state received approximately $4 billion of federal funds for operations.

FIGURE 10.4
Overview of New Mexico Finances: FY 04

(Millions of dollars)

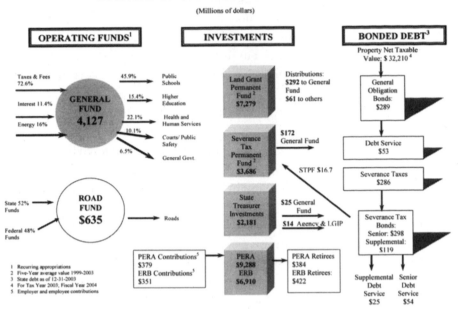

Pursuant to the Ferguson Act enacted by Congress in 1898 and the state constitution of 1912, federal land was conveyed to the state of New Mexico to benefit twenty public institutions (see Article XIV, Sections 1 and 2). A significant share of the state's oil and gas resources occurs on these state lands and royalties from production are deposited in the Land Grant Permanent Fund (LGPF). As shown in Figure 10.4, average assets of the LGPF have grown to more than $7 billion. Eighty-three percent of LGPF investment income is distributed to the general fund for public schools—$292 million in fiscal year 2004. (An important 1996 constitutional amendment eased restrictions on investment in stocks and modernized the distribution method for beneficiaries.)

Article VIII, Section 10, of the Constitution of New Mexico, adopted in 1976, provides for some severance taxes, again mostly on oil and gas production. These revenues are dedicated to pay debt service on severance tax bonds, with revenue in excess of that needed to pay debt service transferred to the Severance Tax Permanent Fund (STPF). The State Investment Council invests STPF funds. A portion of the fund

(4.7 percent of the average five-year value) is transferred to the general fund. STPF balances reached $3.6 billion, generating $172 million for the general fund in fiscal year 2004.

Other major state investment funds include the Public Employees and Educational Retirement Funds with fiscal year 2004 assets of approximately $16 billion and state treasurer's investments of approximately $2 billion.

Finally, Figure 10.4 shows the state's two major capital outlay/bonding programs. Article IX, Section 8, of the New Mexico Constitution authorizes issuance of General Obligation (GO) bonds backed by property taxes up to 1 percent of the state's net assessed valuation. On December 31, 2003, $288.5 million in GO bonds were outstanding. Also, severance taxes discussed above are deposited in the Severance Tax Bonding Fund for debt service on severance tax bonds; $416 million were outstanding on December 31, 2003. Over the last decade legislation gradually expanded the use of severance tax revenue for debt service from 50 percent of total severance tax revenue to 95 percent. Surplus severance tax revenues not needed for debt payments are transferred to the Severance Tax Permanent Fund.

THE NEW MEXICO APPROPRIATION PROCESS AND ACCOUNTABILITY IN GOVERNMENT ACT

In New Mexico, the appropriation process officially begins in mid-June when the state Budget Division of the Department of Finance and Administration sends budget request instructions to state agencies. As part of their request, agencies are required to provide information such as actual and anticipated revenues and actual and anticipated expenditures from all sources for the previous fiscal year, the current fiscal year, and a budget request for the next fiscal year, as well as other information such as an organizational chart, strategic plan, and information technology plan. Agencies submit their budget requests no later than September 1 to both Department of Finance and Administration and Legislative Finance Committee.

The Legislative Finance Committee is an interim committee of the legislature charged with examining the laws governing the finances and operations of departments, agencies, and institutions of New Mexico and with reviewing the policies, costs, and effect of laws on the functioning of governmental units.

New Mexico is fairly unique in that both the governor and the Legislative Finance Committee propose a comprehensive state budget to the full legislature. The dual executive and legislative recommendations help to ensure a system of checks and balances and to incorporate the different perspectives of the two branches into the budget process.

From September through December, both State Budget Division and Legislative Finance Committee staffs analyze agency budget requests and develop the governor's and Legislative Finance Committee budget recommendations. Also during this time, economists from the Legislative Finance Committee, Department of Finance and Administration, the Taxation and Revenue Department, and Department of Transportation develop a consensus general fund revenue estimate. Like most states, New Mexico must balance its budget each year without incurring a deficit (see Article IX, Section 7, of the New Mexico Constitution). To provide a buffer against unexpected revenue shortfalls or expenditure overruns, the state maintains a reserve that has been traditionally set at about 5 percent of recurring revenues. In years when the revenue estimate seems particularly prone to risk and sufficient revenues are available, reserve balance targets have been increased to as much as 9 percent.

State law requires the governor to submit a budget to the Legislative Finance Committee and each member of the legislature no later than January 5 in even-numbered years and no later than January 10 in odd-numbered years. The Legislative Finance Committee finalizes its budget recommendations in December.

On the first day of the legislative session, the executive Budget in Brief and the Legislative Finance Committee Budget Recommendations are made public. Simultaneously, the General Appropriation Act, also known as the "state budget," is introduced in the House of Representatives. Typically, the introduced version of the General Appropriation Act represents the governor's budget recommendations in summary by agency. The House Appropriations and Finance Committee and Senate Finance Committee are the primary entities that shape the state budget for the coming fiscal year. If the budgets passed by each House differ, a conference committee is appointed and determines the final version.

The governor may sign the General Appropriation Act, veto it, or make item vetoes in the bill (Article IV, Section 22, of the New Mexico Constitution). Following a veto of the General Appropriations Act in 2002, in unprecedented action, the legislature convened itself and overrode a governor's budget veto for the first time in state history.

It should be noted that not all appropriations are made through a single bill. Article IV, Section 16, of the New Mexico Constitution limits the appropriations in the General Appropriation Act to those expenses "required under existing law." For example, various one-time capital outlay projects or tax bills that might generate additional revenue will not be included in the General Appropriation Act.

Following passage of the General Appropriation Act, agencies are required to submit their plan (or operating budget) on how they will spend funds appropriated on or before May 1 to the State Budget Division. The Legislative Finance Committee also receives a copy of the agency operating budget.

Accountability in Government Act

The state adopted the Accountability in Government Act in 1999 to place greater emphasis on results. The primary feature of the Accountability in Government Act is implementation of performance-based budgeting, requiring that agencies submit performance-based budget requests with targeted levels of performance. Select performance measures and corresponding targets are included in the General Appropriation Act immediately following program appropriations. Already, a few agencies have been able to improve the link from their budget to performance. For example, the Children, Youth and Families Department used data to show the benefits of the department's efforts on rehabilitation as opposed to incarceration. Higher education institutions used "gap analysis," the difference between their current performance and comparative group performance, to develop action plans to address improvements and to develop realistic performance targets.

Recent efforts have sought to focus on key measures for large agencies, improve the quality of measures, and implement quarterly reporting of agency performance. In the near future, agency quarterly performance reports will be available on state Web sites.

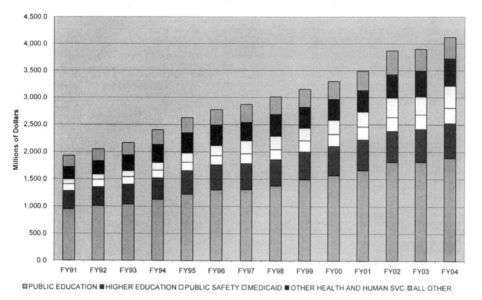

FIGURE 10.5
General Fund Appropriation by Major Function

☐PUBLIC EDUCATION ■HIGHER EDUCATION ☐PUBLIC SAFETY ☐MEDICAID ■ OTHER HEALTH AND HUMAN SVC. ☐ALL OTHER

STATE GOVERNMENT EXPENDITURES

The first priority of state government spending for operations in New Mexico is education. Figure 10.5 shows general fund recurring appropriation trends over the past several years. Public schools and higher education recurring appropriations represent 61 percent of the total in FY 2005. The next largest component of general fund recurring expenditures is health and welfare, with the Medicaid program driving spending growth. The public safety budget is about 6.5 percent of the state's recurring budget. Combined, the legislative, judicial, general government, commerce and industry, agriculture, and energy categories represent only about 10 percent of the state's budget.

PUBLIC SCHOOLS

There are eighty-nine school districts in New Mexico, ranging in size from Mosquero, with an average daily membership (ADM) of less than 50 to Albuquerque, with an ADM of 87,909 in New Mexico. Statewide public school enrollment in the 2005–6 school year was 316,243.

The state provides nearly all funding for school operations, with funding levels determined by the public school funding formula as specified in state statute. The present state education distribution formula for public schools was enacted in 1974, with several significant modifications made since that time. The state's public school funding formula emphasizes a policy that all students are entitled to an "equal educational opportunity." The formula focuses on funding enrollment plus fixed costs. This approach is commonly referred to as the "cost of opening the doors." Approximately 90 percent of school districts' operational revenue is derived from the state equalization guarantee (SEG) appropriation; New Mexico typically ranks among the lowest in the nation for its percentage of school funds from local sources. A school district's SEG is the amount of money the state guarantees to provide equal access to programs and services appropriate to their educational needs regardless of geographic location or local economic conditions. School districts have the discretion to spend their formula dollars according to local priorities. However, they must comply with statutory requirements and relevant directives from the Public Education Department. In calculating the SEG, the state takes credit for 75 percent of property tax revenues, federal forest reserve revenues, and certain operational federal impact aid fund revenues received by the school district.

The formula begins with a basic unit of education equal to 1.0. However, due to adjustments made over the years, all but one student category has a different weighting factor. For instance, pupils in kindergarten have a factor of 1.44, and grades seven through twelve are given a weight of 1.25, respectively implying costs of education equal to 44 and 25 percent higher than for a basic unit. Additional weights are added for special education classes, bilingual education, fine arts education, at-risk students, and special factors for school and district size and rural isolation. Finally, additional weight is given to both the experience and formal education of the faculty. The weighted ADMs of various schools in a district are then added together to obtain a total for the school district. Currently the formula results in an average of about 1.9 units per member.

Each year, the state legislature sets a dollar value per weighted ADM and, depending on available general fund revenues and other budget priorities, appropriates funding for public school support. The Secretary of the Public Education Department sets the unit value based on appropriations and estimated program units. A final unit value is determined in January each year based on program units reported by school districts.

As shown in Figure 10.5, state spending on public schools rose from just over $800 million to under $2 billion from 1989 to 2005. Maintaining the share of general fund spending for public schools at 50 percent has been a point of the fiscal policy debate of the state. In recent years, although public schools have received significant, real (inflation adjusted) funding increases, the share has drifted down to about 45 percent, as state spending for Medicaid and other health and human services has increased. However, it can be argued that the 50 percent target is an artificial construct that only superficially measures the state's commitment to education.

In 2003 Article 12, Section 7, of the state constitution was amended to increase distributions from the Land Grant Permanent Fund to designated beneficiaries, with public schools receiving 83 percent of the increased distributions. The annual distribution increased from 4.7 percent to 5 percent of the five-year average of year-end market values of the fund. For fiscal years 2005 through 2012, an additional distribution of eight-tenths of 1 percent (a total of 5.8 percent) and from fiscal years 2013 through 2016, the additional distribution reduces to five-tenths (a total of 5.5 percent). After fiscal year 2017, the distribution remains at 5 percent. This provided an additional distribution to public schools of $67 million in fiscal year 2005.

In 2003, the state adopted the Public School Reform Act to improve teacher quality by implementing a three-tiered licensure program—a progressive career system in which teachers are required to demonstrate increased competencies and undertake increased duties as they progress through three licensure levels and receive compensation increases accordingly. In the first phase, all teachers were provided with a minimum salary of $30,000. In the next phase, qualifying teachers reached levels two and three with associated salaries of $35,000. In July 2005, the minimum salaries for these teachers will be $40,000. In subsequent years, the minimum for level three teachers will be $50,000. Latest analysis indicates the three-tiered licensure ladder could cost over $100 million when fully implemented with additional costs for retirement contributions.

Also, in part due to the federal No Child Left Behind Act of 2001 (NCLB), there has been increased focus on student progress and on successful schools. For fiscal year 2005, the Public Education Department released the final assessments of public schools under NCLB and the New Mexico School Reform Act. For the 2003–4 school year, 521 schools made adequate yearly progress, while 244 did not. Particularly worrisome, only 45 percent of the state's high schools made adequate yearly progress.

HIGHER EDUCATION

Public, postsecondary education in New Mexico consists of three research universities, three comprehensive universities, nine branch community colleges, and eight independent community colleges. There are also three public special schools. Total fall 2002 enrollment was 113,650 students, of which 55 percent attended community colleges and 45 percent attended universities. Of total degrees awarded in the 2001–2 academic year, just under 64 percent of associate's degrees were awarded to women, while nearly 60 percent of bachelor's and graduate degrees were awarded to women.

In most states, higher education funding has fallen due to declining statewide revenues; however, New Mexico spending on higher education has remained strong compared to national trends. As shown in Figure 10.5, over the last fifteen years state general fund recurring spending for higher education has increased from the high $200 million to the high $600 million level. Over the same time period, the share of general fund recurring expenditures on higher education has drifted slightly downward from about 17 percent to about 15 percent. In 2002, New Mexico ranked in the top five nationally for state and local spending for higher education on a per capita basis as well as on a percentage of general spending basis.

In contrast to public schools, the funding formula for higher education is not contained in statute. Rather, various laws direct the Commission on Higher Education to develop a funding formula and provide general guidance on the state's priorities. In 2002, a blue ribbon task force modified the state's higher education funding formula by developing a simple "base-plus-incentive" funding model to determine an institution's base expenditure level. The model begins with the current appropriation, which recognizes increases or decreases in workload driven by enrollment changes and the mix of courses offered. Formula-generated transfers, such as building renewal and replacement, equipment renewal and replacement and 3 percent scholarships, are added, then revenue credits, such as land and permanent fund, mill levy, and tuition revenue credit, are subtracted. The formula adjusts for compensation increases and recognizes changes in fixed costs such as utilities, library acquisitions, health insurance, and risk management premiums. This model is similar to the public school funding formula that is based on the basic costs to "open the doors." The model is largely input driven, although the task force recommended five incentive funds to address other components of institutional missions. One of these funds, the Performance Fund, is intended to offer performance awards to institutions based on achieving targeted outcomes.

In 2005, the Commission on Higher Education was replaced by a cabinet agency, the Department of Higher Education.

HEALTH AND HUMAN SERVICES

As shown in Figure 10.5, health and human services programs have grown significantly in the last fifteen years, driven significantly by increasing Medicaid costs. As is the case in many other states, eligibility demands and changes in federal Medicaid policy put strong pressures on state spending. Total general fund recurring spending for health and human services has risen from over $200 million to about $1 billion over the last fifteen years or from about 15 percent of recurring spending to about 23 percent.

The Medicaid program has shown dramatic growth in recent years as reflected in Figure 10.5; total expenditures (state and federal matching funds) increased from $1.5 billion in fiscal year 2001 to $2.7 billion in fiscal year 2006, driven primarily by increased costs for care, increased utilization of services, prescription drugs, new technologies, and growing enrollments, particularly in the state's implementation of home-based personal care services. Changes in the share of cost paid by the federal government (the federal medical assistance percentage rate) create uncertainty in state funding requirements for the program from year to year.

Within the other health and human services category, an important program is the Temporary Assistance for Needy Families program, which replaced the federal Aid to Families with Dependent Children program with the enactment of welfare reform. The new program is financed largely with a federal block grant. However, states must demonstrate that they have maintained state funding at a level at least equal to that prior to welfare reform. This so-called maintenance of effort is presently about $32 million for New Mexico. Other programs in this category include services to the developmentally disabled, behavioral health services, juvenile justice, child care, foster care, and adoption responsibilities.

PUBLIC SAFETY

The public safety component of general fund appropriations mostly goes to the Department of Corrections and the Department of Public Safety. The Corrections budget is driven by inmate population growth that had surged due to annual increases above 5 percent. More recently, inmate population growth has slowed, due to alternative sentencing considerations.

OTHER

While appropriations to other categories have increased over time, these components have remained relatively stable as a percentage of total general fund recurring spending. The other components of state government spending are small in relation to the total operating budget. Efforts to constrain spending within these components result in only marginal savings.

CAPITAL OUTLAY AND DEBT

FUNDING SOURCES

Figure 10.6 shows capital outlay appropriations and funding sources for the last five years. Funding ranged from $250 million to $628 million. The principal sources of funding are severance tax bonds, general obligation bonds, and general fund cash. Severance tax bonds are revenue bonds, where revenue from taxes on the value of natural resource extraction, primarily oil and gas, is dedicated to repay bonds. General obligation (GO) bonds are backed by the full-faith and credit of the state and paid for by a statewide property tax levy. Projects financed by GO bonds must be approved by the voters. The general fund and other state funds also are used to pay for capital projects on a cash basis. Revenue from

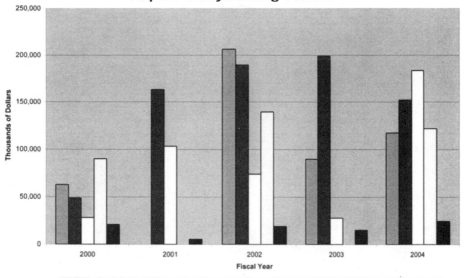

FIGURE 10.6
Capital Outlay Funding Sources

☐ Severance Tax Bonds ■ Supplemental Severance Tax Bonds ☐ General Fund Cash ☐ General Obligation Bonds ■ Other

these sources, however, can be uneven. Roads and other transportation projects are financed from the Transportation Projects and Revenue Enhancement Fund.

In addition to annual appropriations, a continuing appropriation of supplemental severance tax bonds is authorized for public school construction. This program was initiated in the late 1990s due to equity concerns raised in litigation by predominantly Native American school districts. Fiscal year 2004 supplemental severance tax bonds were $152 million, and 2004 awards to districts were $85 million.

STATE DEBT

Outstanding state debt for New Mexico has increased significantly over the past decade, reaching $2.7 billion in 2004, with annual growth averaging about 16 percent (see Figure 10.7). This compares to the national average growth rate of 7 percent. Historically low interest rates, state fiscal downturns, and several large jumbo deals (i.e., pension obligation bonds) have prompted states' and local government's debt issuance to rise rapidly in recent years. Two common ways of measuring debt levels are

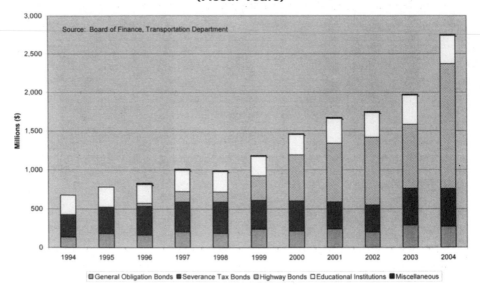

FIGURE 10.7
State of New Mexico Debt Outstanding
(Fiscal Years)

debt per capita and debt as a percentage of personal income. According to a report by a major bond rating agency, New Mexico's net tax-supported per capita debt in 2003 was $962 compared to the national median of $701. New Mexico's net tax-supported debt as a percentage of 2002 personal income was 4.1 percent compared to the national median of 2.4 percent.

New Mexico's GO bonds have grown modestly over the past decade compared to revenue bonds. State transportation bonds account for most revenue bond growth. Starting in 1996, the state's issuance of transportation bonds increased dramatically to build badly needed infrastructure improvements. Secondarily, policy makers saw the increased infrastructure expenditures, accommodated by debt issuance, as a way to further economic development. Innovative financing techniques introduced by the Federal Highway Administration, which included a direct pledge of federal funds for bond repayments, also encouraged the issuance of transportation bonds.

In addition, the legislature has established several revolving loan funds and grant programs to assist local governments with their capital needs by providing zero- and low-interest loans or grants. For example, the New Mexico Finance Authority administers an annual distribution of 75 percent of the state's governmental gross receipts tax deposited into the public project revolving loan fund to make low-cost, low-interest loans for infrastructure, equipment emergency projects to state and other governmental entities, or grants to disadvantaged entities.

LOCAL GOVERNMENT FINANCES

MUNICIPALITIES

There are currently 102 incorporated municipalities in New Mexico, with the distribution by population indicated in Figure 10.8. New Mexico municipalities are very different with respect to size and economic base. Few of the 35 towns with a population of less than 1,000 can be considered to have a strong economic base. Small city fiscal problems are distinct from those faced by large cities such as the city of Albuquerque, with almost 450,000 residents in 2000.

Despite the obvious scale differences, New Mexico law offers very similar financial options to all municipalities. Major sources of revenue for all New Mexico cities are shown in Figure 10.9. The gross-receipts tax, including both the state-shared distribution to cities and the local-option gross-receipts taxes, account for a vast share (over 70 percent in fiscal year 2003) of total local general fund revenues. The statewide gross-receipts tax rate of 5.0 percent includes a 1.225 percent distribution to municipal governments. Prior to January 1, 2005, the state rate was 5.0 percent, but a 0.5 percent credit was provided on goods and services purchased in municipalities, implying an effective rate of 4.5 percent within municipal boundaries. As noted earlier, the credit was ended to offset the revenue loss associated with the elimination of the gross receipts tax on food and certain medical services in 2005.

The state distribution of the 1.225 percent of the statewide gross-receipts tax to municipalities is based on transactions in each municipality. The first local-option municipal gross-receipts tax was authorized in 1955, repealed in 1969, and again authorized in 1975. Currently municipalities may impose a gross-receipts tax of up to 1.25 percent in 0.25 percent increments on top of the effective statewide rate. Over the years,

FIGURE 10.8
New Mexico Incorporated Municipalities by Population, 2000

POPULATION SIZE	NUMBER
Under 1,000	35
1,000–5,000	33
5,000–10,000	15
10,000–25,000	8
Over 25,000	10
TOTAL	**101**

Source: U.S. Bureau of the Census, 2000 Census of Population and Housing.

FIGURE 10.9
Revenues of New Mexico Municipalities, Fiscal Year 2003

GENERAL FUND	IN MILLIONS OF DOLLARS
Property (current)	40.5
Franchise	30.5
Gross Receipts—State Shared	283.5
Gross Receipts—Local Options	199.5
License and Permits	14.9
Gasoline Taxes	3.0
Motor Vehicle	2.2
Small Cities Assistance	2.9
Other	108.1
Subtotal	**685.1**
Correction	41.7
Environmental Gross Receipts	4.4
Fire Protection	7.5
Law Enforcement	8.4
Lodgers' Tax Act	23.6
Municipal Street	31.2
Recreation	6.2
Intergovernmental Grants	153.1
Capital Project Funds	813.6
General Obligation	71.5
Revenue Bonds	7.9
Debt Service Other	19.2
Enterprise Funds	1,433.0
Other Funds	310.7
TOTAL REVENUES	**$3,617.1**

Source: New Mexico Department of Finance and Administration, Financial and Property Tax Data, Fiscal Year 2003 Annual Report.

FIGURE 10.10
New Mexico County Revenues, Fiscal Year 2003

GENERAL FUND	IN MILLIONS OF DOLLARS
Property Tax—Current	193.4
Property Tax—Other	48.5
Gross Receipts Taxes	57.2
Other	68.6
Subtotal	**367.7**
Correction	15.9
Environmental Gross Receipts	11.6
Road Fund	38.5
Fire Protection	14.0
Intergovernmental Grants	9.6
Indigent	37.2
County Fire Protection	10.6
Community DWI Program	6.1
Jail—Detention	6.3
Capital Project Funds	105.0
General Obligation	14.6
Revenue Bonds	9.8
Debt Service—Other	11.8
Enterprise Funds	44.3
Other Funds	125.0
TOTAL	**828.0**

Source: New Mexico Department of Finance and Administration, Financial and Property Tax Data, Fiscal Year 2003 Annual Report.

the state also has authorized various special purpose gross receipts taxes, such as the "quality-of-life" tax in Albuquerque. Special purpose gross receipt taxes often require that municipal governments put the proposed tax increase and use of the proceeds to a vote. Property taxes are the second largest revenue source of municipal revenues, accounting for less than 6 percent of municipal general fund revenues. In short, New Mexico municipalities have an unbalanced revenue structure, and are extremely dependent on a single tax—the gross receipts tax.

Expenditures by New Mexico cities follow the national pattern. Major expenditures support police protection, fire protection, streets, and sanitation. Other services, most importantly water and sewer, often are provided by cities and financed as government enterprises.

COUNTY GOVERNMENTS

There are thirty-three counties in New Mexico, including the Los Alamos city/county. Fiscal Year 2003 revenues are summarized in Figure 10.10. The property tax is the major source of tax revenue for county governments, accounting for about two-thirds of total general fund revenues. In 1983 the county gross-receipts tax was enacted, authorizing counties to impose a gross-receipts tax by ordinance of a maximum of 0.375 percent (in three increments of 0.125 percent). Gross receipts taxes raise about 15 percent of general fund revenues. Proceeds from the first increment can be used for general county purposes. The additional two increments replaced the prior county sales tax, and a portion of the proceeds must be dedicated to indigent health care. There are also a number of limited county local option taxes available for earmarked purposes such as county hospitals and jails. However, these are often limited to specific counties under special circumstances. Counties also received a distribution of the state gasoline tax, which goes to a county road fund. Major expenditures by the counties are for hospitals, streets and roads, and law enforcement.

NOTES

1. This chapter was written by staff from the New Mexico Legislative Finance Committee. Participants included David Abbey, director; Cathy Fernandez, deputy director; Bill Taylor, assistant director; and Arley Williams, Linda Kehoe, Gary Chabot, Mark Weber, David Soherr-Hadwiger, and Olivia Padilla-Jackson. It represents an update of the 1989 version authored by Brian McDonald and Juliana Boyle of the University of New Mexico Bureau of Business and Economic Research and the 1981 chapter authored by Professor Gerald J. Boyle, who passed away in July 1991. LFC staff would like to acknowledge a debt of gratitude on behalf of the entire state to Professor Boyle, for many years a guiding force in New Mexico public finance, who left a lasting imprint by training and helping to place numerous distinguished fiscal professionals with the state, including John Gasparich, John Kormanik, James O'Neill, Aug Narbutus, Charles Turpen, Janet Peacock, and others.

2. U.S. Department of Commerce, *Governmental Finances: FY 2001–02*, Table 1. State and Local Government Finances.

3. Comparative 2004 tax data extracted from CQ's State Fact Funds.

Chapter Eleven

Governing New Mexico's Schools

by David L. Colton and Luciano Baca

Until the middle of the 1900s most Americans believed that their public schools were somehow separate from government and politics. The U.S. Constitution does not mention schools. Schools rarely were the subject of partisan political interest. National political party platforms paid little attention to school issues. Teachers did not see themselves, nor did others see them, as a political interest group; in fact, political activism by teachers was deemed to be "unprofessional." The voting age was twenty-one, so there was no significant student voting bloc. There were no "education presidents" and no "education governors." Of course, local voters regularly went to the polls to elect school board members and to vote on school-tax levies, but such events usually were low-turnout affairs and not issue oriented. Teachers and schools, like mail carriers and post offices, were seen as apolitical service providers; they operated under the auspices of government but were insulated from the political struggles that most people viewed as characteristic of government. Indeed, the politicization of school matters was seen as antithetical to American democratic traditions.

Events of the last half century have forced new views. In 1954, the United States Supreme Court's decision in *Brown v. Topeka Board of Education* made schools the crucibles for overcoming the nation's emotion-laden problem of racism. Sputnik, launched by the Soviet Union in 1957, led American policy makers to look to the schools for the brainpower to combat the Communist threat; a "National Defense Education Act" was quickly approved by Congress. In 1965 President Johnson and the Congress launched a "war on poverty," wherein schools were to become agencies for the eradication of domestic poverty and injustice. In the 1980s, the national agenda shifted from school equity to school excellence. A government report entitled *A Nation at Risk* asserted that dramatically better schools were needed if America was to maintain its international economic competitiveness.[1] Governors and state legislators were exhorted to lead and direct the schools toward better performance. In 1990, "national goals" for education were announced by the White House. By 2000 Congress and the White House had jumped into the education arena with both feet, passing comprehensive education legislation that increased federal funding, imposed education mandates, and established sanctions for mandate violations. Thus, in the course of a few decades, schools lost their apolitical character.

Though the change appears dramatic, what was lost, in fact, was a facade. Educators have been involved in politics and government since the inception of the common-school movement in the mid-nineteenth century.[2] Inspired by their belief that education was the key to individual and social well-being, educators worked with citizens and lawmakers to create an immense public school enterprise in every state.[3] In New Mexico that enterprise today consumes almost half of the legislature's annual general fund appropriation, provides fifty thousand professional and nonprofessional jobs, and enrolls more than 90 percent of the state's school-age youth.[4] In nearly every community, political agendas include school issues: school calendars, hiring, curriculum materials, school locations, school responsiveness, test scores, and athletics. On occasion such issues precipitate major controversies, sometimes resulting in board-recall elections, incumbent defeats, and superintendent turnover. The politics of education are pervasive, as they always have been. In fact, some now argue that democratic control of the schools is excessive; education's problems may be the result of too much government and politics.[5]

This chapter examines the governmental framework in which school politics are played out in New Mexico. That framework is highly fragmented. There are no clear hierarchies of authority, no unifying ideologies or technologies, no fixed boundaries, and no issue-management mechanisms such as political parties. All levels of government are involved in school policy making: national, state, local, and tribal. Educational policy is created in the executive, legislative, and judicial branches of government. Professional groups, citizen groups, and special-interest groups outside of education are heavily involved in shaping school policy. In the first half of the chapter, the formal and informal systems of school governance are described. Three case studies of educational policy making are then presented, illustrating the manner in which these systems work. A concluding section discusses future issues in school governance.

THE FORMAL SYSTEM

Although much of the work of schools is shaped by social norms, by professional educators, and by private interests such as textbook publishers, governmental policies are also significant. The forums for governmental policy making affecting schools are found at national, state, local, and tribal levels.

NATIONAL GOVERNMENT

The national government was a major player in the establishment of New Mexico's public school system. Prior to statehood public schools were a rarity in New Mexico. However, proponents of statehood understood that Congress expected the states to assure the widespread availability of free public education. The Northwest Ordinances of 1785 and 1787 reserved lands for the support of schools in the Northwest Territory and declared that "schools and the means of education" were forever to be encouraged in territories and in the states formed from them. Later legislation extended these principles to western territories, including New Mexico. Writers of the state's constitution in 1910 dutifully provided for the use of school land grants and for the establishment and maintenance of "a uniform system of free public schools."[6]

From 1910 until mid-century, the national government's role in New Mexico education languished, except in the case of Indian education. Then two social upheavals in the 1950s and 1960s precipitated major new education initiatives by the national government. The first was World War II and its aftermath, the Cold War. These events triggered a vast mobilization of war-related labor and industry, producing surges of schoolchildren around military bases and weapons laboratories. These same establishments often nationalized land, removing it from property tax rolls just as school revenue needs increased. To compensate for these nationally instigated disruptions, Congress appropriated "Impact Aid" funds, which provided significant non-categorical revenue (that is, money with few strings attached) to affected districts.[7] Impact aid remains an important source of school revenue in New Mexico, providing from 3 to 4 percent of statewide school operating funds. Impact aid and its distribution has also been the source of a number of school funding disputes.

The second upheaval was the civil rights revolution, which began with the Supreme Court's decision in *Brown* in 1954, and which culminated in the 1960s and 1970s with a broad array of congressional enactments designed to improve educational opportunities for women, minorities, the poor, and the handicapped. In laws such as the Elementary and Secondary Education Act of 1965, the Bilingual Education Act of 1968, the Education of All Handicapped Act of 1975, and the Improving America's Schools Act of 1994, Congress sought to influence local school practice by providing fiscal support contingent upon compliance with federal guidelines and standards. These guidelines and standards were developed and administered by a growing cadre of executive agency officials in the U.S. Department of Education and in regional federal offices.

Although federal aid provides less than 10 percent of the operating revenue of New Mexico schools, state and local officials expend much energy in preparing proposals and in maintaining and monitoring federal programs in areas such as bilingual education, migrant education, vocational education, drug-prevention education, and compensatory education. At times the growth of federal education regulation has provoked resistance. For example, New Mexico's State Board of Education, arguing that federal regulations were excessive, for several years refused to accept federal funds available through Public Law 94–142, the Education for Handicapped Children Act. However, the holdout ended in 1984, when lawsuits and legislative pressure caused the board to change its position.

The growth of federal legislative and executive activism after mid-century was paralleled by the growth of judicial activism. Abandoning their earlier hands-off posture vis-à-vis school issues, a generation of federal judges extended protections established in the Bill of Rights to students and school employees. The Supreme Court set the tone through its reviews of lower court decisions involving free speech, race, gender, and due process issues in schools.[8] Suits filed by New Mexicans sought to capitalize on the new judicial posture.[9] As a result of judicial activism, school district officials, whose discretionary power had previously been limited primarily by custom and by community norms, were confronted by new constitutionally based limitations, often requiring the enactment of new rules involving matters such as student conduct codes, student records, student press, and teachers' rights.

Many educators protested that the growth of legislative, executive, and judicial rules eroded their professional autonomy and local control of the schools. Comparable protests arose in other sectors of American society. Exploiting these complaints, the Reagan administration sought to de-emphasize federal regulation, and to curb the national government's domestic spending. Several federally funded programs were consolidated, and the rate of growth in federal support for education subsided.[10] An era of national government exhortation began. With the U.S. Department of Education publication of *A Nation at Risk* in 1983, and the subsequent pronouncements of Education Secretary William Bennett (who viewed his position, in the style of Teddy Roosevelt, as a "bully pulpit"), the federal government sought to affect state and local educational practice with rhetoric rather than resources, asserting that the nation's success was threatened by low school standards, rather than by insufficient school funding. The solution was said to lie in higher standards, more accountability, and clearer goals. By 1990, this new approach had sparked developments that would have been inconceivable in previous decades. National goals for education were enunciated.[11] Planning for national tests to measure progress toward these goals was initiated. The role of state and local government, traditionally preeminent in education, was called into question. By 2002 the question had changed from should the national government have a role in education to how much of a role should the national government play? The answer was significant. In January 2002, President Bush signed into law the No Child Left Behind Act of 2001 and the landscape of educational governance changed dramatically.

State Government

The Tenth Amendment to the United States Constitution provides that powers not delegated to the national government are reserved to the states. Traditionally, the establishment and operation of schools has been considered one of those "reserved" powers. In New Mexico, as in most states, responsibility for the exercise of that function is shared by the legislature, the governor, a state public education commission, and the local school boards.[12]

The legislature performs two principal tasks in education. First it enacts laws regulating the establishment, governance, and operation of schools.[13] Over the years the legislature has adopted laws guiding the operation of a state public education department and local school districts and boards, establishing curriculum and graduation requirements and setting forth conditions for the employment and termination of school personnel. Such provisions are under continuous legislative scrutiny; every legislative session witnesses statutory changes reflecting new political pressures and educational demands. Later in this chapter the reader will find a case study of a 1986 effort to strengthen legislative control of schooling.

The second major legislative function is the provision of funds for school operation. Most state legislatures assign a major share of school funding responsibility to local districts and taxpayers. That responsibility customarily is exercised by levying local property taxes, with tax rates (and hence, the level of school spending) subject to voter approval. However, in New Mexico the legislature has assumed virtually full responsibility for financing school operations; less than 3 percent of school operating funds are raised locally. Thus the financial burden is borne at the state level. Just less than half of New Mexico's annual general fund appropriation is allocated to the support of public elementary and secondary schools.

The allocation of state revenues to local schools is a matter of intense and continuous interest on the part of educators, parents, and citizens. To minimize the effects of partisanship and personal loyalties on funds distribution, and to obviate lobbying by individual school districts, "funding formulas" are utilized to distribute state funds. The adoption of one school funding formula is discussed later in this chapter.

Much of the legislature's development of educational policy is carried out through the activities of two interim legislative committees, which include representation from both the House and the Senate: the Legislative Education Study Committee (LESC) and the Legislative Finance Committee (LFC). The LESC is charged with the task of studying educational issues and making recommendations for necessary statutory changes to the legislature. A permanent staff of professional policy analysts gathers data and solicits testimony about the items on the LESC agenda, then formulates a set of recommendations for the legislature each January. The topics chosen for study may originate among members of the LESC itself, or in the legislature as a whole. The topics vary widely. In its 2001 report to the legislature, for example, the LESC addressed matters as diverse as full-day kindergarten, teacher preparation programs, innovations in educational technology, and charter schools.[14]

The LFC concerns itself with the state's budget, including both incoming revenues and expenditures. Each year this committee, aided by its staff of professional budget analysts, reviews funding requests for most state programs, including education. These requests are compared to incoming revenue estimates. Funding recommendations are then developed for consideration by the legislature and its committees. Although the recommendations of the LESC and the LFC are important factors in shaping the ultimate statutory environment of schooling, neither is decisive, for the legislature is obliged to consider not only the recommendations of its own committees, but also those of the governor, state agencies, interest groups, and citizens.

The idea that governors should take a leading position on educational issues is a recent development. In fact, in New Mexico and most other states the policy system long has been designed to insulate school policy from executive politics. As recently as 1986, New Mexico voters amended their constitution to remove the responsibility for administering state school funds and approving local school budgets from the governor's office. The move was short lived, however, as voters were persuaded to amend the constitution again in 2003 to firmly establish control of education in the governor's office.[15]

Recent governors in New Mexico have exercised great influence over educational policy. Issues of taxation, economic development, family and youth services, and health, areas subject to a governors' influence, are inextricably linked to schools. In addition, school issues have come to acquire central importance to parents and citizens generally, virtually compelling position-taking by governors. Thus governors' annual messages to legislative sessions, and lobbying by the governor's staff, often include significant proposals intended to shape educational legislation.[16]

In New Mexico as in most other states, the desire to insulate school governance from the partisan politics characteristic of legislative and executive bodies resulted in the formation of an independent branch of government. For many years, responsibility for school oversight and direction was assigned to a State Board of Education, a body consisting of five members appointed by the governor and ten members elected to four-year terms by voters in the state's ten state school board districts. Typically elections were low-turnout affairs; elections often were uncontested. Although positions on the board were considered prestigious and powerful, relatively few New Mexicans understood the role of the state board or its duties with regard to school governance and policy. Nonetheless, the legislature historically assigned virtually every aspect of school operation to the state board including the formulation of curriculum standards; the establishment of licensure requirements for teachers; school accreditation and approval; the administration of federal funds for schools; the oversight of regulations governing school activities such as athletics; budget approval; and the regulation of home schools. When local boards failed to meet their obligations, the state board was empowered to take over local school district management functions.

In the years between 1986 and 2003, board members were frequently criticized for decisions about policy, funding, and governance of the State Department of Education, decisions often out of step with legislative and gubernatorial preference. In 2003 the legislature proposed a constitutional amendment to redefine, rename, and restructure the State Board of Education. Voters authorized the constitutional change in a special election in September 2003, leaving the future duties of the newly created Public Education Commission (formerly the State Board) to legislative enactment. The future role of the public education commission appears destined to be more advisory than managerial. Still, the constitutional language gives the legislature great latitude and undoubtedly, the role of the Public Education Commission will continue to evolve.

From 1923 until 1986, the regulatory power of the State Department of Education was constrained by the fact that the governor's office, rather than the department, had authority over school-district budgets; "purse" and "program" responsibilities were divided. In 1986 a constitutional amendment moved financial responsibility from the governor's office to the department, ostensibly setting the stage for more effective and efficient state leadership. However, the consolidation of purse and program responsibilities created new tensions in school governance. A series of disputes focused on projections of school enrollments and on what some legislators perceived as slackness in setting the rules establishing local district funding entitlements (and hence, involving the taxes needed to support these entitlements), strained the relationship between the department and the legislature. In 1991, the legislature retaliated by cutting the department's budget. Thus during the first few years of its consolidated control of program and purse, the department's power was not appreciably enhanced. During the remainder of the 1990s, relations between the state board, the state department, the legislature, and the governor remained uneasy as the board and the department attempted to deal with intractable problems, rising expectations, and reducing revenues. The situation prompted many historical critics to fix blame rather than fashion solutions. Gradually, proposals to return control to the governor's office gained popularity, and when the 2003 legislature decided to remake the State Board of Education they also chose to restructure the governance of the State Department of Education. Voters were asked to approve the necessary constitutional changes and in the fall of 2003 Article 12, Section 6, of the Constitution of New Mexico was amended to abolish the historical post of Superintendent of Public Instruction (appointed by the State Board of Education) instead establishing a secretary of education appointed by the governor.

Though the administration of the Public Education Commission and the Public Education Department (formerly the State Department of Education) has undergone constant revision in the last two decades, one governing body remains consistently powerful and controversial. That body is a relatively unknown source of school policy in New Mexico—the New Mexico Activities Association (NMAA). The association promulgates and enforces rules and regulations governing interscholastic activities, including sports and curricular activities such as science fairs and band competitions. The NMAA is a quasi-governmental organization, consisting of member school districts whose dues are used to finance operating costs. The NMAA's budget and policies must be approved by the Public Education Commission before they can be enforced. Disputes involving NMAA actions occasionally become agenda items for the commission.

Local Government

In all states except Hawaii, elected local boards of education are the basic governing unit for public schools. Most of New Mexico's eighty-nine school districts have five-member boards with members serving staggered four-year terms. Board members are elected at-large, except in the larger districts, where members run in geographic districts. School board elections are nonpartisan and are scheduled separately from the elections of other public officials.

Local school board members serve without salary. However, they have a formidable list of duties, including the stewardship of all school funds, the acquisition and maintenance of school properties, and the implementation of legislative statutes and Public Education Commission regulations governing the operation of schools. To perform these duties, each board hires a district superintendent, who becomes the board's chief executive officer and who is responsible for administering the daily affairs of the district in accordance with the law, as well as for keeping the board apprised of developments in education. Particularly in the state's many small school districts, the superintendent may be personally responsible for providing leadership on matters as diverse as employment, curriculum, testing, budget, transportation, maintenance, textbook selection, real estate acquisition and sale, school construction, report forms, legislative issues at the state and national levels, parental complaints, student discipline, and the multitude of other issues that invariably develop around school operations. The division of responsibilities between boards and superintendents is a delicate and controversial matter and one subject to statutory change. Superintendent turnover is consequently high with anywhere from 19 percent to 30 percent of the state's superintendent positions changing hands in a given year.

Employment practices are a frequent source of controversy. Because the school district often is a community's major employer, it may be looked upon as a source of jobs as much as an educational institution. Board members, on their own or as a result of constituent pressures, may seek to have certain individuals hired or fired, with minimal regard for their professional qualifications. Discontent and lawsuits often result from suspect personnel practices.

In contrast to most other states, local boards in New Mexico do not invest great energy in persuading local voters to support local property tax increases for school operations, inasmuch as school operating funds are derived almost entirely from state sources. In recent years much thought and discussion has been given to proposals to permit voters to reinstitute property tax levies for schools. Proponents argue that such levies would generate additional revenues and would enhance the capacity of local taxpayers to exert influence on school policy and practice. The legislature has not supported such measures, in part because of questions of maintaining equity in school funding, because it would affect the tax base upon which other governmental functions depend; and it would significantly alter the role of local boards vis-à-vis their constituents.

A closely related problem of school governance involves school district consolidation. In the decades before school transportation became feasible, school districts tended to be small and compact; at one point New Mexico had nearly five hundred districts. However, most of these districts enrolled few students, producing economic inefficiencies and limiting the scope of services that any single district could provide. Around the middle of the twentieth century a school consolidation movement gained momentum. It rested on the argument that fewer and larger schools were needed, in order to promote the most efficient use of school funds. The advocates of small districts unsuccessfully argued that transportation was dangerous and costly, that small schools had virtues that were lost in the anonymity engendered in large schools, and that consolidation would cause the affected communities to disappear, thereby altering the social fabric of an entire region. Although the formal arguments centered on economic issues, the real conflict may have reflected competing lifestyles and values.

Even after the consolidation movement, many of New Mexico's eighty-nine districts remain very small, thanks to the low population density of much of the state. More than one-third of the state's districts enroll less than five hundred students each. The smallest district, Mosquero, enrolled only sixty students in 2003–4; the Albuquerque district, by contrast, enrolled more than ninety thousand. Albuquerque's large size has engendered its own controversy. While portions of the state have been scrutinized for consolidation possibilities, Albuquerque Public Schools (APS) has been the focus of several school district size reduction movements. At several points in the 1990s the district was the focus of numerous discussions regarding the need to split APS into multiple smaller districts. Though studies have been conducted, the legislature has chosen to leave the district intact and APS remains the state's largest district by far.

Differences in district size and community lifestyle produce major tensions in school governance. One such tension is embedded in the school funding formula. In order to help make it possible to ensure that students in small districts are not disadvantaged educationally, the state has for many years provided supplemental funding to these districts, to compensate for the high per-student operating costs associated with low enrollments. However, large districts have argued that their size and the problems of urban living create special costs that also warrant special funding. In 1989 a "large district" or "density" factor, placed in the formula at the behest of urban legislators, resulted in major conflicts among large, medium, and small districts. Medium-sized districts were eventually mollified when the factor was redesigned to also provide funding to them. In 1997 the factor was eventually converted to an "at-risk" factor. Another source of tension is generated by Public Education Department standards and regulations, which somehow have to accommodate the differing needs and capabilities of districts with widely varying characteristics. Such differences, along with the inherent tensions between teachers and administrators, parents and schools, old and young, employers and educators, give rise to a kaleidoscopic array of disputes within the arena of local school district and interdistrict politics. Alliances form and fail, issues are transformed, and educational progress is made or delayed as those disputes are played out.

Finally, while the state and local school districts wrestle with education issues, they also wrestle with each other and the question of who should decide school policy. Site-based management, a phenomenon of growing interest in the late 1980s and 1990s, may alter the nature of governance issues within districts. Site-based management is a concept grounded in an opposition to "big-government," "central-control," and "top-down" approaches to the management of public functions, and supports the idea that the people in closest proximity to problems ought to be empowered to develop and implement solutions. Thus the concept raises questions about the role and function of both state government and local district government in education. In addition, it raises questions about the nature of decision-making structures at the building level, where principals, teachers, parents, and community agencies all assert claims justifying their involvement in the determination of school policy. During the 1990s, the debate over school control coalesced in support of a new type of local school governance, that of charter schools. Beginning in about 1990, the legislature amended the Public School Code to allow the development of local and individual programs to restructure the curricula and administration of individual public schools. In 1993 the Charter School Act was created to provide a vehicle for the establishment of alternative curricular programs. Though the original act only authorized the establishment of a few schools, amendments in 1998 expanded that number to allow the creation of up to seventy-five per year. Separate legislative enactments in 1998 even allowed the creation of several charter districts. Whether charter schools or charter districts, the charter acts free schools (or districts) of many of the restrictions and obligations of the state Public School Code. In 2006, there were sixty-four charter schools in New Mexico, almost half of them in the Albuquerque Public School district. The notion of site-based management continues to be a popular theme into the twenty-first century.

Other dilemmas of school governance at the local level involve relationships between schools and other agencies that affect young people's lives. These include health providers, family-support services, adult education, juvenile programs, and the like. Local relationships between school districts and other entities involve local property taxation, safety and security matters, the joint use of facilities such as libraries and parks, zoning and property development, and the use of bonding capacity for school and nonschool purposes.

The future of local control of education is very much at issue in New Mexico and elsewhere. Proponents of local school boards contend that they are democracy's best defense against the perils of state and federal control, on the one hand, and professional educators' self-interest on the other. Critics argue that local boards meddle in school affairs, impede the development of interagency relationships essential to effective family services, and limit the responsiveness of individual schools to their constituents and communities. These arguments reflect, in the schooling context, ancient and so far unresolvable issues about the proper relationship between government and society.

Government and Indian Education

The federal government, through its constitutional obligations and treaty relationships with Indian tribal groups, has a special responsibility for Indian education. Until World War I, federal Indian education policies were overtly assimilationist in purpose. Indian languages and cultures were systematically undermined by missionary schools and by Bureau of Indian Affairs (BIA) schools, in an effort to incorporate Indians into the dominant culture and economy. Since the 1960s, however, growing support for the concept of cultural pluralism, coupled with abundant evidence of the widespread failure of assimilationist policy, have produced a number of educational policy initiatives that reflect various combinations of assimilationist and pluralistic orientations. In recent years "self-determination" has been the dominant theme of federal Indian policy.[17]

Today Indians living in New Mexico are served by a variety of school governments. A majority of Indian students attend regular public schools, where their unique cultural roots receive varying degrees of recognition. The state Public Education Department maintains an Indian Education Division. The division is charged with the task of providing assistance to school districts and fostering educational opportunities for Indians in public schools. Some Indians attend public schools in districts in which the enrollment is predominantly Indian. The Zuni district, for example, was carved out of the Gallup-McKinley district in 1979. Members of the Zuni tribe operate the district, but do so within the constraints of laws and regulations pertinent to all state school districts. Finally, many Indian students attend Bureau of Indian Affairs–funded schools in New Mexico. BIA schools currently are of two types: "contract" schools operated by Indian communities on the basis of formal agree-ments with the BIA; and BIA-operated schools, including day schools and boarding schools.[18]

Few people profess to be satisfied with the effectiveness of any form of Indian education. Proposals for reform abound. While many of these proposals focus on matters such as curriculum, instructional strategies, and teacher qualifications, others focus on governance arrangements. As is true of all schools, no altogether satisfactory governance arrangement has yet been devised.

THE INFORMAL SYSTEM

In education, as in virtually every other important policy arena, govern-ment agencies do not work in isolation. Well-established special inter-est groups provide information and exert pressure designed to shape policy outcomes in ways favorable to their members. Other groups, organ-ized in an ad hoc fashion, occasionally arise around issues of the moment and may engage citizens normally outside the policy process.

ESTABLISHED INTEREST GROUPS

One cluster of interest groups represents teachers, administrators, and other school employees. Three groups compete for teachers' loyalties in New Mexico. The two largest of these are the New Mexico affiliate of the National Education Association and the New Mexico Federation of Teachers, representing local unions belonging to the American Federation of Teachers. Both the NEA-NM and the NMFT maintain permanent staffs at the state level. Particularly at the state level, the two groups work coop-eratively joining efforts to lobby the legislature, the Public Education Commission, and other government agencies whose policies may affect teachers and schools. Both the regulatory environment and the fiscal sup-port of schools are objects of great attention by these teachers' groups. A third, much smaller teachers' group is the New Mexico Association of Classroom Teachers. Historically this association has concentrated its attention more on issues of teaching and learning than on fiscal matters.

School administrators in New Mexico are represented by a fourth pro-fessional group, the New Mexico Coalition of School Administrators (NMCSA). The Coalition, formerly the New Mexico School Administrators Association, was established in the early 1970s in response to efforts by the national teachers' unions to limit membership to teachers and limit or exclude school administrators' participation. The Coalition advocates public education policy and provides professional development and networking for its members. The Coalition maintains a Santa Fe office that monitors revenue projections, budget proposals, and regulatory proposals that may affect local administrative functions. Other groups represent other categories of employees, e.g., cafeteria workers, clerical workers, and school librarians. Some of these groups are able to support professional representatives in the state capital; others rely on volunteers to monitor and testify on matters of policy interest.

Sometimes these educational employee groups form alliances that work together on matters of common interest, such as increased appropriations for public education. Often, however, they have different views about the manner in which available revenues should be allocated, and about the distribution of powers of governance. Collective bargaining by teachers, for example, has proven a particularly divisive issue.

Another key lobby is the New Mexico School Boards Association (NMSBA), representing citizens elected to serve as board members of New Mexico's school districts. NMSBA members are faced with a variety of competing pressures from teachers, administrators, parents, taxpayers, and constituents. They are also embroiled in efforts by state and federal agencies to influence or curtail their discretion.

Interest groups not representing school employees frequently turn their attention to educational policy issues. Historically taxpayers' associations have been significant lobbies attempting to hold down taxes and, consequentially, educational revenues. Business-oriented groups often find themselves caught in lobbying dilemmas; on the one hand they recognize the importance of well-prepared employees and the significance of offering nationally competitive salaries for school employees, but on the other they are not inclined to support tax increases for schools. Consequently, business groups frequently find themselves advocating "accountability" measures and market-oriented reforms, which are supposed to improve schools without increasing their costs.

Students of politics, including the politics of education, argue endlessly over the appropriate relationship among interest groups, governmental institutions, and the public interest. Schooling provides one of the most active arenas of interest group activity, and should not be ignored by students of government.

AD HOC GROUPS

Normally, established educational interest groups are the primary unofficial actors in the corridors of powers. On occasion, however, singular issues arouse some segment of the public in ways that trigger ad hoc governmental responses. Most often this occurs at the local district level, where petitioners may seek a hearing with local school officials or the local school board. Here all manner of disputes and concerns are aired and resolved, avoiding the need to involve judicial or legislative forums. Often complaints and suggestions will be met with proposals to create temporary task forces, which study the issue and then make recommendations that may or may not elicit action from the local board.

Some issues either transcend district lines or may not be resolvable locally. In such cases, ad hoc groups may seek to invoke legislative interest. Although New Mexico does not provide for citizen initiatives such as those in California, legislative memorials provide a convenient and commonly used device for managing episodic issues. A friendly representative often will agree to sponsor a constituent's concern via a memorial that expresses the sense of the legislature (or of a single house) on the matter at hand and most often requests an agency such as the Public Education Department or the Legislative Education Study Committee to study the matter and to report its findings back to the legislature. An example is provided in the first of the following case studies of school government at work.

CASE STUDIES

The following case studies illustrate the manner in which formal and informal systems of school governance operate in the face of real issues. The three cases, involving curriculum materials, school funding, and educational-excellence standards, reflect a governance system that is complex and fragmented.

SATANISM IN THE CURRICULUM

Public schools operate in a milieu filled with competing perceptions of truth and morality. Horace Mann and other progenitors of the public

school system sought a curriculum of "common" learning, and emphasizing essential literacy and citizenship skills and leaving divisive religious
and political issues to the home and the community. However, it is easier to advocate such a curriculum than to secure agreement about the
particulars of what should be in it. Much of the politics of education
involves efforts by various groups to include or exclude particular views
in school textbooks. Battles over evolution, religious holidays, school
prayer, health clinics, and a host of related matters regularly erupt in the
forums of school government.

In the mid-1980s, Christian fundamentalism was on the rise in the
nation. Fundamentalists worried about the apparent upsurge of Satanism
among young people and about New Age ideas featured in the media.
U.S. Education Secretary William Bennett called for the restoration of
"moral education" in the schools. Groups such as Phyllis Schlafly's Eagle
Forum and the National Association of Christian Educators organized
themselves to combat "secular humanism" and what they perceived as
the anti-Christian orientation of the schools. In Tennessee a parent group
went to court, claiming that the schools violated their first amendment
rights by using materials featuring witchcraft (*Macbeth*), magic
(*Cinderella*), and religious relativism (*Diary of Anne Frank*). The trial court
affirmed the parents' view, and awarded damages, though the trial court
decision was reversed on appeal.[19]

The Tennessee trial court verdict made headlines in New Mexico.[20]
It heartened an Albuquerque-based Christian-oriented parents' group
that had been formed several weeks earlier. A leader of the group had
removed her children from the public schools, contending that they were
encouraging students to discuss "philosophical issues" rather than limiting their work to the teaching of "basics."[21] Visiting with teachers and
inspecting curriculum materials, members of the group found evidence
that the schools were using materials that involved mythology, fantasy,
and internationalism. Global education materials shared with teachers
at seminars in Taos were viewed as propaganda promulgated by the peace
movement and promoting New Agers' religious designs for "one world
government."[22] With vocal support from a like-minded member of the
State Board of Education, the group sought to influence local and state
textbook review committee decisions. However, most teachers and school
officials on these committees saw the issue as one of censorship. Rather

than permitting a particular parents' group to veto instructional materials, the educators advocated procedures that would permit students to select options to materials that parents found objectionable. Faced with these views, the concerned parents met with little success.

The concerned parents then sought legislative help. At the 1987 legislative session, five senators cosponsored Senate Memorial 45, which expressed the Senate's opposition to school use of "mind-altering techniques" such as "transcendental meditation, guided imagery, altered states of consciousness or the occult." At a hearing there was conflicting testimony about the purposes and extent of use of the disputed materials and techniques. Several senators felt that the matter should be resolved at the local level; perhaps it was necessary to review the procedures for securing parental input. In committee, language was added to SM 45, requesting the State Board of Education and local boards to review the Senate's concerns and to develop appropriate guidelines. SM 45, as amended, was passed by the Senate.

In response, the state superintendent of public instruction advised school districts that they were to develop guidelines for obtaining public views about instructional materials being considered for adoption. In addition the state board appointed a task force to study the matter and to conduct hearings. The Department of Education's instructional materials coordinator, reporting to the board on the status of textbook litigation around the nation, cautioned that nationwide censorship efforts were leading to "watered down texts."[23] Board members inquired as to whether the memorial applied to private schools, whether the materials to which the parents objected actually were in use in the schools, whether the memorial would interfere with teaching cultural values, and whether counseling and psychological services would be adversely affected.[24]

The concerned parents wanted the state board to modify its "educational standards" regulations governing school accreditation to include prohibitions on the acquisition and use of "occult" materials. However, changes in education standards regulations must be preceded by public hearings. At the hearings, SM 45 advocates stressed the importance of parental control over the inculcation of moral values. Opponents argued that the proposed changes would jeopardize the work of counselors, librarians, and nurses, and would result in the censorship of hundreds of books.

In June 1988, the state board took final action. A motion to change the education standards was rejected; the board adopted its task force's recommendation that local districts be advised to ensure that local parents had ample opportunity to be heard in local instructional materials adoption processes. Subsequently, the superintendent of public instruction issued a memo advising local districts of their responsibilities along these lines and enclosing sample policies for local consideration. There the matter ended for the time being, leaving the schools' instructional materials intact, but providing easier access for aggrieved parents to press their case upon local school boards. Since most education disputes like most government disputes rarely disappear, it should be noted that in 1997 the legislature provided for the distribution of instructional materials directly to local school boards, bypassing the historical first stop at the State Department of Education.

EQUITY IN SCHOOL FUNDING

Every state develops "state-aid" policies that provide for the distribution of state appropriated funds to local school districts. In 1974 New Mexico adopted a state aid policy that was, and remains, among the most equitable in the nation. The essence of the policy is its guarantee that the elementary and secondary education provided in every New Mexico community is a function of the wealth of the state as a whole, rather than the wealth, or poverty, of the community in which the child lives.[25] Because of this guarantee, New Mexico has been spared the expensive, divisive, and prolonged litigation that has plagued many states with less equitable state aid policies.

A propitious set of circumstances made the 1974 policy achievement possible. Since statehood New Mexico had utilized property taxes as a major source of school support. In response to the 1910 constitution's mandate requiring the establishment and maintenance of "a uniform system of free public schools," the legislature did what other states had done: it authorized local communities to tax property for school purposes. In 1930 more than 75 percent of the money used to operate New Mexico's school was raised locally.

However, in 1933 Depression-plagued New Mexico voters placed a cap on local property-tax rates. Cash was scarce and New Mexicans worried that tax delinquency would result in people losing their property.

With property taxes capped, schools faced major program reductions or closure. People looked to state government to fill the school-revenue gap. Sales and income taxes, as well as revenue from lands reserved for school support, were tapped to meet the need. The state's share of school funds jumped from less than 25 percent in 1930 to approximately 75 percent in the ensuing decades.

As the state's contribution grew, so did the significance of the criteria governing the distribution of state aid. These criteria largely determined the size of each district's budget and hence the range and quality of the programs it could operate.

For many years the criterion most significant for state aid distribution was student enrollment. Large districts, which enjoyed economies of scale, sought distribution formulas based directly on enrollment. However, districts operating small schools pointed out that their costs were fixed; teachers had to be hired and classrooms heated even if there were not enough children to fill those classrooms. Therefore, state aid ought to include some sort of "weighting" factor providing extra funds to small schools.

After mid-century another consideration entered policy discussions about state aid distribution. Inequities inherent in local property taxation had become increasingly apparent, as some communities prospered and others stagnated. Property-rich districts could raise significant school funds through property taxation, but poorer communities could not. Children in communities blessed with railroads, oil wells, mines, and commercial enterprises attended schools far better built, equipped, and staffed than did children from communities less well endowed. Educational policy analysts advocated state policies that would ameliorate these wealth-related differences by distributing more aid to poorer communities.[26]

For a time New Mexico rejected such proposals, preferring to distribute state aid purely on the basis of school enrollment.[27] However, in the mid-1960s, inspired by the civil rights movement and by the Johnson administration's War on Poverty, a significant lawsuit was filed in California. In *Serrano v. Priest*, the plaintiffs claimed that disparities in districts' local wealth were associated with disparities in the education available to children. These disparities, the plaintiffs argued, violated the state constitution's mandate that "equal" education should be provided. The California Supreme Court concurred and ordered the legislature to design a state school funding system that was "fiscally neutral," that is, one that disconnected the quality of a child's education from the wealth of the community in which the child lived.[28]

New Mexico took notice. A study of the existing formula showed that it actually was *dis*equalizing; wealthier districts received more state aid per pupil than poorer districts.[29] A *New Mexico Law Review* article warned that New Mexico's existing school funding formula could not withstand a *Serrano*-type attack.[30] The Legislative School Study Committee (a precursor of the LESC) reported:

> One of the wealthiest districts in New Mexico is assessed at $53,000,000 and raised $755 per student from all local/county sources for schools; one of the poorest New Mexico districts is assessed at $2,361,764 and raised $42 per student from all local/county sources. Even after all federal revenue and state operating and equalization funds have been allocated, this same wealthy district has $2060 to spend per pupil compared to $1018 per pupil which the poor district is able to spend. If [*Serrano*] is upheld, the New Mexico legislature will be forced to revise the state's methods of public school financing."[31]

The LSSC's warning was issued at a time ripe for policy change. Redistricting after the 1970 federal census had strengthened the hand of the "Mama Lucy" coalition of legislators. The Mama Lucys, taking their name from a Las Vegas eatery where they gathered, represented urban and northern liberal interests, as distinct from southeastern oil patch and other more conservative interests previously dominating the legislature. Many in the group were determined to overcome what they perceived as the formula's bias against poor districts. Following the 1973 legislative session, Governor Bruce King, then midway through his first term, appointed a large advisory committee of legislators, state officials, and schoolteachers and administrators. The committee's task was to study and make recommendations about state school funding.

The task was not easy. Like any such group, this one had to deal with a number of fundamental issues of school governance. One involved control. Intergovernmental transfer payments such as state school aid are often accompanied by "strings" designed to induce local compliance with state policy. However, New Mexicans have had a strong aversion to central-government controls; it appeared that a formula change that expanded state control would be unacceptable. The governor's advisory committee therefore adopted a general, non-categorical approach to state aid. (In the mid-1980s, as noted in the next case study, the control issue was seen differently.) Funds would be distributed on a formula basis, and districts could make their own decisions about the use of distributed funds.

A second issue was taxation. Who should pay? In the 1970s New Mexico was well ahead of the national average in terms of the extent to which the state paid the bill for public schooling. Local property taxes were relatively low in the state. However, property taxes, and the inequities they created, had been the source of difficulty in the California case. Thus the advisory committee decided to rely on state income and gross receipts taxes, rather than on property taxes. Entrenched New Mexican hostility toward property taxes, the threat of *Serrano*-type litigation, and the availability of a surplus in the state treasury made it plausible to think about increasing state aid to cover the costs of a new formula, even though the governor declared that sufficient funds were not available.

A third issue involved the determination of need. Different types of educational programs (such as vocational, bilingual, pre-school, handicapped) required different amounts of money. Relying heavily on the work of a national school finance study then underway, the advisory committee adopted a weighting scheme that estimated the relative costs of educating different types of students (elementary students versus high school students, handicapped students, English-as-Second Language students), different sizes of schools, and different levels of teacher training and experience.[32] Using these factors, each district would develop a student profile unique to its own characteristics; the profile would determine each district's share of total state aid. Thus state funding could be based on need, not wealth. The problem, of course, was that a need-based formula could provide an equitable way to distribute available funds, but it could not determine the overall level of funding required. That problem was left to the legislature and the governor.

Fourth, and of critical importance in the *Serrano* context, the advisory committee had to determine how to deal with local differences in property tax yield. The committee decided that every district would levy property taxes at a fixed rate, and that 95 percent of the yield would be credited against the state funds awarded under the state's need-based formula. Through this mechanism, income disparities based on property tax wealth differences were virtually eliminated. The price was that districts no longer had an incentive to raise local school property tax revenues. The school tax burden thus came to fall entirely upon the legislature.

A final issue involved federal aid. Many of New Mexico's districts benefited from federal impact aid, which compensated districts affected by the presence of federal installations such as military bases. Because the federal government viewed these funds as substitutes for lost local revenues, states were prohibited from taking credit for them in state formula distributions. However, under the formula envisioned by the advisory committee, impact aid would have a substantial disequalizing effect if not credited against the state's allocation. It was decided to take credit despite the federal prohibition and to seek a change through federal legislation or in the courts.[33]

With these issues substantially resolved by the advisory committee, the proposed formula was presented to the 1974 legislature for action. Though many procedural and substantive obstacles remained, there seemed to be significant overall support in both houses. One problem was the Senate Education Committee, which was not inclined to favor the bill. Another was the governor's assertion that school revenue increases could not exceed $20.5 million. A third involved thirty districts, including several in the politically powerful southeastern oil patch, that would receive reduced state funding under the proposed new formula. If these districts were to be "held harmless," that is, if nonformula funds were to be provided to ensure that the next year's allocation would not be reduced, a considerable portion of the governor's proposed and already insufficient allocation would be used up outside the formula, thereby limiting its attractiveness.

Legislative strategists went to work. In an unusual move, the bill was first heard in the House, which passed it overwhelmingly, after adding a district-sparsity factor (for which no need had been shown, but which benefited many of the districts previously in the "hold-harmless" category). A deal was then made to maneuver the bill through the Senate Education Committee. With each new step, the costs of implementing the formula increased. Eventually HB 85 was passed by the legislature and signed by the governor.[34] The regular session then adjourned, having adopted a new formula but no school appropriation. A special session was called to address the problem. During the special session, conservative interests from the Senate were able to secure some concessions not previously agreed to in exchange for an appropriation considerably higher than that initially proposed by the governor.

The final product was a school funding formula that set a national standard for equity in school funding. However, by the mid-1980s the formula was under severe strain, and its future was in doubt. Some legislators, anxious to avoid the onus of tax increases at the state level, sought ways to restore local property taxation for schools. Other legislators protested the formula's non-categorical nature, arguing that stronger state fiscal control was needed if schools were to improve. Frustration led to an attempt to legislate excellence in schools.

Excellence by Mandate

The Reagan administration came into office determined to diminish and dismantle the federal role in education. However, Education Secretary T. H. Bell had a different idea. He created a National Commission on Excellence in Education and asked it to prepare a report on the quality of American education. The commission's report, *A Nation at Risk: The Imperative for Educational Reform*, brought school reform to the center of the nation's policy agenda. Ringing rhetoric set the stage for public receptivity: "If an unfriendly foreign power had attempted to impose on America the mediocre performance that exists today, we might well have viewed it as an act of war."[35] Claiming that the quality of schooling had declined in the preceding decades, the report asserted that individual and national survival required the restoration of standards of excellence in schools. High school graduation requirements, curriculum content, teacher qualifications, and college entrance standards must be raised significantly, according to the commission's report. State policy makers, particularly those disenchanted with the equity agenda of preceding years, those opposed to the idea that pumping more money into the schools would alleviate their problems, and those distressed by the mounting evidence of social maladies seized upon the commission's agenda.

Conditions in New Mexico were ripe for policy innovation. Declining state revenues in 1982 and 1983 had meant that solutions to school problems no longer could be addressed simply by increasing appropriations, unless taxes were increased too. The issue of educational standards appeared to provide an alternative to traditional funding issues. Conservatives in the political arena, enjoying strengthened electoral power built on President Reagan's immense popularity and on the growing unpopularity of Democratic Governor Anaya, saw in the school reform agenda an opportunity to build their political base.

In 1985 a conservative coalition seized control of the legislature. The 1985 session was unusually rancorous; neither the governor nor the coalition was in a mood to compromise. The coalition determined that it would focus on school issues during the interim. Bypassing traditional educational policy-setting groups such as the Legislative Education Study Committee and the State Board of Education, coalition leaders created an interim Public School Reform Committee. The committee was dominated by legislators sympathetic to the view that school reform was urgently needed and that reform required the imposition of new standards of excellence.

During the summer and fall, hearings were held by the reform committee. Testimony from established groups was politely received. Meanwhile a comprehensive reform package, later to be known as Senate Bill 106 (SB 106), was hammered out behind the scenes by members of the committee. The proposal, officially known as the Public School Reform Act, implemented a number of policy changes. Teacher tenure was repealed, high school graduation requirements were raised, teaching times for various subjects were established, teachers' nonteaching assignments (such as lunch duty) were limited, academic standards for participation in extracurricular activities ("no pass, no play") were defined, training requirements for prospective teachers were set, and new tests of student accomplishment were established. The act also changed school funding formula provisions pertaining to class size and salary schedules. Suddenly, the legislature was involved in the nitty-gritty of school governance—a task historically reserved to state and local school boards.

When the legislature convened for its thirty-day session early in 1986, coalition leaders were faced with a difficult task. On the one hand, it appeared that a tax increase would be required to sustain basic state functions, despite stout opposition from some members of the coalition. The cohesion of the coalition could be sustained only if major reforms were tied to the tax increase. However, the proposed reforms were threatened by the prospect of a veto from the governor if they were too offensive to one of his key sources of support, teachers. A deal would have to be struck between the governor and the coalition, among the interests supporting and opposing tax increases, and among the proponents and opponents of school reform.

Teachers were split by the bill. Some opposed it because of its abolition of tenure and its prescriptions for classroom management. Other teachers supported the bill, because it limited class size and restricted the assignment of nonteaching duties to teachers. All, of course, were interested in the bill's impact on prospective salary increases. Ultimately the division among teachers was reflected in a split between the NEA-NM and NMFT; the latter, convinced that the abolition of tenure could be ameliorated by the adoption of strong due process procedures, avoided a direct confrontation with the coalition, which tended to view the abolition of tenure as a nonnegotiable issue. The NEA-NM remained committed to retaining tenure.

The NEA-NM was not alone in its opposition to SB 106. There was a great hue and cry from some supporters of athletics, who claimed that the "no pass, no play" eligibility requirements would hurt students whose interest in school was motivated by their participation in interscholastic sports. Vocational educators objected to the increase in academic course requirements for graduation. Educators and parents representing gifted students objected to the bill's restrictions on eligibility qualifications. Representatives of the State Board of Education offered muted criticism of SB 106, reminding legislators that the board had already initiated several school reform projects, that funding for many of the reforms proposed in SB 106 was not available, and that the legislature was trespassing on the board's prerogatives. Representatives of local school boards and school administrators objected to what they saw as new intrusions upon local autonomy.

However, the conservative coalition was not prepared to accept major changes in its school-reform bill. Tax increases and reforms must go hand in hand. Citing public dissatisfaction with schools, emphasizing the compromises already accomplished during the reform committee's deliberations, and backed by indications of popular and business support for strong school-reform measures, coalition leaders held their ground. To those who noted that SB 106 created major unfunded financial obligations, the coalition responded saying that funds would be found later, if the reforms could be adopted now. Provisions were included in the bill for a gradual phase-in of the most expensive reforms (class-size reductions in the primary grades and in English classes).

While SB 106 was proceeding through hearings, a tax increase package was adopted, creating the possibility of a salary increase for teachers. However, coalition leaders insisted that there would be no salary increase for teachers unless the reform package was adopted too. In the House, teacher advocates won amendments protecting teachers' tenure and then refused to accede to the Senate's request to rescind the amendments. The dispute was referred to a Senate-House conference committee dominated by coalition loyalists.[36]

An across-the-board salary increase for teachers became a key issue, along with the tenure dispute. Behind the scenes, an agreement was struck: a $2,200-per-teacher salary increase was to be adopted at a cost of $33 million, tenure was to be abolished but some procedural protections were to be added, and the remainder of the reform package was to be safe from gubernatorial veto. As the session drew to a close, the conference committee agreements were presented to both houses of the legislature. The SB 106 school reform package, virtually intact, was adopted by both chambers of the legislature and then signed by Governor Anaya. Significant change in New Mexico's statutory environment for schooling had been accomplished, with virtually no participation by established educational policy making bodies.

The ensuing years demonstrated the difficulties of change by mandate. Some of those difficulties arose from New Mexico's continued economic straits. Despite several tax increases, reluctantly agreed to by the Carruthers administration in the late 1980s, revenues were barely adequate to sustain existing levels of public services; funding for new obligations embedded in SB 106 had to be deferred. In 1992 the legislature had made little progress in providing funds for class-size reductions, which teachers deemed to be the cornerstone of effective reform. Implementation of expensive remediation programs was deferred. After the conservative coalition's control of the legislature was broken in the late 1980s, the legislature restored teacher tenure, eventually even extending that provision to noncertified personnel. However, some of the bill's provisions began to have an effect on school practices.

By the end of the 1980s, the need for school reform still was widely acknowledged. National goals were established, along with state-level adaptations of them. However, the limits of "top-down" reforms such as those represented in SB 106 were beginning to be acknowledged throughout the nation. "Bottom-up" reform efforts materialized, embedded in "restructuring" movements designed to enhance participation in decision making at the school building level. Efforts to reconcile and merge these two strategies for school improvement posed new challenges for New Mexico's educational policy makers in the future.

SUMMARY AND PROSPECTS

The governance of schools, like that of other public functions, necessitates recognizing that competing interests and expectations of individuals, society, and government are not easily reconciled. Solutions that are satisfactory at one time or place may be unsatisfactory at another.

In the decades of the twentieth century, New Mexicans repeatedly made adjustments to their policies for school governance. At the state level, there was frequent tinkering with the distribution of authority between the governor's office, the legislature, and the State Board of Education. Locally, relationships among school, municipal, and county governments varied. Relationships between state and local agencies, and between them and federal education initiatives, also underwent change to meet new conditions.

School governance will continue to evolve. One fundamental issue for New Mexicans will be the delineation of an appropriate role for the national government in education. As the national government places additional burdens on educational institutions, will it provide assistance? And will national government involvement impede or assist New Mexico's quest for school improvement?

A second fundamental governance issue will involve, as it always has, the proper distribution of authority within and among governmental units within New Mexico: individual schools, school districts, other local governments, regional agencies, the governor, nonschool state agencies, the legislature, and the new state Public Education Commission and Public Education Department. Historically at odds with one another, and constrained by changing constitutional arrangements, various state and local agencies can work with one another to design collaborative approaches to the improvement of schooling, or they can neutralize one another's efforts to resolve problematic issues in education.

Underlying these two enduring governance problems is yet a third. It asks not how, but whether government should direct schooling. Advocates of market mechanisms argue that government itself is the greatest impediment to effective and efficient education.[37] By giving parents greater say in choosing schools, market advocates say, control over school policy can be shifted from government to consumer, with dramatic improvements in responsiveness. Some would go farther, creating voucher systems, to allow families to decide whether to place their children in public, private, or church-related schools.

Opponents of the market approach argue that the problem with schools does not lie in their control; it lies in their lack of resources. The problem is that citizens and their elected representatives simply have not been willing to levy the taxes necessary to finance effective schools. Rather than diverting attention to "choice" plans, the central need is deemed to be that of securing sufficient investment in schools.

And so the issues go on. Each fall, meanwhile, twenty-five thousand or so young New Mexicans enter the first grade, experiencing the benefits and the liabilities of educational programs they have had no voice in designing, choosing, or financing, and which will affect the quality of their lives. Responsibility for the educational effectiveness of their experience lies with the generations that preceded them.[38]

NOTES

1.   National Commission on Excellence in Education, *A Nation at Risk: The Imperative for Educational Reform* (Washington, D.C.: U.S. Department of Education, 1983).

2.   Thomas H. Eliot, "Toward an Understanding of Public School Politics," *American Political Science Review* 52 (1959), pp. 1032–51.

3.   There are many excellent histories of American public schools. See David B. Tyack, *The One Best System* (Cambridge, Mass.: Harvard University Press, 1974). Also, see the multivolume history by Lawrence A. Cremin, beginning with *American Education: The Colonial Experience, 1607–1783* (New York: Harper, 1970). For a history of education in New Mexico, see Tom Wiley, *Politics and Purse Strings in New Mexico's Public Schools* (Albuquerque: University of New Mexico Press, 1968).

4.   The governance of nonpublic schools is not considered in this chapter.

5. John E. Chubb and Terry M. Moe, *Politics, Markets, and America's Schools* (Washington, D.C.: Brookings Institution, 1990).

6. New Mexico Constitution, Article XII, Section 1.

7. For an account of the origins and operations of impact aid, see I. M. Labovitz, *Aid for Federally Affected Public Schools* (Syracuse, N.Y.: Syracuse University Press, 1963).

8. For examples see *Tinker v. Des Moines*, 393 U.S. 503 (1969); *Brown v. Topeka Board of Education*, 347 U.S. 483 (1954); *Goss v. Lopez*, 419 U.S. 565 (1975).

9. For examples, see *Serna v. Portales Municipal Schools*, 499 F.2d 1147 (1974); *Garcia v. Miera*, 817 F.2d 650 (1987); *Norton v. Board of Education*, 553 P.2d 1277 (1976); *New Mexico Association for Retarded Citizens v. New Mexico*, 495 F. Supp. 391 (1980). These cases deal with bilingual education, corporal punishment, student fees, and special education, respectively.

10. For an overview of the long-term rise and fall of federal spending for schools, see Richard Rossmiller, "Federal Funds: A Shifting Balance?" in Julie K. Underwood and Deborah Verstegen, eds., *The Impacts of Litigation and Legislation on Public School Finance* (New York: Harper and Row, 1990).

11. See the special issue of *Phi Delta Kappan*, December 1990, for a description and analysis of these national goals.

12. For an account of the development of education governance structures in New Mexico, see Wiley, *Politics and Purse Strings*.

13. School-related statutes are compiled in the Public School Code, *See New Mexico Statutes Annotated*, Sections 22–1–1 *et seq.*

14. Legislative Education Study Committee, "Report to the Second Session of the Forty-fifth Legislature" (Santa Fe: Legislative Education Study Committee, January 2001).

15. In a statewide special election held in September 2003, voters approved proposed Constitutional Amendment no. 1 by a vote of 101,542 to 83,155.

16. Governors' views are outlined in their annual messages to the legislature. For the text of these messages, consult the *Journals* of the New Mexico House and Senate available from the Legislative Council Service, State Capitol, Santa Fe, New Mexico.

17. Bureau of Indian Affairs, "Report on BIA Education," (Washington, D.C.: U.S. Department of the Interior, 1988), Chapter 1.

18. Legislative Education Study Committee, "BIA Schools Study," (Santa Fe: Legislative Education Study Committee, June 15, 1987).

19. *Mozert v. Hawkins County Schools*, 647 F. Supp 1194 (1986). The ruling was reversed on appeal. See 827 F.2d 1058 (1987).

20. *Albuquerque Tribune*, Oct. 24, 1986; *Albuquerque Journal*, Oct. 25, 1986.

21. *Albuquerque Tribune*, Nov. 24, 1986.

22. Personal communication; documents from Susan Gurule to David Colton, January 1988.

23. New Mexico State Board of Education, *Minutes* (Santa Fe: State Board of Education, October 8–9, 1987), p. 32.

24. New Mexico State Board of Education, *Minutes* (Santa Fe: State Board of Education, November 18–20, 1987), pp. 92–95.

25. "Wealth" in this context refers to real estate rather than income or intangible property.

26. For example, see Paul R. Mort, "Toward A More Dynamic Fiscal Policy for New Mexico Schools," Report to New Mexico State Board of Education (Santa Fe: Department of Education, October 1961).

27. Wiley, *Politics and Purse Strings*, Chapters 6–8.

28. *Serrano v. Priest*, 5 Cal 3rd 584 (1971).

29. Jose A. Perea, "A Comparison of the Equalization Effects of Federal and State Public School Fund Distributions in New Mexico" (Ph.D. diss., University of New Mexico, 1971).

30. William F. Carr, "*Serrano v. Priest* and Its Impact on New Mexico," *New Mexico Law Review* 2 (July 1972), pp. 266–85.

31. Legislative School Study Committee, "Report to the First Session of the Thirty-First Legislature" (Santa Fe: Legislative School Study Committee, January 1973).

32. Lawrence Huxel, "A Computer-based Simulation Model for Public School Finance in New Mexico" (Ph.D. diss., University of New Mexico, 1973).

33. Jo Ann Krueger, "The Politics of School Finance: New Mexico Passes a State Funding Formula," *Journal of Education Finance* 1 (Summer 1975), pp. 86–95.

34. For additional information on the passage of HB 85, see Stan Pogrow, "School Finance Reform in New Mexico," *Division of Government Research Review* 83, no. 2 (Albuquerque, 1974).

35. National Commission on Excellence in Education, *A Nation at Risk*, p. 5.

36. *Journal* of the House of Representatives, 37th Legislature, 2d Session (Santa Fe: Legislative Council Service, 1974); *Journal* of the Senate, 37th Legislature, 2d Session (Santa Fe: Legislative Council Service, 1974).

37. Chubb and Moe, *Politics*.

38. Historical developments and future trends are included in John B. Mondragon and Ernest S. Stapleton, *Public Education in New Mexico* (Albuquerque: University of New Mexico Press, 2005).

Chapter Twelve

A Concluding Note

The government of New Mexico described in the preceding pages is the result of decades of both planned and unplanned growth and change. Much of its complexity has been due to a lack of central coordination and long-range planning. Governmental structures have developed in response to demands and pressures emanating both from inside and outside government. Those interests wielding considerable political influence have incorporated their ideas and values into the state's governmental processes and institutions. Relatively little attention had been paid to the government's responsiveness to the general public interest, and there have been only a few concerted efforts to shape the whole into an efficient, effective, and coordinated unit of governance.

New Mexico is not atypical in these respects; many other state governments are in the same condition. However, the requirements of a modern, changing, technological society are pressuring sometimes obsolete governments to adjust to new circumstances. Over the past three decades, about half of the states, including New Mexico, have either attempted or accomplished major governmental reforms.

The necessity for timely and responsible governmental reformation and reorganization is particularly acute in New Mexico. This state is in a precarious condition of flux, alternating between stagnation and emergency responses. Dramatic changes are occurring in its economic, demographic, social, cultural, and environmental settings. The state's economy continues to evidence serious problems, including an imbalance between government and private employment, low per capita income, a widening gap between the wealthy and the poor, and increasing intensity and duration of poverty for some of our citizens, particularly ethnic minorities and children. New Mexico's vast and pristine natural environment, long one of its most valued qualities, is threatened by abuse, neglect, and degradation. Public services are at a discouragingly minimal level. The areas of education, law enforcement, rehabilitation of offenders, transportation, services for children, and physical and mental health care are beset by serious problems.

At the same time, the state is experiencing a tremendous influx of new residents. From 1980 to 2000, New Mexico's population grew considerably faster than that of the rest of the nation. Within the state, the urban centers (especially Albuquerque/Bernalillo County, Las Cruces/Doña Ana County, Santa Fe County, and Sandoval County) are faced with the highest growth rates. The common problems of these metropolitan areas and the increasingly well-known difficulties of boom areas add to the strain.

Our public schools from kindergartens through universities remain a subject of controversy among various segments of the population. The state's most expensive public service is criticized for its instructional procedures, its curricular content, and its level of financial support. On any one of these particulars, one can find diametrically opposed viewpoints. Attempts at reform have been largely unsuccessful due to faulty premises, little or no economic underwriting, or opposition by defenders of the status quo.

Government at the state level is one of the few social institutions that can resolve statewide problems. Where problems are best handled by other agents such as local governments, private organizations, or individuals, state government can assist, encourage, or promote these activities. In any case, an efficient, effective, responsive, and responsible state government is a necessity for a sound commonwealth and an emotionally and physically healthy citizenry.

To meet the legitimate expectations of the citizenry that state government deal efficiently with the above issues is one of the major challenges of the twenty-first century. The last major reorganization occurred in 1975, when the governor eliminated unneeded or obsolete state boards and commissions. A set of government reorganization bills was pushed through the 1977 legislature, which consolidated a multitude of agencies into twelve cabinet-level departments, each headed by a gubernatorial appointee. While this arrangement helped to streamline a large portion of the executive branch, and in its basic configuration continues today, much more can be done. There remains the fragmentation of executive authority caused by the constitutional establishment of several other executive officers of state government. Many of the numerous state occupational licensing boards still exist. The legislature did, however, enact a "sunset law" to accompany the governor's reorganization acts. That law periodically terminates agencies automatically, unless each agency is able to persuade the legislature that it deserves to have its mandate renewed (which virtually all have succeeded in doing). Changes in the composition of numerous occupational licensing boards have been made, and a few boards have been allowed to die.

Cabinet department changes were minimal and largely a reshuffling of responsibilities amongst existing departments until the administration of Governor Richardson, when major changes occurred. Six new departments were created out of previously existing noncabinet agencies with the most significant action being the establishment of the Public Education Department and the dissolution of the Department of Education and its governing board. Though some of the Richardson changes are consistent with administrative theories to improve both efficiency and responsiveness, others reflect the governor's desire to exercise policy and programmatic control in the executive branch.

Governors in New Mexico are limited in what they can do with the governmental apparatus, because of the state's fragmented executive system, the separation of powers, bureaucratic inertia and irresponsibility, and other formal and informal constraints. Yet this office is both the most visible and potentially the most influential of all state agencies. The constitutional amendments of 1986, allowing for two four-year terms of office and removing the prohibition against executive officials running for other executive offices, should help. The many independent and sometimes contrary elected state executives could be reduced to a still smaller number. Those whose positions do not necessitate independence from the chief executive or who do not require a direct popular electoral base should be subject to the direction of the governor. Central and visible coordination and control would help to focus the energies and activities of the executive branch.

In the previous editions of this book a persistent theme propounded by the authors and the editors has been that New Mexico government needs structural and procedural reform in order to meet the contemporary problems facing state government efficiently and responsibly. The 1995 report of the Constitutional Revision Commission proposed more than one hundred changes to both the constitution and statutes that would effect some of the reforms urged by experts. Approximately a third of the highest priority reforms recommended by that commission have been adopted.

Since the mid-1960s the state legislature has made some progress in the improvement of its performance as the people's representative assembly, assisted by competent staff services and redistricted in line with the dictates of the "one person, one vote" reapportionment decisions in the early 1960s. The New Mexico Legislature has improved considerably in comparison with other state legislatures; however, several problems continue. Though the constitution continues to limit the length of regular sessions, the legislature has effectively become a full-time body. With a plethora of interim committees, task forces, and special sessions, part-time legislators are engaged in full-time work. Voters continually refuse to authorize a salary for legislative service, leaving legislators to craft their own rewards through legislative retirement and constant interim committee per diem. Unfortunately, the lack of salary has increasingly pushed citizen legislative service beyond the reach of all but retirees and the independently wealthy.

While pay for service is certainly important, other constitutional revisions would improve the work of the legislature. Such revisions could include the allowance of more time for the governor to consider legislation and the establishment of an independent fiscal auditor. These changes were recommended by the 1995 Constitutional Revision Commission but have yet to be adopted. Perhaps on a more global, but related level, it seems doubtful that the legislature will acquire the ability to be proactive instead of reactive. A part-time, unpaid legislature must continually deal with the brush fires of society, leaving little time for preservation or improvement of the forest.

Our legislature also suffers from a malady common to most states. The parochial, regional, and private interests of some legislators too often detract from their ability to perceive the general public interest. The seniority accruing to legislators from "safe" districts sometimes distorts the equitable distribution of political power, especially in the Senate. These and other shortcomings have been reflected in approval ratings in statewide surveys of citizen attitudes. The legislature scores the lowest ratings of public officials, rarely getting above 25 percent "excellent" or "good." Thus in the early 1990s serious public interest coalesced around the issue of limiting the number of terms state legislators could serve.

In light of the fact that the state of Nebraska does well with a one-house legislature, we do not accept the inevitability or necessity of supporting 112 legislators in two houses representing similar constituencies and performing duplicate functions. The presence of two legislative chambers encourages buck-passing and greatly increases citizen difficulty in pinpointing responsibility for legislative decisions.

Judicial reorganization in the mid-1960s helped improve the quality of justice in New Mexico, but improvements can still be made. The 1988 constitutional amendment establishing a hybrid merit-selection system for judges of the metropolitan, district, and appellate courts will require several decades of operation before its effect on the quality of New Mexico's judges can be adequately evaluated. Constitutional revision scholars and legal advocates have since recommended reform of New Mexico's limited jurisdiction courts.

Perhaps the major problem facing our courts and law-enforcement agencies is the tremendous strain on their resources. Courts are understaffed and some judges are overworked; the state prisons and county jails are overcrowded and are often marked by deterioration of both the physical facilities and the people incarcerated in them. State attention must be focused not only on improved law enforcement but also on meaningful rehabilitation programs for those who can benefit from them. Consideration should also be given to creating a sophisticated statewide unit capable of coping with white-collar criminals and organized crime. Such a unit in the Department of Public Safety would need to work closely with the state police and the attorney general's office. Such crime is best addressed by well-trained and well-funded investigators with a statewide focus, rather than by numerous local law-enforcement agencies.

Local governments must be assisted in their efforts to provide citizens with essential everyday services. The legislature should refrain from its tendency to micromanage local governments and to impose tasks on them without providing the means to meet increased costs. Small town and village governments should be promoted and strengthened as the focal points for community development. Metropolitan areas need to be granted the authority and the revenue resources to meet the complex and ever-growing needs of their populations.

New Mexico needs an educational *system*. This state's development depends upon employing its financial and human resources with maximum efficiency and effectiveness; New Mexico cannot afford to continue to perpetuate a hodgepodge of educational institutions and programs. Educational and financial considerations should be foremost, ahead of politics. Measures of educational needs and evaluations of outcomes must be developed and implemented. These must be used to design an education-delivery system that will provide the knowledge and skills the state's citizens will need to cope with our changing economy and society.

Governmental reform is a difficult and occasionally perilous task. Yet, as the first decade of the twenty-first century unfolds, the necessity of reform becomes increasingly evident. Let us hope that the citizens will find the will and the courage to take whatever steps are necessary to shape a state government that is capable of meeting these new challenges while preserving and maintaining the unique cultural and environmental heritage of New Mexico.

Index

Page numbers in italics indicate illustrations.